THE
ALIEN JIGSAW

Katharina Wilson

Introduction By
BUDD HOPKINS

The Alien Jigsaw

Copyright © 1993 by Katharina Wilson
Introduction copyright © 1993 by Budd Hopkins
All rights reserved. No part of this book may be reproduced or transmitted in any form or by any means, electronic or mechanical, including photography, recording or any information storage and retrieval system, without permission in writing from the author. Inquiries should be addressed to: Katharina Wilson, Puzzle Publishing, P.O. Box 230023, Portland, OR 97281-0023.

Library of Congress Cataloging-in-Publication Data

Wilson, Katharina, 1960-
The Alien Jigsaw / Katharina Wilson; introduction by Budd Hopkins

Includes illustrations, bibliography and index.

ISBN 0-9639916-0-4: $24.95

Library of Congress Catalog Card Number 93-94321

First Edition: 1994

Printed in the United States of America

Cover Design: Katharina Wilson

Dedication

This book is dedicated to my loving husband.
If not for your love and support
this book could have never been written.
Thank you for believing in me.

Table of Contents

Dedication 5
Table of Contents 7
Introduction 9
Preface 15
Prologue 17
Acknowledgments 19
Childhood Experiences 21
The Sighting 29
The Loss 33
The Awakening 41
Regressive Hypnosis 59
Visions of the Future? 77
Theatrics and Hints of The Government 103
They Repaired My Heart 127
Teacher or Student? 145
New Beings and Another Military Base 177
1992: The Year of The Government 205
It Continues 237
The Guys 271
Why Are They Here? 279
Government Agencies,
the Military, and the Aliens 283
Earth Changes 287
So You Think You're More Aware? 289
Epilogue 291
Correspondence 295
Notes 297
Appendix A 299
Appendix B 303
Appendix C 305
References 307
Index 3

Introduction

by Budd Hopkins

Over the past eighteen years I've worked intensively with many hundreds of people who have described to me their bizarre experiences with the occupants of UFOs. I've received letters and phone calls from thousands more, and have interviewed abductees in places as far from my native New York as Rio de Janeiro and Brisbane, Australia. During these years of travel and research I've sensed, in those reporting such encounters, an enormous degree of pain and confusion and terror. For the most part, the nature of my work cannot be characterized as happy, though it is always deeply rewarding to provide support and understanding and some degree of healing for a suffering fellow human being.

But one of the distinct advantages I've found in doing this kind of work is my vivid awareness of the extraordinary bravery, intelligence and strength possessed by so very many abductees. Despite their harrowing, lifelong UFO experiences, most retain their optimism, their resilience, and even their sense of humor. Simply said, over these long years I've met many beautiful souls. If the aliens are, as I suspect, attempting to bolster their apparently anemic emotional and spiritual resources by studying those qualities in the men and women they abduct, they're doing at least something right.

Katharina Wilson, embodying as she does a powerful morality, a natural wisdom and a deeply human spirituality, provides an ideal example for her student captors. If the aliens can learn from any of us, what they can learn from Katharina is of the highest importance. Anyone lucky enough to know her or to read her book will know exactly what I mean.

I first met Katharina in April, 1988, as she describes in her Chapter Four, "The Awakening." My first impression was of a very lovely, shy and gentle young woman who radiated feelings of vulnerability and warmth. As we talked it became evident to me that she had been deeply hurt by something in her life—perhaps by several somethings—and that the process of healing would be anything but instantaneous. But I also realized that she had an enormous advantage in that Erik, her husband-to-be, was completely supportive of her desire to explore her experiences, no matter where they led. A steady support-system at home is one of an abductee's most important assets, and Erik's love for her has obviously been deeply sustaining.

The proof of the huge distance Katharina has traveled between then and now can be easily demonstrated. The strong, forthright woman she has become, the clear-hearted writer who faces the world and fearlessly tells her complex, painful story, is light years away from the shy young woman I met nearly six years ago. At some point during that first meeting she nervously handed me two sheets of paper; on one she had listed what she labeled her "Good" qualities and situations, and on the other, her "Bad." Knowing that the UFO abduction experience tends to engender a low self-esteem, I was not surprised that such a bright and beautiful young woman would present such a sad self-evaluation. Her words form a near-perfect picture of the typical abductee personality. First, printed in a neat and careful hand, Katharina listed her "negative" qualities:

Anxious
Ashamed
Afraid to be alone at night—uneasy during the day
Constantly checking doors to make sure they are locked
Distrustful of most everyone I know
Energetic and excited one moment and fatigued and hopeless the next
Depressed easily by certain things—the treatment of animals mostly
Always feel I'm being watched
Whenever I have to go out of the house I'm afraid to leave for fear something terrible will happen to my cats. (I still check a lot.)
Whenever I'm away I always feel like I need to hurry up and get home.
I hardly ever remember my dreams anymore
Always feel the need to "save" or to take care of animals, whether they are mine, someone else's, or wild—especially abandoned or wild.
Can't deal with children—feel very uncomfortable around them.
I'm impatient.

Revealing as this "negative" list may be, Katharina's list of "Good" features also demonstrates problems of self esteem in her insistent modesty and in her tendency to ascribe her own good features to others. Her shorter and not entirely "positive" list goes as follows:

Basically healthy (except for migraines, anxiety, tension).
Erik—wonderful
Cats—wonderful
I have a job—I don't "love it" but at least I'm fortunate enough to be gaining work experience.
I love animals, nature
I'm sensitive
I no longer contribute to the mass murder of animals by eating meat—
I do steal from them by eating cheese and eggs and by drinking milk. (I still eat seafood)
I try to be nice and considerate of others
Basically content with my physical appearance—could trim up a little.

> I'm creative
> I try to be open-minded

This was Katharina Wilson in the spring of 1988, at the very beginning of a long, complex, unsettling voyage of exploration. The history of that voyage and what led up to it is the subject of this courageous book.

But before leaving this illuminating list of personal strengths and weaknesses, I would like to mention one theme which seems to be of particular importance: the author's concern for the welfare of animals. In fact, she devotes a great deal of attention to this subject in *The Alien Jigsaw*, and is currently caring for many stray cats and a dog at her Portland home. Over the years, I have found that many abductees seem to feel an unusually strong sense of identification with animals, and with their own pets—dogs and cats—in particular. One woman told me that she never left the house without first hiring a baby-sitter for her two dogs, a Beagle and a terrier of some kind. When I asked why she felt this highly unusual need, she answered that she was always afraid something dreadful would happen to her dogs if they were left alone in the house. "I was terrified that someone would break in and carry them off." For abductees, the issue seems to be primarily one of projection; having been taken oneself, one fears the pets will be taken too. As Katharina wrote in her list, she is afraid to leave the house "for fear something terrible will happen to my cats." Another abductee told me that the sight of his dog being inoculated on the veterinarian's metal table brought back the image of himself lying helpless on just such a cold surface inside a UFO; the sudden memory brought him to the edge of tears. It might be said that only someone who has experienced complete physical subjugation at the hands of a "stronger species" can fully imagine and identify with the powerlessness of a dog or cat at the hands of a human being. Ironically, abductees may therefore be the most caring pet owners of all in our traditionally pet-loving land.

Many of the memories, dreams, abduction experiences and speculative ideas which Katharina presents in *The Alien Jigsaw* will be familiar to those acquainted with the UFO abduction literature, but some will be quite unfamiliar. One such experience is the subject of Chapter Three, titled "The Loss." It has to do with Katharina's sudden inability to perform musically after having devoted eight years to the study of wind instruments. She describes what she sees as the direct, unexpected and unwanted result of a UFO experience in this way: "Something had happened to me. The bright yellow light did something to me. It seemed as though a part of my life had ended, but I could not bring myself to believe it or accept it...I started practicing in my room instead of the music school because I didn't want anyone to hear how bad I sounded...The abrupt change of direction with my music career had repercussions that extended into what I believed I could and could not accomplish in my life...[it made] my confidence dwindle. I cannot imagine that these Beings understand the pain they cause in people's lives."

Katharina goes on to relate that after she had told me about her sudden loss of musical skill, I told her of a very similar case in which a young woman with a promising career in popular music suddenly lost her ability to sing after a UFO encounter. These kinds of experiences are not known to the general public and we can be thankful that they are apparently rare; in fact, I'm quite sure that such abduction sequelae are being discussed in print here for the first time in *The Alien Jigsaw*.

I'm aware of only a handful of such cases, incidents which suggest a long-term alien control over the lives and careers of certain people, the purpose of which is unknown. The reason I've never presented this type of report is simple: The problems abduction experiencers routinely face are difficult at best, so I've felt no need to add to their burden of fear by suggesting still other—rarer—patterns of disturbing alien activity. And yet, because Katharina has fully and openly described her musical loss in *The Alien Jigsaw*, some readers may find both relief and answers to old and deeply personal mysteries. Truth, no matter how unsettling, always contains the seeds of its own resolution.

Many things Katharina Wilson recounts in *The Alien Jigsaw* are controversial and readers will not necessarily agree about the meaning of all that she presents. But virtually all abductees and UFO researchers will recognize in her account the complex textures and emotions of the abduction experience, rendered with clarity and truth. There are open questions and unsettled feelings, however, which will always be endemic to this kind of many-leveled encounter: What is literally real and happening in our hard-edged world? What is a dream? What is a mixed experience, a blend of dream-like metaphor and hard-surfaced reality? What is basically an alien-staged or alien-imposed image, a false picture designed to elicit emotion through imitation of the literal, the actual? When do Katharina's own hopes and fears color her memories and subtly alter their content? Is there a government agency playing mind-games with hapless abductees for some nefarious purpose? Are the aliens actually involved with a government agency, or are they merely simulating such a connection to further some study or experiment?

Each of us will have to decide these things individually as we read this fascinating and deeply honest book. But what we can easily agree upon is the warmth and sincerity of its author and the authenticity of her feelings. That Katharina Wilson has suffered at the hands of the aliens, no one can doubt. That she has grown spiritually and emotionally in the years since she first began to explore her experiences is also self-evident. Is that growth, as some would say, a gift to her from the aliens, as if she were an empty vessel into which they have poured wisdom and strength? Perhaps, but I incline far more fervently to the idea that her growth is the result of her own reactions to the troubling UFO experiences she's known since childhood. Her resourcefulness has been able to flourish partly because of the support she's received from her loving husband, from her family, friends and many in the UFO research community, a fact she generously acknowledges in these pages.

The Alien Jigsaw is written with unadorned simplicity. The author's calm and modest voice is one that we immediately and intuitively accept as authoritative. We are fortunate, too, in that Katharina Wilson is able to create drawings which clearly and dramatically illustrate her UFO abductions. Though her experiences with non-human intelligences are vividly presented in words and pictures, for me the most personally rewarding aspect of her book has to do with its remarkable author. I cannot help but remember this frightened young woman I met in the spring of 1988, and marvel at the heroine she has become.

Budd Hopkins, New York, December 1993.

Preface

The decision to write this book did not come easily for me. I am a very private person, and I value my privacy, as well as my family's, very much. In 1989 a MUFON investigator made a suggestion that I write a book. I was told I would be a good candidate because I had kept excellent documentation of my experiences and my case had been thoroughly investigated by a Ph.D. psychologist and a MUFON investigator. I was quite surprised that someone would suggest the idea of writing a book about my abduction experiences, and at that time, I decided against it. Three years later and three thousand miles away, another MUFON investigator made a suggestion that I write a book about my experiences. We were having a conversation about how some of my experiences did not fit what had become accepted as the standard abduction scenario. Although several excellent books had been published on the abduction phenomenon, I seemed to be remembering events that had not been included in published case histories of mainstream UFO abductees. These memories left me feeling somewhat alienated.

Documentation of my abduction experiences spans several years. In 1988 I began meeting with other people claiming to be abductees or experiencers. In 1991 I began hosting abductee support group meetings and it was during this stage of my life that I realized there were other individuals who felt the same way I did. In 1992, and for the first time during my personal investigation, I felt that writing a book about my experiences was the next logical step to take. My intent is to share all of the information I have pertaining to a phenomenon that has touched the lives of many people. I am telling my story for myself and the many other abductees like me.

The terms "abductee" and "experiencer" are often used to describe individuals who have had abduction experiences. I have had both positive encounters and negative encounters, and I have chosen to use the term "abductee" to describe myself, because it is the most commonly used word in the UFO literature to date.

The terms "UFO," "alien craft," and "spacecraft" are used interchangeably in this text. I am not implying they are the same, nor is it my intention to imply all UFOs are alien crafts that come from outer space. It is generally accepted by ufologists and abduction researchers that we do not know where the alien Beings or their unusual crafts come from. In addition, I believe they should remain defined as aerial vehicles under intelligent control and of unknown origin.

It is not my intention to imply the alien Beings are somehow less than humans, or to suggest any other negative connotation by my use of the term "alien." I view the Beings who have interacted with me as not being from here. The term "here" represents this planet, this time-line, this reality, or this dimension.

I have chosen to capitalize the word "Being" to indicate that I am speaking about an alien. I have also chosen to capitalize the specific types of aliens to aid the reader in recognizing these Beings.

Two final notes to the reader: A double-space in a journal entry indicates a pause or a lapse in time, and the letter "I" followed by a number in parentheses "(I-34)" denotes the illustration of the Being or craft I am referring to.

Prologue

Most UFO abduction investigators suspect a person of having undergone an alien abduction after a certain number of unusual experiences have occurred. Research by Budd Hopkins and David Jacobs has determined that there are five key unusual experiences that indicate whether a person may have been abducted. These five indicators are: "(1) Waking up paralyzed with a sense of a strange person or presence or something else in the room, (2) Feeling that you were actually flying through the air although you didn't know why or how, (3) Experiencing a period of time of an hour of more, in which you were apparently lost, but you could not remember why, or where you had been, (4) Seeing unusual lights or balls of light in a room without knowing what was causing them, or where they came from, (5) Finding puzzling scars on your body and neither you nor anyone else remembering how you received them or where you got them." [1]

Although abduction research has shown how important these five indicators are, they should not be the only criteria used when determining whether an individual is an abductee or not. There are many other factors to take into consideration, such as the results of a complete psychological examination, in-depth interviewing, and other anomalous occurrences.

My grandmother was fascinated with dreams and their possible meanings, and when I was a young teenager, she encouraged me to keep a dream journal. It was not until I was twenty-three years old that I began this journal. Initially I used my journal to simply write down my dreams, but it soon became a tool for self exploration and a friend to me. I began writing down my dreams and would follow them up with what was happening in my life and how I felt about it. I also began recording unusually vivid dreams I had had as a young child. These dreams seemed to be so vivid that even after almost twenty years, they felt as if they had occurred only yesterday. It seemed to me that writing these experiences down was a natural step to take. I believed it would help me lessen the vividness of the experience by getting the memories out of my mind and onto the paper. My journal came to be my silent, and therefore, most trusted, companion.

To understand my story, you need to know that my journal contains "dreams" that have many of the hallmarks of ordinary conscious reality. So much so that they really lie part way between ordinary dreams and ordinary reality. If I could describe them using one idea it would be this: Imagine, if you can, going to bed at night and falling off to sleep. And, although you don't remember how you got there, you find yourself in a different location and you are experiencing the most unusual events. You are aware you are no longer asleep in your bed, and you are also aware that the Being you are looking at is not human.

When I record a memory, I usually write in the first person. I do this because it is extremely difficult, if not impossible, for me to remember what happened to me without reliving the experience. It is a very draining procedure to endure, but nevertheless, it is the way the memories of such unusual encounters seem to flow forth. My journal entries appear in italics and are recorded verbatim except for very minor edits for clarity.

The events contained in this book are the memories of a psychologically stable and mature woman. I have undergone a brain CAT scan independent of any UFO investigation, and during a MUFON investigation of my UFO experiences, a CAT scan of my sinus cavity was performed. I have also undergone extensive psychological examination and investigation. I was diagnosed as a normally functioning adult according to these psychological testing procedures. These are the same tests that mental health professionals use in the day-to-day evaluation of the population at large. I believe the incidents contained in these journal entries are best interpreted as real events. This is a true story.

Acknowledgments

I have many friends to thank for providing me the encouragement and support that I needed in order to write this book. First and foremost, I would like to give special thanks to my loving husband and best friend. He has always taken the time to listen to me, has always supported me, and loved me unconditionally. I extend a very special thanks to Budd Hopkins for his support and his many years of friendship. If not for his enduring drive for the truth and his dedication to helping others, there would not have been a place for this book in our society. My special thanks also go to the MUFON investigator of my case, Vicki Lyons, for her friendship, perseverance, confidentiality, and her help in editing the manuscript. My sincere thanks also go to Keith Rowell for his many useful suggestions and the long hours he took away from his family to edit the manuscript. I wish to thank Boots Eckert, Art and Mary Hufford, Bruce and Anne Morrison, Donald Ware, Patti Weatherford, Larry and Bobbie Hutchison, and Leah Haley for their friendship and enthusiasm. I would like to thank all of the abductees and experiencers who have been incredibly brave and have told their stories or allowed their stories to be told by others. You have helped pave the way for many others sure to follow.

I must also express my gratitude to my parents. Even though my beliefs and life experiences are different from what society considers to be mainstream, you have always shown me unconditional love. Thank you for teaching me to have the integrity and perseverance to stand up for what I believe.

CHAPTER 1

Childhood Experiences

I was born in a small college town in the deep south in 1960, and I became the middle child of what would eventually be a family of five. I feel very fortunate that I had the security and comfort of a loving, stable, and nonviolent family. Although we were not rich by any means, we never went without any of our basic needs being met. All three children received college degrees, married, and are working professionals.

Although sexual or physical abuse during childhood can sometimes remain hidden, I am quite certain there has never been any incidence of childhood (or adult) sexual abuse or any other type of violence within our family. Only now, in light of the number of reported cases of child abuse occurring across our country, am I truly understanding just how fortunate we really were.

I was still living in this small college town when I was about six years old. We lived in a comfortable, middle-class neighborhood. This is where I was living when my brother was born and when the astronauts first landed on the moon. This is also where I was living when I had my first conscious memory of a very unusual event.

During this period my mother always made me go to bed an hour or more before my older sister. It didn't matter how much I pleaded and begged, my sister was three and a half years older and that meant she could stay up longer than I. This was one of the most miserable episodes of my childhood, having to go to bed alone, without my big sister there beside me to make me feel secure.

After several months of personal investigation into the abduction phenomenon, I discovered that many abductees have an unexplained and intense fear of the dark. The following journal entry is a memory from 1967 when I was six years old, and is my earliest conscious memory of feeling as though I were flying through the air. It is also an early example of another extremely prevalent occurrence reported by abductees in many different countries: telepathic communication. This is a fully conscious memory. Although hypnosis was used some twenty-two years later to try to find out what happened, it was unsuccessful at uncovering any new information.

1967

> *I'm scared to death to be in this room alone. I don't understand why I have to go to bed alone—why I have to be first. My flashlight. I can't*

let Mamma know I have it because I'll get into big trouble. I have to get all of the way under the covers—I'm getting into bed—and I have my flashlight. The covers are over my head. I'm shaking with fear. I'm peeking out to see if they are in my room. I'm shining the light frantically around the room. Nothing. I'm back under the covers. I'm so afraid.

Now I'm on my back and I just woke up. My sister is next to me and she is still asleep. I'm looking up at a big piece of chocolate cake. This is great! Chocolate! It's floating above me on a plate! I really want to eat it. I'm lifting myself up—I'm reaching out to it. I'm going to grab it and eat it—Ummph! It's gone! It disappeared. I never get to eat the chocolate cake. I'm angry. Why won't they let me have it? It's never real. I'm going back to sleep.

Now I have that feeling. I know exactly what is going to happen next. It always happens the same way. I'm not afraid. I really like this. I know where I'm going—I'm going to visit God.

I'm flying. I see dark brown gravel. I must be flying over a gravel road. I don't know where I am but I'm not afraid. This always happens the same way.

Now I'm floating and I can hear God's voice. He's talking to me again. I hear his big mechanical voice inside my head. I'm floating toward him. I don't have any clothes on and I'm floating. I remember screaming not too long ago but there was no sound to my voice. I felt myself scream but nothing came out. Now I'm floating over some type of floor that is not solid. It looks like a metal grid. There are big fat cables with oval-shaped objects on the ends of them. I'm definitely with God. This is the place I always come to when he wants to talk to me. The things on the ends of the big cables look like my wooden beads I play with except that they're all shaped the same. Big, giant, oval-shaped pods on the ends of big, giant cables. I don't really mind being here except that I can't move. I'm floating through the air, but I can't move. My throat and chest feel tight. I'm confused a little because as soon as God talks to me I forget what he says. I wish he wouldn't do that. He always talks to me and then makes me forget. (I-3)

At the beginning of this encounter I felt a presence in the room. I had my flashlight, and I was going to see what it was that was about to *get* me. The fear I felt was uncontrollable. The cake was an obvious illusion or possibly even a holographic image, probably created and designed to have me focus my attention on a pleasant stimulus. Chocolate was an exceptional, positive stimulus for me because it was my favorite flavor as a child. This visual image had the effect of not only calming me, but it also made me fix my attention on the piece of cake. I seemed to know at some level that I could not have the cake, but I tried to grab it nevertheless. It was, in fact, always the same. Never did I reach out and actually get to taste, or even touch, a piece of cake.

Today, I do not believe this was actually God talking to me. This was most likely a very early experience of telepathic communication from another Being. I was floating. I was naked. I had a feeling of paralysis and I remembered having screamed, but not having heard any sound from my voice. This type of encounter happened to me many times and although I cannot say exactly how many times it occurred in my young life, it was often enough that I came to know what to expect. I can still feel the sensation of having my little, naked body, floating in thin air. I know what the sensation of paralysis feels like when you scream and scream and nothing comes out of your larynx. I know the frustration of being given a telepathic message, of having a voice inside your head that you are incapable of blocking out, only to be followed by an immediate inability to remember what the message was.

I believe I was inside a very large structure that had a metal grid floor. There were large cables carrying pods, much larger than I was, and the only association I could make with them was to my wooden beads I played with. The two things that I feel these pods could have been were either small crafts being transported within this huge structure I was in, or some kind of pod that carried Beings from one place to another. Of course, there are other possibilities.

From as far back as I can remember, I was a serious child feeling as if I had a very important mission. If I were to have a child today and know she was experiencing the inner thoughts and emotions that I experienced as a six year old, I would be absolutely crushed. While outside, I would often stare up into the sky and have mental conversations with God and sing him songs. From the age of six on, I knew I was here for an important purpose, and I knew I was not here to have children, or a family, or to gain wealth, fame, or fortune. I had a feeling that there was something I had to do that was more important than anything else in the world, and it surpassed every career and lifestyle choice in our society. I would end up suppressing these feelings for almost twenty-five years. I would be several years into my personal investigation of my abduction experiences before I could consciously accept that the interaction I was having with the Beings was what I had been feeling I had to do since I was six years old.

Another strange occurrence that seems indicative to me of abduction experiences seemed to revolve around my Brownie Scout meetings. I was about seven years old. In order to get home from school, my sister and I had to walk by the church where our scout meetings were held. On more occasions than I care to remember, because I always got punished afterwards, I would decide not to go to my Brownie meeting.

What was so unusual about my behavior was knowing I would be punished for skipping my meeting, and once inside the house alone, knowing I would be absolutely terrified because no one would be at home. This fear was just as intense as having to go to bed alone at night for that hour or so before my sister came to bed. One of my most vivid memories after entering the house was having to sit at the table for what seemed like an eternity while waiting for my mother to return. This was totally illogical. Why would I skip a Brownie meeting so I would have to sit terrified and alone in the house, while I waited for my mother to return home just so I could be punished? I would have rather been almost anywhere than in that house alone.

{In 1988, Budd Hopkins performed a hypnotic regression on me concerning this. We learned that I felt as if I should not be at the church, but instead should go straight home. Nothing astonishing was revealed; however, my memories of these events were much more salient than before the hypnosis session.}

The usual scenario after I got home was as follows: I would put my books on the kitchen table, and then suddenly I would hear a shuffling sound and a low sound like a closet door slowly rolling closed. I would become terrified and would stand for a moment next to the table while trying to decide what to do next. Since I had such a long walk home, I invariably had to use the bathroom, but I didn't dare go down the hallway to the first door on the right to use the bathroom. "They" were in the house. At this point I would slowly and cautiously move toward the record player and play the same album every time, an album of Strauss waltzes. I would run back to the table and listen to the music while it, hopefully, drowned out the strange sounds in the house. Then I would, for some reason, seem to fall asleep at the table, only to be awakened by my mother shouting at me.

> "What are you doing home and how could you have forgotten your meeting?"
> "I don't know Mamma, I just did. I forgot to go."
> "How could you forget to go to your Brownie meeting with your uniform on?"
> "I don't know. I don't know!"
> "But you have to walk by the church in order to get home!"

Although these discussions always brought me out of my sleeping rather quickly, I was always left feeling very groggy. I have no idea how much time elapsed, but the album was always finished playing by the time she awakened me.

My seventh year of life was unusual in another way. I began going through puberty. I developed a very bad case of acne that required me to go to a dermatologist twice a week. My body was apparently going through some kind of change and I know my mother was very concerned and confused. Nevertheless, by the age of seven, I was seeing a dermatologist twice a week. This, of course, was followed by the natural progression of puberty: oily skin and hair, breast development at nine years, and menstruation at eleven years. My childhood was over.

Anyone who understands the basics of adolescent psychology and physiology knows that these early pubertal changes are not unheard of. However, for many of the women who were successful at forgetting what this "hormonal warfare" was like, the following passage represents a good review of a point I'm trying to make: "Menarche, the beginning of menstruation, is a relatively late development in the sexual maturation of girls. Hence, it is incorrect to use menarche as a marker for the onset of puberty among girls. A great deal of pubertal development has taken place long before the adolescent girl begins to menstruate. Regular ovulation, and therefore full reproductive function, follows menarche by two years."[2] Even when taking into consideration that the onset of puberty can occur as early as eight years, and as late as thirteen years in girls, I seemed to be pushing the lower limits by a solid year. This may, or may not, prove to be significant as further research is conducted, but another interesting thing occurred during this time. It also appeared I had an understanding of adult sexual behavior by the age of seven.

One afternoon I told another child that I knew all about sex and how "it" was done. Somehow, I knew how two people "did it." When my mother found out, she spent the next hour trying to pump me for what "it" meant. I remember crying because I wasn't supposed to tell her. No one, well, no human being had ever explained sex to me. I had never seen anyone "do it," and my sister who was ten years old, and my brother who was four years old certainly didn't tell me. My parents never talked about sex to me or around me. It was just something I *knew* about, and it was as if it dropped out of the sky one day and into my brain. The saddest thing of all was I somehow believed I would actually die if I told her or anyone else I knew how a man and a woman "did it." After about an hour of crying and believing I would die if I told her, I relented. I'll never forget her gasping and getting up and walking out of the room without saying a word. To say I was relieved is an understatement. I had *survived*. I was sure that I would die if I ever told anyone about "it," and she didn't even get mad at me. Certainly she was confused, but she was not angry with me. I had yet to realize a turning point was approaching in my life. My "sex education" didn't occur until many years later.

Today, although many will believe this is utterly impossible, I believe I learned this information from the alien Beings I had contact with. I also believe my interactions with them may have accelerated my puberty. The reasons for my believing this will be evident as you continue to read my story.

I alternated between being an excessively serious child and being a child full of mirth. Oftentimes I contemplated adult themes. When I was in the third grade, I began to focus my attention on world pollution. I did a third grade project on the subject, and would often lecture my young friends about how bad it was to litter. It was a source of anger in my young life. I continuously wondered how and why adults could pollute our world. It was inconceivable to me.

We moved to Pensacola, Florida, when I was nine years old, and it was in the front yard of our new house that I met Sandra. We became best friends. However, it was within this house that I remember something else occurring that points in the direction of abduction experiences.

My sister and I were still sharing a bedroom, but we had separate beds now. On several occasions, I remember waking up in the middle of the night in a totally reversed position with my feet where my head should have been, and my head where my feet should have been. I would often be so groggy the next morning that I could barely walk into the bathroom. Then, for some unknown reason I would throw my underwear away, only to come back into the bathroom a little while later, see them in the waste basket, and quickly take them out. Again, for some unknown reason, I would squeeze tooth paste out onto my hands and wash my hands with it! It was as if I wasn't totally conscious of what I was doing. I was very confused and embarrassed after I would realize what I had done.

Another behavior that has surfaced in much of the abduction research is a fear, unexplained discomfort, or even dislike of babies. It appears that experiences with babies are the core of many abductees' encounters.

I began baby-sitting to earn money when I was eleven. I never had an experience during which any of the children were ever injured or where any other unpleasant experience occurred. I only knew that for some reason, I could never trust children, especially babies. To me, babies seemed to be the most deceitful little things on the planet. I didn't dislike them, I just knew I couldn't trust them. I felt extremely uncomfortable with babies until I was twenty-eight years old and my nephew was born. That important event, coupled with the fact that I was aware of my abduction experiences, helped me overcome that extremely uncomfortable feeling I had when I was around babies.

When I was thirteen years old, something happened to me, and I firmly believe the turning point had been reached. I do not know what prompted my behavior, but I became extremely agitated and I walked outside, down the driveway, and told my sister, "When I get old enough, hopefully in a few years, I'm going to have everything removed from me. I'm going to have it all taken out." I was referring to all of my reproductive organs. She told me she didn't think I was old enough to make that kind of decision, and I remember becoming angry. Suddenly, I could hardly stand my body.

Ever since I began menstruating at the age of eleven, I was regular, every twenty-eight days. However, when I was thirteen years old, I began menstruating irregularly, almost every two and one-half weeks. It was crazy. My mother decided to take me to a gynecologist. My mother stayed in the corner of the examination room by the door while he examined me. My mother was more than a little over-protective of me. The first thing this doctor asked me while he was examining me was, "Have you ever been pregnant?" Before I could say "no" my mother had already answered for me, and it was a quite stern, "NO." The doctor didn't say much after that and continued to examine me. Afterward, the doctor told me I had a cyst on my left ovary and my right ovary was infected. He said that was why I was menstruating so often. I think I got a prescription for some pills, and that was that. He never told us how or why the infections occurred. However, for the next fifteen years, each time I went to a gynecologist, during the examination I would be asked if I had ever been pregnant. Later, after I began remembering my abduction experiences, I started questioning other women and nurses, and found that the pregnancy question wasn't normally asked *during* an examination. Today, I often wonder why a doctor would ask me this unless they were seeing something unusual that would prompt this question. What is most confusing to me today is why I never questioned the doctors about this.

I believe it would be prudent at this juncture to say that I have never had an abortion. Answering the question, "Have you ever been pregnant?" is much more difficult, and as this story unfolds I believe it will be equally as difficult for the reader to make this determination as well.

This change in my feelings about my body and the physical problems I was having occurred two years after I began menstruating. As research indicates, this is the year I had reached full reproductive functioning. Today, I strongly believe the alien Beings removed something from my ovaries that created the cyst on my left ovary and the infection in my right ovary.

CHAPTER 2

The Sighting

One summer night in 1976, when I was sixteen years old, I was baby-sitting at the end of our street for the Donleys. They came home around midnight. Although the Donleys only lived one block away from us, my mother never allowed us to be outside walking around at night. We walked toward the front door so Mr. Donley could drive me home. The moment the door opened and we stepped outside, we saw two dark helicopters with huge spotlights shining down. The pilots were shining them on the ground and then into the air as if they were looking for someone. They were heading east, and they were flying much lower than I had ever seen a helicopter fly before. Somehow, I instantly knew they were looking for "them." I saw "them" almost immediately. Three objects, with bright lights, high in the southern sky. Mr. Donley saw them too and I will never forget the look on his face. It was a look of disbelief, fear, and shock. He asked me what they were but I didn't even answer him. All I could think about was getting home so I could get a better look at them. It seemed like an eternity before we reached my house. Mr. Donley gave me some money for baby-sitting, and I got out of the car as quickly as I could. I remember seeing him looking up at the lighted objects while he drove, very slowly, back toward his house.

I was captivated with what I was looking at, and somehow I knew exactly what it was. Even at the age of sixteen, I knew they were alien. There were three intensely lit, bright white objects in the sky. And standing there in our cul-de-sac were several children I baby-sat for sometimes. I thought it was unusual that these children were outside so late at night. We all watched the three crafts hover for about ten minutes. Then I ran into the house, grabbed my telescope, and told my entire family. I pleaded with my father to come outside and look, but for some odd reason, he calmly looked at me and said, "I know you think you are seeing something, but I know it isn't real."

My father then went back to his reading. His behavior was perplexing to me. I couldn't believe he wasn't interested in seeing the lighted objects in the sky. I ran back outside. Only my mother came out with me at that time, but I remember my brother being with us some time later.

I watched the three lighted objects hover with my little telescope. I realized they were spacecrafts and they looked identical to one another. They were silver and hamburger-shaped with a row of red, blue, and yellow lights moving around their midsections. They were hovering in a triangle formation approximately forty to forty-five degrees up from the horizon in the southern sky. Then the craft on the top of the triangle and the craft on the left of the triangle began to move in a way that was totally different from anything I had ever seen before. They moved very smoothly and quietly. Then suddenly, these two crafts made right angle turns, shot off like arrows, and "blinked out." The third craft remained, and I watched it through my telescope while it moved slowly toward the west. (I-42) The entire sighting lasted about forty-five minutes. I was so happy to have seen what I knew had existed for so long.

What I have just described is what I call an "awakening." I believe it was time for me to see them in a fully conscious state. I also believe they had their own reasons for *allowing* me and the other children in our cul-de-sac to see them. I do not believe there was anything accidental about this event. I know too many credible abductees who have had a sighting of an unusual looking craft, only to discover they were the only person to see the craft in the sky. Sometimes, the vastness of size and the obviousness of the event make it unlikely that only one person, or one family would have been the only witnesses. I firmly believe these types of sightings are either "performed" for the witness or abductee, or the abductee is attuned to a level of "sensitivity" that most other people are not. There is no doubt in my mind that it was their intention that I see them at that particular time. The words that best describe what I was feeling while viewing these three crafts were *familiarity* and *confirmation*.

The following day I went to school and began telling all of my friends what I had seen the night before. After all, I thought the entire world had been changed. Certainly everyone in Pensacola must have seen these incredible UFOs in the sky. They were bright, high in the sky, and obvious. There I was, "sweet sixteen," a year I shall always remember because it was the year I saw "them." Unfortunately, my excitement was quickly extinguished after telling several of my friends in school the following day. They were either very quiet and felt pity for me, or they outright laughed in my face. Sadly, I shut-up about the UFO sighting and I didn't tell anyone else about it for ten years.

Two years later, in June of 1978, I graduated from high school and went to Europe to visit my mother's family as a graduation gift. It was my second trip overseas. The visit in 1978 was enlightening, but tough. When I returned I began my freshman year at college. I chose to pursue a performance career in music. This turned out to be the beginning of a very humbling year.

At eighteen I experienced my first migraine headache. The pain was so bad I thought I was dying of a brain tumor. I had never experienced even a regular headache in my entire life, and now I was on my way to the hospital. My boy friend was taking me. I was given a shot in the emergency room for the pain and told *not to worry so much* by the doctor. On the way home, I vomited continuously from either the pain, the medication, or both, and eventually passed out.

Music school was tough but I beat the odds, over and over again. Within a year, I was on a partial music scholarship and a partial academic scholarship. Nothing seemed as important, however, as learning how to play the saxophone and making it into one of the elite jazz bands. My sophomore year, I accomplished this, too. I found myself playing and practicing between six to ten hours a day. Since I made one of the jazz bands, I also had to learn how to play the flute. My flute instructor told me I was a "natural." This was also the year my music professor told me he felt I was by far the best clarinetist in the school of music. I was meeting my goals.

The migraines continued to flare up periodically and when I wasn't enduring a migraine I had a low-grade headache twenty-four hours a day. One night in the latter part of March, during my sophomore year, I received a phone call. It was my father. He said, "Sandra is dead."

I will never forget those words. Sandra had been my best friend for eleven years, and now she was gone. Apparently, she decided to stay home after she and her brothers hosted a barbecue with friends. It was exceptionally windy, and the wind blew some hot coals into their garage where her father had over fifty gallons of gasoline stored. The entire house burned down. Sandra and her cat, one we had given her, had died. She was buried on her twentieth birthday. Sandra's death hit me very hard.

Shortly after Sandra's death, there were times when I would be practicing that I would receive a very strong impression I was being watched. It would overwhelm me, and I would have to leave the practice room and find another one. It was a very uncanny feeling. Sometimes I would leave the music building all together. I felt as if someone was watching me and I was terrified.

Much time went by and I continued working hard. I usually practiced until one o'clock in the morning, and my day began at five o'clock in the morning. I planned to skip the second semester of my junior year so I could take all of my non-music courses at a local university closer to home. I had just broken up with my boyfriend of almost three years, I had my junior recital to get through, and after that was accomplished, I thought the break away from school, and him, would do me good.

My father drove, and my mother flew up from Pensacola to hear my recital. Shortly after the subsequent celebrations, I packed up my belongings and was on my way home. I remember being with my father in his green, full size pickup truck. We had been driving all day and we were still driving into the early hours of the morning. Our trip was mapped out at almost eight-hundred miles. It's a long drive but it can be made in approximately fifteen to sixteen hours. This is what I remember:

February 1981

We are driving on some back roads because I-65 isn't finished yet. This is always the toughest stretch to drive. The last hour and a half. Suddenly I see fog everywhere. We have gotten into some really heavy fog. It seems to be everywhere. Oh my God! There are deer everywhere! Oh! We almost hit one! My father is driving very slowly and the truck seems to be swaying back and forth in the fog. Somehow we stop. I saw a deer standing on the left hand side of the road. Now I can see one looking at us through the front windshield, and there is another one looking at me through my window. He is very close to the truck. I can see his huge, beautiful black eyes. His head is quite large and he is so beautiful. There is fog—and there are deer—all around us.

We arrived home at about three o'clock in the morning and went straight to bed. I was twenty years old when this experience occurred. Nine years later I realized just how unusual these "deer" really were when I saw an adult deer grazing along the side of I-10 in Florida. This *real* deer had *ears* and it was much shorter than the "deer" I saw looking at me. For some reason, I never considered the possibility that deer had ears. It was then, I realized this real deer did not resemble the "deer" I had seen so many years ago. Today it is clear to me that these were no ordinary deer. It would be impossible for a deer to peer through the front window of a full sized pickup truck without standing on top of the hood and bending down a considerable amount. I feel certain that these deer were really gray, or tan-skinned, large-eyed alien Beings, and they were really floating around or near our truck. After I realized this, I asked my father what he remembered about the trip. He remembered seeing the deer, but unfortunately, that is *all* he remembers.

The idea that alien Beings can somehow make us see them as animals, and make us see other objects that are not really there, is what has been called a "screen memory" by many researchers. I prefer the term "camouflage," but both terms represent similar occurrences. My interpretation is that the aliens appearing as deer represents a form of camouflage. The fog, the swaying of the truck, and any subsequent "implanted" memories are what I call a screen memory. In my interpretation, a screen memory is all-encompassing. On the other hand, camouflage is a technique an alien Being uses to change or distort his physical appearance.

CHAPTER 3

The Loss

Soon after I returned home to Pensacola, I was registered for school again and studying all non-music courses. It was different studying for humanities, math, and philosophy. And the heat...wow! I had forgotten how hot and humid this place was! Whew!

A very strange event occurred to me shortly after I returned home. I was sleeping in my old room. I still had most of my belongings at home since I was moving from house to house each year up at school. One night I was sleeping, and then I remember seeing a very bright yellow light in my room. It was above my head where the ceiling and the wall meet. It was moving along the wall, but for some reason it seemed to stay near the area where the ceiling and the wall come together. I don't remember anything else, other than being terrified. The following day I could not stand the thought of being in my room, and I even left my house because I didn't want to be near it. Although it would take me eleven years to realize it, it would become evident to me that my life had just been manipulated by an alien presence.

My sister had married a couple of years earlier, and she and her husband were living in Milton, Florida where he was attending flight school. I went to visit them after I returned home and discovered an entire new world—Flight School and The Military. I met a man named Mike. He was in a transitional stage in his life and was completing his flight training. Obviously, something about him attracted me to him, but I cannot say what it was even to this day. We became friends.

While we were talking one day, I told Mike about the frightening occurrence involving the bright yellow light. He had recently begun attending a new church, and he wanted me to go with him to a friend's house where they would be having a Bible study group. I was a confirmed Lutheran, but ever since I left for college my family had only been going to church during Christmas. Subsequently, our family was excommunicated from our church for "not giving enough money and nonattendance." I wasn't really keen on going back to church, but I wanted to be with Mike so I went. I was then drawn into the most unusual group of people I have ever met in my life. Because I started going to church with Mike, I became more and more involved with these other people also. One bright, sunny day I decided to accept the Holy Spirit into my life and become a "Born Again" Christian.

It was becoming obvious to me that I needed *divine intervention* in my life. Ever since the bright light appeared in my room shortly after returning home from college in 1981, and scared the hell out of me, I was unable to go near any of my musical instruments. I knew I could not play anymore. Somehow, I knew I could not be a musician. It was an extremely frightening and disturbing realization because I had spent eight years of my life dedicated to becoming a musician. I always knew what it was I wanted to do, and now I realized all of that had somehow changed. Somehow it had been taken away from me. The inner pain I felt at not being able to play, consumed me. Unconsciously, I knew my music career was over, but it would take eleven years for me to understand why, and as of this writing, I am still having a difficult time accepting it.

I walked up to the front of the church with a group of other people who had decided to be saved that Sunday. While all of the ceremonial words were being uttered by the preacher, I noticed people falling down all over the place. Right onto the floor! I bent down to help one lady and Mike said, "No, it's okay."

He kind of smiled down at me. Then I realized just how stupid I was. I stood there feeling totally helpless while people were falling down on the floor and making strange utterances in some language I'd never heard before. I was told later that day that these people were "speaking in tongues." Losing physical control of one's body and falling to the floor was what it was like to be "filled with the Holy Spirit." Since I couldn't "speak in tongues" and I didn't fall to the floor, I obviously wasn't going to be saved that day or, I feared, any other day.

During the short time I was home, the light had returned two more times. I was terrified of it. I continued to go to the meetings for several weeks, and I ended up telling the Bible group about the experiences I had with the bright yellow light in it. This was their explanation: "Satan" was trying to take me away and the light was Jesus trying to protect me. "Well," I thought, "Jesus sure was scaring the hell out of me!" The day the people in this Baptist Bible group decided that my family was not saved, that I should move out of my parent's house, and that I shouldn't complete my education at the university, I became extremely uncomfortable with them. My encounter with the Bible study group and the Baptist church lasted six months. Becoming a "Born Again" Christian did not protect me from the light, nor did it help me regain control over my music career. That experience, coupled with our family being excommunicated from the Lutheran church, left me with extreme doubts about my need for organized religion.

I continued with classes at the local university and visited my sister in Milton from time to time. It was there that I met my first husband, Mark. He was a second lieutenant in the Marine Corps. While I continued my studies at the university, Mark and I saw each other on the weekends. I was twenty-one and knew absolutely nothing about military life, but I did know one thing, I was in love.

Finally the time came for me to go back to the university to finish my last year of music school. This was during the Fall of 1981. It was the hardest thing I have ever done. Something had happened to me. The bright yellow light did something to me. It seemed as though a part of my life had ended, but I could not bring myself to believe it, or accept it. I forced myself to play, even though it was sometimes impossible. I started practicing in my room instead of the music school because I didn't want anyone to hear how bad I sounded. My professor was extremely disappointed that my level of playing wasn't up to professional standards anymore. There were times when I did not feel I could go on. However, I continued to force myself to play every day, no matter how difficult it was or how much physical pain I had to endure. I managed to keep my scholarship and I graduated with a 3.5 GPA.

I believe I had three experiences involving the yellow light. There was a presence associated with it, but other than intense fear, I remember nothing else about the experiences involving the light.

Until the experience with the bright yellow light there had never been a time in my life when I doubted myself or my ability to achieve anything. It is not by coincidence that the change in my career coincided with the appearances of the yellow light in my room. Eleven years later a prominent abduction researcher named Budd Hopkins stayed at our house while lecturing in Portland, Oregon. He began questioning me about the sudden change in my career and the experience involving the bright yellow light. After he allowed me to come to my own conclusions about what occurred, I listened and shuddered inside while he explained a similar experience that happened to another abductee he has been working with for several years. He told me about a woman who had a promising career in music. After an abduction experience involving a light, this woman suddenly found she could not sing anymore!

I began to wonder, if this could happen to me and to this other woman, how many other people has this happened to?

The abrupt change of direction with my music career had repercussions that extended into what I believed I could and could not accomplish in my life. My inability to understand the reasons for the sudden change in my career, and subsequently my life, made my confidence dwindle. I cannot imagine that these Beings understand the pain they cause in people's lives. Certainly, they cannot know what it is like to feel this way and to be left for so many years, not knowing.

Mark and I were married in June of 1982. His new orders took us to New River, North Carolina, the air base near Camp LeJeune. We had a new house built not too far from the base, and we settled in after a short honeymoon in New England. Mark wanted to fly jets on the west coast, but instead he got helicopters on the east coast. This was the military. You never get what you want. You like what you get. If you don't, you're going to be miserable. Mark didn't like what he got.

My guilt level was extremely high because I was not pursuing my music career. I decided to compromise by teaching private music lessons. I thought I could play well enough to teach and to demonstrate to my students, even though it bothered me greatly that I could not play as I used to. If that wasn't enough to deal with, something strange began to occur shortly after we moved into our house. I began to experience anxiety before going to bed at night, and while alone in the house during the daytime. My anxieties worsened. It wasn't long before I began checking the front door after Mark would lock it. This would infuriate him, but I just couldn't help myself. For reasons unknown to me, I began to feel unsure about things I never gave a second thought to. I also started checking the stove and oven, and I became more and more protective of my two cats.

The following October, a year and a half after we were married, Mark had to go on "float." That meant his squadron had to ship out for seven months on a Navy vessel. They were on their way to the Middle East by way of the Mediterranean. During the time from approximately two months before Mark left, to the month he returned, I did not menstruate. I didn't know what was going on, but I remember telling Mark about it before he left to go on float. He told me if I was pregnant I would have to have an abortion or he would leave me. Needless to say, I was flabbergasted by his statement, even though at that time I was certain I was not pregnant. I was taking birth control pills, and I *never* forgot one. When I questioned him about his remark, he became furious. He said, "This isn't a discussion. You have two options: an abortion or a divorce."

I countered with, "What about the baby? What about what I'm going to have to endure going through an abortion? Don't you care about those things?"

Again, he angrily stated, "This is not a discussion! You can get an abortion, or a divorce! That's it!"

Shortly before he left, our marriage became more shaky because Mark seemed obsessed with talk about killing. One night while we were in bed he told me he had constant thoughts of killing me. For a moment, I thought of all of the weapons he had around the house, guns and knives mostly. I mentally denied that he would follow through on his threat. I ended up going to sleep without responding to his comment. I had to drive Mark up to Norfolk, Virginia, the following morning because he was to leave out of that port. After we arrived in Norfolk we got into an argument. The night before Mark was to leave he stormed out of our hotel room. We spent our last night apart from one another. The following morning I met him outside on the dock where his ship was in port. He wouldn't even kiss me good-bye. I got a quick hug and a pat, and that was all.

After I returned from Norfolk, Virginia, I was very depressed. It was a four hour drive and I had cried all the way home. I loved Mark, and I already missed him terribly. I remember walking back into the house and feeling a great emptiness inside me. One night, shortly after Mark left, I awakened with a terrible memory. I suddenly became terrified to be alone in our house at night. I began to lock my two cats in the bedroom with me so they would be safe. I began checking the doors and windows periodically. I was afraid of something, or someone from the outside coming into the house. At this time, when I was twenty-three, I began keeping a journal because it gave me someone to "talk" to and I wrote down this memory:

Winter 1983:

> *I'm lying on a table of some kind, and there are two nurses and a doctor around me. I don't really see their faces. Somehow, I've just had a baby. No! No! I can't! I don't want it! They are trying to show me my baby. Somehow I know they are happy for me, and they want me to hold the baby. I'm screaming. No! No! Get it away from me! I don't want to touch it! I don't want to look at it! Get it out!!!*
>
> *They're taking the baby out of the room. I'm crying—I'm hysterical—I'm terrified.*

I found myself in my bed in the middle of the night, unable to sleep and feeling terrified. I was afraid that someone was going to come into our house and assault my cats and me. This fear lingered for several days. I remember calling a friend and telling her about what I remembered. It felt so vivid, and we couldn't determine why I would be remembering something such as this. Even though I felt Mark was being very unreasonable, I never really planned to have children. However, if I had become pregnant, I never would have had an abortion. At the time, the memory was so real I couldn't relate it to my not menstruating. I thought I had stopped menstruating because I was taking the pill, and I read that this occurred to some women who took birth control pills. Then, about three months later, *they* came back. I was shown a baby by a medical team again. It was just as real and just as terrifying.

Ever since these two experiences, I've never felt any house I've lived in was safe. I also have constant, lingering doubts that I'm not going to be able to protect my pets...my family.

In 1988, about five years after this occurred, I told my doctor I was constantly worried about making sure my house was safe. He told me he thought I had a mild case of obsessive-compulsive disorder. I tried hypnosis some time after his diagnosis, and although the Ph.D. psychologist who was working with me at the time felt he had cured me of this disorder, it did little to ease the anxiety, or stop the behavior.

I have met other abductees who have similar fears and anxieties. One man told me he puts furniture in front of his doors and checks his windows at night before he goes to bed. I have spoken with women who put their children in their bedroom with them at night so they can protect them from the Beings. Other abductees have fears about leaving their pets at home when they to go to work. And still another abductee I know is afraid to venture out alone for fear of "getting lost and being forgotten." Probably the saddest situation was a female abductee who moved her children across the United States trying to elude the aliens.

I am not an isolated case, and I certainly empathize with other people who feel this way. We continually feel the need to check even though we know there are no aliens in our houses. We feel responsible for our families and pets, and this is the only way we can gain anything that even remotely resembles control over our lack of knowledge and understanding of our experiences. We can never be quite sure when the next time will come for us. How many times have we asked ourselves, "Is what I'm seeing really there?" Sadly, I can only imagine how many people are suffering from these unusual anxieties and do not even realize they are abduction related. How can our mental health community help alleviate the stress these behaviors cause when they refuse to admit to the reality of the abduction experiences which create the behavior in the first place?

When Mark left, his squadron was going to replace the men who were killed in the bombing of the barracks in Beirut, Lebanon. After they had been in the Atlantic for three days, they received their "other orders." His ship was diverted to Grenada to help rescue American students who had sought refuge at the university. We lost three men in our squadron during that incident.

Mark's request for a divorce came in a letter two weeks after Christmas. I was devastated. I couldn't figure out what I had done wrong. I knew our marriage had some problems, but I was willing to work them out. No one in my family had ever gotten a divorce, so it was never an option in my mind. I stared at the words he had written. He obviously wasn't willing to try anymore. I received many letters over the next several months stating that he was still obsessed with feelings of wanting to kill me and that he still wanted a divorce.

It is important to mention here that although Mark was somewhat manipulative and mentally abusive, he never once harmed me physically. After seven months, Mark finally returned. He was a "self-proclaimed" changed man. He wanted to remain married to me. I had also changed. I had been alone for many months. I had been ostracized by the wives in our squadron because rumors of our divorce came back to the wives by way of Mark's ship. I had come to terms with the idea of divorce. It was very difficult, but I left. I went back to Pensacola with my cats. Our divorce became final a year later. I haven't seen Mark since 1984.

I believe I had two alien encounters during the seven months that Mark was away. Including the two months before Mark left, I went nine months without menstruating. After the second memory of what I believe was an alien medical team trying to show me a baby again, I went to a doctor at the hospital at Camp LeJeune. With much insistence from me, I persuaded the doctor to give me a pregnancy test, the results of which were negative. I thought it was very odd, as did he, to believe I was pregnant, especially since I was taking birth control pills and my husband had been away for several months. Nevertheless, I had a very strong feeling that I was pregnant. Logically, it didn't make any sense.

Today I believe these events and Mark's behavior were engendered by my alien encounters. I am not trying to place blame onto others for my career or marriage failures. I strongly believe my life, my present husband's life, and my ex-husband's life have been manipulated by some of the alien Beings interacting with us. It may have been to separate my ex-husband and me, therefore allowing Erik and me to be together today. Or, it could be something I am totally unaware of. However, the people referenced in this text are certainly not alone when considering this manipulation factor. I have heard similar stories from friends who are also abductees.

CHAPTER 4

The Awakening

After Mark and I separated, I moved back to Pensacola. I took an apartment and began working a temporary job in a bank. After the person I was substituting for returned to work, I went back to school and began working on an MBA degree. I met my present husband, Erik, in a business management class.

It was during this time that my migraine headaches flared up again. I began to think there might be something physically wrong with me again. One afternoon in 1985, during a particularly bad migraine, Erik and my mother decided to take me to a neurologist. He hospitalized me for three days while tests were run on me. I don't remember much about being in the hospital other than the constant, intense pain in my head. A CAT scan was performed and after three days of testing, my headache finally subsided. The neurologist could not detect any abnormalities, and again I was told to *stop worrying so much*.

Shortly after I came home from the hospital, I decided to seek a psychologist's help. I wanted to find out what could be causing my horrendous headaches. For three months we charted everything I did, everything I ate, how I felt on a daily basis, and where I was during my monthly cycle. It was very methodical and I was very honest. I wanted the pain to stop so I could get on with my life. After three months, he determined that I had a serious case of premenstrual syndrome. I was miffed. This certainly took me by surprise. "PMS? Great." I thought, "This sounds like another way to tell me to stop worrying so much."

As miffed as I may have been, this psychologist was kind and understanding, and I believe in some ways he helped me. He taught me certain things I could change with my diet that made me feel better. However, I still continued to have migraine headaches, and I was still filled with anxiety. Interestingly, there was one particular day when I asked this psychologist if he believed in UFOs. The question surprised me almost as much as it surprised him. I had no idea why I would ask him a question such as this at that time, but today it is somewhat obvious to me. He told me he had never seen a UFO nor knew anyone who ever had. I never mentioned the subject of UFOs to him again.

When I think back to this period in my life, the only thing I had ever read about UFOs was an article in our newspaper about Charles Hickson and a fishing buddy named Calvin Parker who were taken on board a UFO in Pascagoula, Mississippi, in 1973. I still didn't believe it really happened.

Extraterrestrials and UFOs were not something I spent time thinking about. I had not spoken about the three UFOs I saw since my friends at school embarrassed me into silence back in 1976. By this time, nine years had passed since that unbelievable sighting of the three hamburger-shaped crafts.

Two years after Erik and I met, we moved in together. He had a rental house, and we renovated it together in our spare time between work and school. It was a lot of hard work, but it was fun. It was in this house that my anxieties became the most debilitating.

In 1986, I dropped out of school and started working full time. I was having vivid nightmares, and it seemed I was afraid all of the time. I was so afraid of someone breaking into the house at night that I began propping a chair against the front door. I persuaded Erik to put nails in all of the windows to prevent whatever was outside from getting us.

I also found myself becoming more sensitized to our local domestic animal population problems. I had always loved animals and was always trying to lend a hand whenever I could. I was aware of the cruelty that society was inflicting by its apathy toward unwanted dogs and cats. It seemed as though my need to help became more pronounced in 1985. I joined the local SPCA and humane society and did what little I could do to help in the education process. I rescued two kittens in 1986, and Erik and I now had four cats. We had a kennel built for them and had it attached to our house. This would allow the cats to come in and out freely, but they would still be protected from whatever it was that was *out there*. A short while later, I came across two more kittens in two different circumstances, which we ended up rescuing also. We were working our way toward quite an unusual and large family.

In 1986, I was becoming extremely frustrated with my anxieties and unusual fears. This was prior to having much conscious memory of my alien encounters. Looking back, it seems I was a time bomb ready to explode. I had no idea what was happening to me, but it wouldn't take too much longer for the flame to be found to light the fuse.

One night I woke up from an especially vivid memory. Besides the content of the memory, another aspect was fascinating—I remembered this occurring several times during my childhood. It was so familiar to me that I had to write it down.

1986

> *I'm standing in front of a large building that has many steps leading up to it. In front of these steps is a beautiful fountain with a pool of water around it. As I look into the water, I seem to know what lies within and beyond the water. It is a door, an opening, into another world.*

I'm approaching the pool of water, and I'm looking at some steps that lead down into the water. It is like an underwater staircase. I want to walk down the staircase, but I'm not sure if I can hold my breath long enough to get to the other side. The steps seem to go on forever. Suddenly, I see a figure underwater. It is a male. He is lifting his head out of the water and he is looking up at me. I immediately trust him. He is youthful, like a child, but he is not a child. I'm stepping into the water. I'm going to go down the steps with him—I'm walking down the steps. Something tells me he has webbed feet. He wants me to follow him. He is going to take me somewhere. As I descend into the water, it reaches my face, and I am somewhat hesitant to go under. I hope it is like before—Yes, I can breathe. I inhale a deep breath and I feel more at ease now. I am breathing normally now and I'm underwater. This Being is leading me along some steps underwater. He is moving very gracefully, almost like he his floating. It is not easy for me walk underwater so I have to move slowly.

Suddenly, I am no longer underwater. I'm on another planet! I'm turning around to look at the Being I was underwater with. He is still in the water, and he is looking at me with a very peaceful and loving expression. He cannot come with me. I'm watching him as he disappears into the water.

This place is incredible and very familiar to me. I somehow know the Beings who inhabit this planet are advanced spiritually as well as technologically. Even though it is dark here, it is a beautiful planet. I feel as though I am HOME, and it is such a peaceful feeling. I can see tall structures illuminated in soft white and blue hues. There are vehicles moving gracefully along elevated structures that circle their city.

I am very close to water again. It is another fountain. This fountain is much more modern looking than the fountain I just traveled through. It is large and wide, but shallow. This fountain has beautiful designs on the bottom. The designs appear to be made out of tiles, I think. In some places, the water comes up to my knees, and in other places it only comes up to my ankles. I am looking at the deeper section with the steps again. The Being that brought me here is watching me again. I sense he is happy that I came.

I'm not sure what I am seeing now. My mind tells me something unreal just occurred. Suddenly, I see two male Beings wearing white, but I cannot see their faces. I feel that they are males. I have just noticed several other people here with me. They are all standing in this shallow water with me. They appear to be asleep, but they are still *standing up. They look as though they are hypnotized. The Beings in white are standing in an elevated area of the fountain. It is almost as if they are floating just above the water. They are speaking to us using a medium that I can only describe as telepathy. Although I know I am being given information, it is almost as if it is bypassing my conscious mind and it is being put into my unconscious. I should be able to remember what they are saying immediately after I hear it, but somehow it is lost somewhere in my mind.*

I am suddenly overwhelmed with the feeling that what the Beings have just told me is more important than anything else in my life. I cannot let them down. I'm looking at my sister now. She is standing next to me. I feel that something is coming to an end.

My anxiety level stayed very high, and within another year I began another unusual behavior. I found myself being drawn outdoors at night. Suddenly, for what seemed to me to be for no apparent reason, I was looking for aliens in my backyard! I also found myself looking up into the night sky expecting to see a UFO again. If I had seen aliens, I would not have known what they were supposed to look like. This was the climax. I thought I was going crazy. Shortly after this behavior began, one cold January night, I had an abduction experience.

1-19-87

There is a black square. It appears to be two to three feet square. I'm here in my living room, and I'm receiving some sort of message from this square. I can't actually hear it, but I am receiving a message. It is a telepathic message. I'm terrified. It is reinforcing my fears of having to check and re-check all appliances, doors, and windows in the house. I have some furniture up against the front door. I'm afraid someone or something is going to get in.

Every time I look into this blackness I am more and more afraid and unsure of myself. I know everything is okay. I know the door is secure. I'm looking around. Oh! I'm becoming hysterical with fear! I'm calling out for Erik.

We are outside now, and the front yard looks as if it has been burned— not all of it but some of it. There is frost on the ground around the burned area—I'm looking around—There is also a white car floating over the large arborvitae bush next to our bedroom window. Some supernatural force must be at work here, and this doesn't feel like a positive force either.

I'm outside now on my front porch. Someone is communicating with me. I think they are on my roof. They are telling me that I paid a Tibetan monk to do this to me! I'm very angry now.

The following day after I recorded this I also wrote: "I feel strange energies around me today. I am fighting off fear from this—still."

Today, I believe this was a screen memory. I felt a strong presence in my house. The floating white car next to our bedroom window was probably a screen memory of a craft. I have been forced to ask myself, what could the aliens gain by inducing such strong fears in me? Were they trying to induce an obsessive-compulsive behavior in me? What could the aliens gain by having me suffer from this disorder?

I did have a large wing chair up against the door that night for added protection. The yard was not scorched the following morning, but there was a heavy frost on the ground. I believe it is possible that what occurred to me was a form of conditioning by the Beings. I also believe this type of conditioning may have been performed on me in 1982 after Mark and I moved into our new house in North Carolina when I first began these unusual behaviors.

The morning after this experience I recorded my memory involving the black square, but it was not until five years later, in 1992, that I re-read the journal entry. The implications were astonishing to me because a similar experience would occur yet again, in 1992. Although I no longer put furniture in front of my doors and no longer nail my windows shut, I still do not feel that my husband or my pets are safe in our home. I always feel a constant need to protect them.

Seven months later, the weekend of July 4, 1987, I sat down to read a book. It had taken me half an hour the day before to finally decide to purchase it. After all, I had *never* bought a book about UFOs before. The name of the book was *Intruders: The Incredible Visitations at Copley Woods*. It was written by a man named Budd Hopkins. I had never heard of Budd Hopkins, nor had I heard of aliens being here before either, except on television.

I read the book in three days, which was fast since I have to admit to putting it down several times because it was so frightening to me. I never imagined that if we were to one day meet someone from another planet, it would be so terrifying. The only science fiction movies I recalled seeing prior to reading this book were *Close Encounters of the Third Kind* and *Star Wars*. I also suddenly became interested in watching *Star Trek* (a show I had always disliked, but now enjoy immensely). Regardless of how bizarre the story seemed, what bothered me the most about this book was feeling as if I was reading about *myself*. After I finished the book, I remember asking Erik to read it, thinking he would scoff and tell me it was crazy fiction. He read it, and when he finished it we both just stared at one another. We didn't talk about it very much. We didn't have to.

On September 12, 1987, I was abducted. This journal entry, along with a questionnaire, would be the catalyst for Budd Hopkins' investigation of me.

I'm in a hospital or some type of health clinic. I'm walking through a corridor, and I see a baby crawling across the floor. It looks weak, and it obviously needs help. I'm picking it up—I'm handing it to a nurse. I'm thinking to myself, I must see what this is—something has gotten my attention down here. I'm walking toward a wider area of the hallway. It's an incinerator, but I don't know how I know this. People are putting dead or dying babies into it. Somehow I know that this device doubles as a rejuvenator also. It can also heal babies. A male humanoid Being wearing a white jacket—he is explaining the process to me. He has just explained the rejuvenation process to me.

I am looking for the little baby I picked up off the floor a few minutes ago. I see a nurse and I ask her, "Where is the baby I just handed you?" She replies, "Your father-in-law said it was dead and to put it in the incinerator." I'm furious. I begin to yell at her. "He is an old man with Parkinson's disease and can hardly speak! He doesn't know anything about babies!" I'm walking toward the incinerator, and I see a female Being about to put the baby into the incinerator. I'm taking the baby away from her. Oh! The baby is wrapped in a light, clearish-blue plastic bag! I'm frantically trying to remove the bag away from the baby and when I do it gasps for air. "Thank God," I say to myself.

Oh, now it has stopped breathing again—it seems it is taking forever to breathe again. Suddenly, it is breathing again. My heart is pounding and racing. It's alive and it's a girl! I'm showing her to everyone. "Look, she was alive! Look, she is alive!" I'm showing her to anyone I can get the attention of. No one believes me! No one seems to care! I'm hearing a voice, "Throw her away! Put her into the incinerator!" I can't believe this!

I'm taking her into another room. I'm putting her on a shelf of some kind. The shelf is about four feet long and right at eye level. There is nothing else on this shelf except her. The room is empty except for a few of these shelves. The room is a light, pale blue color. I'm talking to her in a sweet soft voice. She is sitting up on the shelf, and she is looking at me. I'm speaking to her, "Hello, are you okay? You're safe now, everything is all right." I'm looking at her eyes. They are very large and appear to be closed. (I-12)

I have the sensation that some time has elapsed—Something is different. I'm still talking to her, but now she appears to be older. Her skin is a very, very pale bluish-gray color and her eyes are still closed.

I don't see pupils, just big round eyes. She is communicating with me telepathically. I am very close to her and I'm looking into her eyes. I still think they are closed. They are very large and round. I feel as though she is not finished being formed because of the color of her skin, and she appears to be extremely fragile. She is so delicate, I'm afraid to touch her. I don't want to hurt her. I feel so close to her. I am very anxious for her to grow up so I can see what she will look like. She is speaking to me telepathically: "I always have blue-gray eyes when I incarnate into the Earth plane." Something—maybe it is she—is telling me this is her fourth or fifth time to incarnate into our Earth plane. I'm so happy, but I'm astonished at the same time. She is speaking to me telepathically again: "Ask Erik about his vision."

Suddenly, I am up in the air looking down at my body. It's the middle of the night and I'm watching myself walk across our front yard. I'm going back into my house. It must be over now.

This memory was just that, a *memory*. There was nothing obscure about it other than my inability to remember how I got "to and from" wherever this experience occurred. It felt just as real as when I would float and visit God as a child, or when I flew above the gravel road, or when I reached for the piece of chocolate cake. It was just as real as the time I was hysterical over being shown my baby.

I purchased the November-December 1987 issue of *Omni* magazine because there was a questionnaire in it about UFOs and alien abductions. I filled out the interview titled, *Hidden Memories: Are You an Abductee?* It sat around the house for a while, and finally Erik insisted that I mail it. Filling out something such as this and mailing it are two very different things. I eventually mailed the questionnaire directly to Budd Hopkins because I thought the fewer people who read it the better. I figured my life was so messed up the next logical step was for me to be declared "insane." It was terribly frightening. I ended up sending him pages of answers. I didn't realize how desperate I was to have somebody to talk to about this. I waited in dread for "the men in the white coats" to arrive, because I thought Budd was going to send a couple of "shrinks" to my house to have me committed to a mental institution.

I wrote to Budd Hopkins on November 29, 1987. He telephoned me shortly thereafter and told me he would be in Pensacola in April, and asked if he could meet with me when he was in town. Now, I thought, this wasn't the way this was supposed to work out. The "men in the white coats" never showed up to take me away, and here was this stranger actually telephoning me? To add to my luck, I found him to be extremely kind and sincerely interested in talking to me. It didn't make sense. It was too good to be true.

On April 24, 1988, I met Budd Hopkins. He interviewed me for over two hours. I remember trying to read every expression on his face when I would answer his questions. I wanted to know if he believed me or if he thought I was crazy, but it was impossible. Budd didn't volunteer any information to me, and he never showed any reaction to my answers other than being sincerely interested in what I had to say. I didn't know whether I was answering the questions "right" or "wrong," and this made me very nervous.

Later, after the interview, Erik came home and I introduced him to Budd. He asked me if I would be interested in trying hypnosis, and the three of us agreed to meet later that evening. I didn't do a lot of talking during the hypnosis session and Budd was very patient. We looked into the time I was supposed to go to my Brownie meeting. The following day during another hypnosis session we looked into the abduction experience that occurred on 9-12-87. The main thing we learned during the second session was there was a blue-skinned baby and a blue-skinned Being. Again, although we didn't uncover anything astonishing, my memories were very salient.[3]

After my first hypnotic regression with Budd, Erik and I ended up going to bed around one o'clock in the morning. I kept waking up periodically during the night only to find that I had been crying. I was actually crying in my sleep, but it was a good kind of crying. I remember feeling an enormous relief. It was as if twenty-eight years of pain and confusion were being released from my unconscious mind. It is almost impossible to find the words to describe the feelings I was experiencing. For the first time in my life, I was releasing this, and I knew I was going to be okay.

I continued to keep the journal I began in 1983. I recorded what happened that weekend and my feelings about it. I felt extremely fortunate to have had this opportunity. It was a very positive experience, and Budd was very kind and sensitive. I owe much to him. He reached out to me, a stranger, and offered to listen. I believe my life would be very different today had he, and my husband Erik, not been there to help me through this final stage of my awakening.

Budd told me he had recently met a woman who lived nearby who was having experiences similar to mine. He felt it was important for me to have someone I could talk to if Erik were ever out of town. He also told me about a woman who was a MUFON investigator who also lived in Pensacola. Her name was Vicki Lyons. I had never heard of MUFON before, but I was to learn that MUFON stood for the Mutual UFO Network.

The protective wall around my alien encounters had been breached, and it was time for the memories to tumble out. Over the next several months, I would experience the drain spontaneous memories can have on the mind and body. I would also experience more abductions. Today, I firmly believe the aliens gave me a posthypnotic suggestion which acted like a mental block, and inhibited my ability to completely remember my past abduction experiences. After my hypnosis sessions with Budd, I felt a feeling I can only describe as an enormous release, coupled with a feeling of peacefulness.

Shortly after my two regressive hypnosis sessions, my brother came over to borrow our sander. It seemed as though everyone was painting his or her house this summer. On his way to his car, I asked him if he remembered much about the house we used to live in as children. He described the house to me to make sure we were talking about the same one. We were. He told me he remembered happy times in that house. This seemed strange to me because I remembered the many times he claimed, as a very young child, to have seen the "devil" in his room.

"What did you see all of those times when you said you saw the "devil" in your room?" I asked.

"I don't remember seeing anything in my room except those short little shadowy figures—but then they would disappear around the corner." He stated.

I couldn't contain my curiosity so I asked him another question.

"Did you feel they were good or bad? Did you feel any particular way about them?"

"I thought they were laughing or giggling at me. Now, *your* room, that was different. I always heard voices from your room, calling my name. I always thought it was you teasing me, but when I would go into your room, I could never find you."

His answer shocked me. I asked him rather bluntly,

"Do you believe in UFOs?"

He looked at me as if I were crazy and said, "No." His expression was obvious. He thought I was nuts for even asking.

Erik and I were now on our way to meet with and be interviewed by Vicki Lyons, the MUFON investigator Budd told us about. We had spoken to one another on the phone briefly to set up the day and time of the interview. Erik and I were more than a little nervous and embarrassed to be on our way to a total stranger's house to talk about the possibility of alien abductions being a part of our lives.

When we arrived, we introduced ourselves and met another investigator named Michael. We situated ourselves in her cozy courtyard while she poured us glasses of orange juice. I knew she had to be a nice person because she seemed to love animals as much as me. Her cats and dogs were out and about in the courtyard during our visit. Vicki asked me if I would mind if she taped the interview. I became nervous again. I can't remember what I said, but I must have told her it would be okay because, before I knew it, the recorder was on and I was talking. Michael seemed rather quiet and I felt very comfortable around him. The questioning was at times embarrassing, sometimes difficult, and sometimes funny. We had a good talk together, and it was to be the beginning of a long friendship. Vicki is an intelligent, fun, and assertive woman, and I have learned a lot from her over the years.

At the end of our interview, Vicki told me about a psychologist who had offered to work with some other abductees in the area, and she thought he would be willing to work with me also. I knew I wanted to try hypnosis again. I also knew I would be put through much psychological testing. It was time to find out if I was insane or really experiencing something extraordinary. I told her to talk to him, and she later telephoned me to give me his phone number.

Shortly after our meeting with Vicki, we were invited to attend a get-together at another MUFON investigator's house. His name was Daniel Ronnigan, and he was the state director and the president of the Pensacola MUFON organization at that time. I had been talking to the woman in Pensacola that Budd told me about. Her name was Mary, and she was a very sweet person. I was to find out that she would be my "buddy." It had been decided that each abductee would be put in contact with an investigator and another abductee, who would act as a buddy, so they could provide support for one another. It was a good idea and, to this day, I feel it is extremely important. However, it was somewhat awkward because we were not supposed to talk about our experiences. Since we were soon to be undergoing regressive hypnosis, we weren't supposed to contaminate ourselves by listening to other abductees' personal accounts. Today, I believe this was also an excellent idea, and it proved to be worth the wait. I was not to read anything or listen to anything anyone said about his or her experiences. Now, I wondered, what am I supposed to do at this party?

We had been given directions to Daniel's house the day before the party, but I seemed to already know exactly how the house was going to be situated, what it looked like, and what he looked like. When we arrived, I realized I was extremely accurate. It was extremely uncanny. Perhaps it was just a coincidence.

The party was really a get-together, and it consisted of four groups of people: MUFON investigators, abductees, interested spouses, and uninterested spouses. It was rather easy to put everyone in his or her appropriate group. Most of the abductees looked nervous, the MUFON investigators seemed to know who everyone was, the interested spouses were interested, and the uninterested spouses were miserable.

I was to come to know much better many of the people at the get-together that night. Most of them are still deeply involved and dedicated to research into UFOs and the abduction phenomenon. The help they provided me with was very important in my coming to terms with the abductions I had undergone, and other abductions I would experience in the future.

Although I was still experiencing a lot of anxiety, at least now I felt as though I had the first working theory upon which to base my unusual memories. In May, I remembered another experience, and although I didn't remember how I got to and from this place, this was as real as anything else I had experienced in my life.

5-1-88

I'm in a small room with about eight Beings. I can't see their faces clearly. I'm also looking at two beds with some kind of partition separating them from the rest of the room. Most of the Beings are to my right. I'm looking at a humanoid female. She looks almost human, but I feel as though there is something different about her. She is plump and has dark hair. "I have to go and have a baby" she says, and she leaves the room.

Some time has passed, and she is coming back into the room with five children. I'm not amused. I don't like this. There are enough of us in here already. The oldest child is a male and looks about five years old, the other is a girl and is about two or three years old. The other three are babies between three and six months old. Somehow, I know it is my job to pretend as if I like these children. I'm walking over to a bed to pick up one of the babies. When I do, its head flops to one side and I hear a "gasp" from someone. It's as if I have an audience scrutinizing my every move with the child. I am repositioning its head to make it more comfortable.

I feel as though I am playing a very familiar role. I can't believe she really expects me to believe she just walked out into the hallway and had five children. Do they really believe I'm that ignorant? Somehow, I know this is something I HAVE to do. I do not have a choice.

Babies, I was to find out, are a central theme in the abduction phenomenon. I thought this was the silliest thing to have occurred, but I definitely felt that familiar presence I had come to associate with the aliens. Ten days after this happened, a terrifying experience occurred. Unfortunately, Erik was out of town, and I was unbelievably frightened when I sensed something was about to happen. This is what I recorded the following day.

5-10-88

I felt terrified before going to bed last night. Erik was out of town, and I was so afraid to go to sleep that I ended up barricading the front door with a chair. I called my abductee buddy, Mary, and she stayed on the phone with me for an hour. I remember telling her that I knew the aliens were coming for me. After our phone conversation, I eventually fell asleep. The last thing I remember before waking up in my bed was standing outside in a large open area with trees and shrubs around me. There may have been a structure or a large object off to my left, but I really do not know for sure. I had the feeling there were others near me although I never really saw them. I felt relieved to be awake, and I remember awakening in an unusual position. My head was practically on top of the little table next to our bed, all of the sheets had been pulled out, and I was lying diagonally across the bed. After taking a shower, I came back into the bedroom and tossed my nightgown onto the bed. It was then I noticed a spot of blood on the sheet near where my neck and shoulders were when I was sleeping. I checked my nightgown, but there wasn't anything on it. The blood was still bright red. I grabbed the camera and took a picture of it. I thought to myself that I must be going nuts. My night seemed so "full," but I couldn't remember a thing. I was late for work so I left the house. That evening after work, I was undressing, and I noticed two little puncture marks on the right side of my neck just over my right jugular artery. They were pink, puffy, and sore.

I immediately felt very uneasy when I saw the small puncture holes in my neck. I felt they were connected to something that happened to me in the middle of the night, even though my memories were practically nonexistent. I felt strongly that I was invaded or violated on some level. I wanted to know what happened and what could have caused the blood on the sheet and the puncture wounds in my neck. All I knew was "they" had come, and for some reason I wasn't remembering what happened.

Two months later, another event occurred that also involved babies. This was extremely upsetting to me at the time, but today my feelings about it have changed somewhat.

7-10-88

I'm in what appears to be a dirty clothing store. I'm looking for a dress to wear to a baby shower. I have retrieved a white lace dress off a rack of what looks like used clothes, and I'm walking down a hallway looking for a dressing room. To my left are individual rooms.

Something makes me feel as though I have to hurry. It is time for the baby shower. I'm looking into the little rooms—It's terrible. There is a baby lying on the floor—it is lying in filth. I continue on to another small room. I'm looking into that room now—This baby is lying on the floor also. All it has on is a dirty diaper. I continue on to another room and here again is another infant, this time wearing only a thin, dirty shirt. I can't do this! I'm going to another room—I can't believe this, there is a baby lying next to a toilet that is leaking raw sewage. The infant is lying in the sewage. All of these infants—all of these babies are alive. These babies are all alive. This last baby is looking at me. I feel compelled to help them all but a voice tells me, "Do not interfere." I'm furious. I can't believe this is happening!

I did not reach out to help the babies because I was told not to. It was, and still is, inconceivable that I would not help them. It goes against my beliefs. If this were to happen to me in my normal reality, then I would surely intervene, even if the babies' mothers were present and demanded that I not. It was devastating for me to see this and not be permitted to do anything. Looking back, it seems clear that they were somehow mentally manipulating me to the extreme. I feel it must have taken a lot for them to control me because I am anything but passive. This is purely my own conjecture, since neither I nor anyone else, knows the true level of their control over us. I remember believing and somehow knowing while I was looking at these babies, that this is what happens when you allow ignorant, selfish, and uncaring people to reproduce. This, in itself, sounds unusual, but at the time I strongly believed it.

I often wonder today if this wasn't a real event occurring somewhere on our planet. I believe that interpretation is just as plausible as it having been an event they created to measure what my response would be. I believe these babies were shown to me in order for the Beings and me to learn something important. "This is what happens when you allow ignorant, selfish, and uncaring people to reproduce," and "do not interfere" were the messages I received. It is entirely possible that at some time during their study of humans, these Beings have witnessed behaviors our society has determined to be acceptable and unacceptable. They may have witnessed babies being treated this way and are simply curious about the behavior. It doesn't take much intelligence to determine that a baby is not going to gain much by lying in its own, or otherwise created filth. For an outsider, especially an alien from another planet (or dimension), to witness such extreme inconsistencies in behavior when dealing with the same stimulus, i.e., a baby, must be terribly confusing. Imagine studying a new species and seeing one set of parents nurturing their baby, another set of parents acting indifferently to their baby, and yet another set of parents inflicting physical harm on their baby. Since you may know very little about this new species, you would have to wonder, which behavior is correct? You have your set of rules by which you treat your young, and this species has their set of rules, which as you've noticed, vary greatly. Especially intriguing is the theory in abduction research, that the aliens are here creating a hybrid species that consists of genetic material from our species as well as their species. Again, which is the correct behavior?

If this was a holographic image designed to instill deep emotional responses in me, I have to ask why. If they wanted to measure my responses, they could simply tune into me while I'm listening to the news. Enough sickening descriptions and images are beamed into my living room every night by way of the nightly news. And these are images I know to be real.

Although not the first researcher to link episodes of missing time with abduction experiences, Budd Hopkins wrote about missing time as it relates to abduction cases. His first book published on the phenomenon had that title, and you will remember that periods of unaccounted-for time are one of those unusual occurrences that is believed to be a sign of possible abduction encounters. I had experienced the phenomenon of missing time as a child and again on my way up to college. The trip normally took fifteen hours. On one particular day, it ended up taking *twenty-three* hours to drive the same route.[4] Just thirteen days after the experience involving the babies, I noticed four hours missing from my night.

7-23-88

> *I'm looking at the clock—it's one-thirty in the morning and I have to go to the bathroom—*
>
> *I'm getting back into my bed—the clock reads—five-thirty in the morning. Oh shit—What happened to me?*
>
> *I was back in bed thinking that I had to find out what happened to me and I began concentrating on relaxing and remembering. The memory was immediate:*
>
> *I'm riding in what feels like an airplane. I'm flying—It's banking really sharply! I feel g-forces against my body. Oh, what's happening! This feels like one-hundred and eighty degrees—now it is leveling out— now it is banking in the other direction! I'm scared. What's this pilot doing?*
>
> *I'm looking across the inside of the plane. It is all white and very spacious. There is my father—The seats are bluish-gray—I'm looking out of a window. There's a tree! We're going to crash! I can see the ground and more trees. I'm waiting to crash. I'm going to die! I'm screaming silently to myself. My heart is racing. I hear a voice, "Everything is okay. I take the land rover frequently—it's safe." Land Rover? We're in a "Land Rover?" I'm looking at my grandmother. She has a "give up and die" look on her face. She is about to start crying. I feel sorry for her. Somehow, my father and grandmother seem a little different. Maybe a little drugged or something. I'm getting out of this damn thing.*
>
> *I'm out of the "thing" and I'm standing on a platform above the vehicle we were in. This is crazy. It really does look like a land vehicle of some type. Nothing I have ever seen before though. I'm standing on what looks like a concrete platform with my grandmother. I can see pine trees off in the distance and pine straw on the ground. This is weird. Where am I? My grandmother is really upset. I have just been told I*

have to get her to her doctor. Suddenly, I feel as though I should try to keep my thoughts from "them." I don't want the Beings to know I'm considering regressive hypnosis. My grandmother just disappeared upward—suddenly she is just—gone.

Suddenly, I'm on an enormous spaceship! There are people all around me. I can't see their faces clearly. Now, I'm looking at a circular lab area. I'm walking by it on my way to somewhere. I'm walking somewhere and there are "others" walking with me. (I-23)

Now, I'm standing in front of a mirror and I'm putting some items inside a cabinet. These are for the next person to use after I'm gone. I don't know how I know this, but it is true. Other people will need to use these items after I'm gone. I'm putting some make-up and a thermometer in a cabinet.

I'm walking around the ship now, and I feel quite comfortable here. THIS is where I belong. I'm very happy here. Oh, I've just remembered a place on the ship that contains things no one else is supposed to know about! There are other people here just like me. They have somehow found out about this secret place and they want me to take them there. I wonder, did I say something to them out loud? I agree to show them, but I know I shouldn't. These people, they are here for the same reasons I am. I'm walking toward this secret place, and my legs suddenly begin to feel like lead. I'm trying to walk normally, but it is difficult. I don't want anyone to notice that I'm having a hard time walking. It is becoming more difficult to walk. "We had the same problem earlier" someone is telling me. I'm struggling to walk up a huge hallway that has a long incline. Oh! There is Linda. She is one of the abductees I met at Daniel's party! Wow—she looks really tired. She is leading us into a large open space. She doesn't look very happy to be here.

It is very dark in here, and we have to be extremely quiet. I hear people whispering to one another. These people with me, they're all humans, just like me. I think we are all here for the same reason. This huge, dark area we are in looks similar to a zoo except, instead of cages, they use big glass rooms. They look like displays. I can walk all of the way around them.

Oooh! I'm looking inside one—I see two gorilla-like Beings and a large cat. The hairy Beings are very tall, and they don't really look like gorillas, but they are all hairy like them. They are asleep. This is very strange. One has fallen asleep reading what looks like a newspaper, and the other is sleeping in a chair. This entire enclosure has furniture in it. A desk, some big chairs, and books. There is a cat on the other side of the room. It is white with orange spots, and it is about two to three feet tall. It must weigh fifty pounds. It was sleeping, but now it is stretching a little and rubbing its face against the glass wall. I'm looking at this and I can't believe it. Are they trying to imitate humans or are these hairy Beings really capable of reading?

I'm walking toward another glass enclosure. The animal in this one appears to be half lion and half reptile. It is lying on its back, and its mouth has fallen open because it is sleeping. I'm looking at its mouth and I can see rows and rows of teeth. I know what this animal is because I'm telling the people standing next to me. I sense the animal has been saved from extinction. Someone next to me whispers, "That is something no one on Earth has ever seen before." I'm nodding in agreement. I am amazed at what I am looking at. These animals are incredible.

There is Erik. He is standing next to me now. I ask him, "Remember the last time we were here? We decided to build Tom's house afterwards?" (Tom was one of our cats.) *Erik smiles at me and says, "Yes, I remember that." He is very happy. We continue to view other enclosures.*

I awakened feeling drugged and dizzy, and I was extremely tired for the rest of the day. I felt as if I had been up all night, and that is exactly what I believed had happened. I had been up all night, and my memory of what happened to me left me feeling amazed, yet uneasy.

I believe the small craft that I saw my father and grandmother in was some sort of shuttle craft just as he said. He did call it a land rover. However, I think this may be inaccurate. It was a very peculiar looking craft, and even as I was standing next to it and looking at it, I did not believe what I was seeing. I have a strong sense that this part of the abduction involved some deception. I felt I was flying through the air and not moving along the ground. I could be mistaken, but this, along with the fact that I was standing on a concrete platform waiting for an elevator with my grandmother, was, in my opinion, somewhat deceptive. I consider this part of the experience to be a screen memory. I almost felt I was on the university campus that I attended when I came home to take my non-music courses, as I was studying the odd shape of the "land rover." Whatever the true appearance of this shuttle craft was, I feel this is probably the craft that took me from my house to the larger craft.

The appearance of my father and grandmother (his mother) is still puzzling to me even several years after the experience. I believe they either *were* really there and were being abducted along with me, or they *weren't*. If they were with me, then I don't remember seeing them again once I was on the larger craft. If it was not really them, then their appearance, by way of a deceptive technique I call camouflage, and others call a screen memory, would make sense. My father's image could have been projected to keep me calm and comfort me since we are very close to one another, and my grandmother's image could have been projected to give me someone to take care of. This would have the effect of keeping my mind focused on someone I cared for instead of focusing on the aliens themselves, the interior of the craft, or something else I am totally unaware of. My gut feeling, however, is that my father and my grandmother were really with me.

After my grandmother disappeared upward, presumably up to another craft, I believe I was then taken on board a craft the size of a three-story mall. The hallways in this craft were approximately twenty to thirty feet wide. The walls were curved, and the area that contained the circular lab had curved walls and was spacious. There were Beings working in this lab area, and they appeared to be very busy working on their tasks when I walked by. They were not at all interested in why I was there, and I do not believe it was an unusual occurrence for them to see humans being escorted through their ship. These Beings were all wearing light blue, loose fitting body suits complete with loose fitting head coverings. Somehow, I knew that this lab area was for biological sciences. I saw machines similar to computers or something shaped like computers, and some of the Beings were working at, or on, these. I did not get a close look at them. There also seemed to be a change in gravity in different parts of the ship. It is possible I was not yet accustomed to the gravity difference inside their ship by the difficulty I was having when walking up the ramp. I also felt as though I had been on this craft before because I knew my way around, and I had a strong sense of familiarity with my surroundings. I am sure the other people with me had also been abducted and were not aliens in disguise by way of camouflage. Although the aliens do use deceptive techniques with me, I am positive these other people were humans, more specifically, abductees.

The animals in the large glass enclosures were very real. Again, I did not sense any deception here. Yes, they were unusual, but I felt at that time, and still believe today, that these animals were very rare and were being saved from extinction. Another possibility would be to compare this area to one of our own zoos. It is also interesting that even today I remember the sex of the reptile-lion was female. While I was in this dark and large zoo area, I did not see any aliens, but I was aware that they were monitoring us. It was clear that we had some freedom to our movements while on their ship, but I always felt they knew exactly where we were. In addition, I only saw a small part of this huge craft. I believe these animals were being helped in some way. Yes, they were captive, but they were healthy and well cared for. The glass appeared to be for one-way viewing, that is, we could see the animals, but the animals could not see us. Somehow, I knew these animals were very special to the aliens and we had to be very quiet when viewing them.

CHAPTER 5

Regressive Hypnosis

The day came for my first meeting with the clinical psychologist Budd Hopkins and Vicki Lyons had arranged for me to see. I remember being extremely reluctant, but I knew I had to find out if my memories were real. I just couldn't go on any longer without an official confirmation, one way or the other. The psychologist I was to end up working with was Dr. Dan C. Overlade.[5] I didn't trust him immediately because at that time, I didn't feel comfortable around doctors, especially doctors in the mental health community. This distrust was intensified by the reason for my visit.

After our initial introductions to one another, Dr. Overlade explained to me that a "blind study" had been undertaken in New York by Dr. Elizabeth Slater. At that time, Dr. Slater had worked with nine people whom she did not know were abductees. She administered specific psychological tests to these individuals to determine if they were suffering from any psychological disorders. Dr. Overlade continued to explain.

> "During Dr. Slater's study of these individuals, she came to the conclusion that her subjects were reporting experiences she could not account for using these psychological tests. That is to say, the psychological tests that were administered to these nine individuals did not show they were suffering from disorders that would account for confabulated fantasies. If they had been lying to the extremes that would be required when reporting abduction related memories, this data would have shown up using these psychological tests."

I sat quietly and stared at the carpet. These nine people knew. They *knew* they were sane. It was all behind them now. I thought, "I still have to face this. I'm not sure about me. What if I'm nuts?" As I continued thinking about what he said about these nine people, I thought to myself, "I don't know if they are lucky to be sane, or are unlucky to have been labeled abductees." Dr. Overlade began talking again and I looked up from my hypnotic gaze at the carpet in his office. I was thankful he wasn't the first psychologist to look into this crazy area of study. He told me he wanted to give me the same battery of psychological tests Dr. Slater gave her clients, and that he had administered to the people he was working with. Then we talked briefly about hypnosis, and my time was up. I made another appointment for the following week to begin the psychological testing. Over the next few weeks, Dr. Overlade administered the following psychological tests to me: The Minnesota Multiphasic Personality Inventory; The Rorschach Ink-blot Test; The Thematic Apperception Test; The Wechsler Adult Intelligence Scale; and The Draw-A-Person Test.

After several appointments, I was finally finished with the testing and the day arrived for the *verdict*. I was extremely nervous, almost to the point of being nauseous. I sat and waited anxiously while Dr. Overlade read the results of my tests to me. I remember thinking that maybe it wasn't so important to know if any of this was real or not. I expected to hear at any moment that I was paranoid, having cultural delusions, or was crazy. Those words, however, never came.

Dr. Overlade went through each psychological test, and one by one, he noted there was no psychosis present. I had no abnormalities beyond some anxieties, more specifically what he called "symptoms" of post traumatic stress disorder, and low self-esteem. The testing showed I was a psychologically stable individual, with an above average IQ, who was not fantasy prone, or suffering from any other psychological abnormalities. In one way, I couldn't believe it was over, and I was okay. A part of me felt that everything was finally over. What was really occurring, however, was that the journey was just beginning. Dr. Overlade then told me he now considered it appropriate and safe for us to begin the hypnosis sessions. Here was the conflict: I didn't want to be crazy, but I wasn't sure if I wanted to remember all of these possible experiences either. I wasn't really sure what it was I wanted. I was weighing the intrigue and excitement of learning about an alien life form with the possibility these alien life forms may not be so friendly. It was time to face the facts. There might really be something to these memories and experiences I had been having. I became nervous again. Dr. Overlade then told me to schedule an appointment for my first hypnosis session. It would be on August 1, 1988.

The initial induction procedure induces hypnosis in a subject. Different psychologists, psychiatrists, and hypnotherapists all have and use their preferred methods. They are all different to some extent, but they have more similarities than differences. Dr. Overlade's chosen preference for hypnosis involved using a digit response system that will be explained shortly. I also learned how to create a muscle fasciculation, or as we usually call them, a muscle twitch. I quickly learned that just as a person's autonomic nervous system was carrying out certain functions without that person always being consciously aware of it, so also was the unconscious mind carrying out its functions. In the same way we can effect our heart rates and respiration through the use of biofeedback techniques, so also can we tap into the knowledge that the unconscious mind holds. Not only is the unconscious mind capable of performing certain functions, it also never forgets anything we experience in our lives. I learned how to create a muscle fasciculation in whatever part of my body I wished. I then learned to move this fasciculation around to different parts of my body while in a hypnotic state. I would simply think about the area of my body I wanted the fasciculation to move to and I would, after a few moments, feel the twitch. At that time I would be so relaxed and in such a good trance state that the session would normally begin.

Another important tool Dr. Overlade used is the digit response interaction between the unconscious mind and the body. Since the unconscious mind cannot speak by itself and since it never forgets anything, it is an important source of information. One way to retrieve this information is to direct the information to the physical body by way of the hand's digits or fingers. I determined which digits would represent "Yes," "No," or "I Don't Want To Answer," to a particular question directed to my unconscious. I chose my index finger to signal "I Don't Want To Answer" to a question, my middle finger to signal "No," and my ring finger to signal "Yes" to a question. There is never an "I Don't Know" because the unconscious mind never forgets an event.

The following excerpt is from my first hypnosis session with Dr. Overlade, concerning possible memory retrieval of an abduction encounter.

> Dr. Overlade began by calmly stating:
> "It's 2:28 on August 1 of 1988. Is there something that wants to come to consciousness and be recorded just now?
> "I'm afraid to."
> "Afraid to speak?" He asked.
> "Yes."
> "Okay. Tell me about the fear."
> "I shouldn't be here." I said.
> "You shouldn't be here?"
> "No."
> "Where should you be?"
> "Home."
> "You should not be here trying to recall memories?" He questioned.
> "No."
> "Okay. Who has directed you not to recall besides yourself?"
> "I don't know." I said.
> "Do you feel as if someone has?"
> "Yes."
> "See if you can tell me what you imagine to be the consequences of recollection." Dr. Overlade asked.
> "Letting...letting somebody down."
> "Do you have a sense that it's a great many people or do you have no sense of it?"
> "Yes. It's a lot of people." I replied.

As the session continued, we discovered that what I was remembering was something I was told when I was a child. I was feeling some resentment and anxiety because of the questioning. I also felt I should be at home, and my arms were tight, as if I was holding on to something.

> "There is something I have to do." I stated.
> "Something the woman or the child has to do?"
> "I don't know. There's something I have to do."
> "Is it already accomplished in 1988?"
> "No." I stated confidently.
> "Is it still to be accomplished? Is that correct?"
> "Yeah."
> "What do you think it might be?"
> "Something really important." I said.
> "Something really important. What might be really important?"
> "The future."
> "And what is it you are to do about the future?" He asked.
> "There's something I'm supposed to know."

The ensuing dialogue indicated that I unconsciously knew what it was I was supposed to remember and do in the future.[6]

Although this first regressive hypnosis session didn't uncover anything miraculous, it did reveal that there was something extremely important I felt I was supposed to do. I didn't feel as though I should be talking about my experiences, and I felt very guilty for undergoing hypnosis. The feeling was as though I was betraying the aliens by talking, and it was exceptionally powerful. One week later I was visited again by the alien Beings. It seemed they were intent upon showing me my baby.

8-7-88

> *I'm in some kind of hospital. I'm not sure why I'm here—Something in my mind is telling me I've just delivered a baby. I'm standing up and I'm looking down at my body. I have regular clothes on—my khaki pants. They're very comfortable. I'm thinking to myself, "It's inconceivable that I could have just delivered a baby here..." I'm confused. There is no way in hell I could have had a baby without knowing about it.*

> *Oh, okay—I did just have a baby. It is clear in my mind now. A male humanoid Being has just entered the room. He is wearing a white jacket and is holding some kind of clipboard—He has dark hair—He's looking at me. (I-4) He must be in charge. "I have just had a baby. I want to see it." These are my thoughts as this humanoid Being is looking at me. I'm very curious. I really want to see my baby. Erik is with me. He is happy and wants to see the baby too. This is strange. I*

wonder why we are feeling this way? We never planned to have children.

We are being shown the baby. It is lying in a glass box. The box is about three feet by two feet and there is a small piece of white fabric in the bottom of it. Just a small piece. The baby is lying on top of this small piece of fabric. There is no other padding or covers for the baby. The glass box has an opening in the front of it. One side of the glass box is completely open. (I-28) (I-29)

This isn't right—this baby is black. This isn't our baby. I'm disappointed. I wanted to believe this baby was ours, but now I'm confused. How can this be our baby? It is a black baby, and we are both white. I'm so confused.

Oh, okay—I have to "accept" it as being our baby. It is as if this information is being given to me directly from someone else's mind, and it is being placed directly into my mind. I'm not hearing voices, and I haven't spoken yet.

I feel terrible. I'm looking at the baby, and it has spots all over its face. They look like large growths of some kind. Maybe they're large moles. They appear to be about half an inch wide. The baby also has a lot of freckles. That's normal, I guess. This male Being—he's The Doctor. He is in the room observing us—now he has gone out.

There he is again. Some time must have gone by. Sometimes The Doctor is here and sometimes he isn't. I'm questioning The Doctor about the child, about the color of its skin and the growths on its face. Whenever I speak to him, he looks down at the clipboard thing he is holding. Now he is looking at me with an empty look on his face—He's walking out of the room again.

I'm leaving Erik in the room. I'm walking out into the hallway. I'm going to find "my" baby, and then I'll prove to them that is not my baby. I'm thinking about this as I'm walking down a long and very wide hallway. They must have lost my baby or misplaced it. Hospitals do that all of the time! My baby must be in another room. I'm walking into another room, and I see a woman with long blonde hair lying in bed. She appears to be human. She looks as if she's had a baby. She is speaking to me. She is tired and very sad. I can't hear her. I can't remember what she said, but whatever it was, it made a lot of sense to me. There is a glass box with a baby in it in her room also. I'm looking at it. This child looks as if he is about four years old, but he looks like a miniature version of a four year old. He is very, very thin and frail.

This must be my child. I'm about to pick him up—Oh! This poor child! This is not my child. Something is wrong with him. He is shaking uncontrollably. His eyes have rolled back into his head, and his mouth is quivering uncontrollably. He must have a nervous disorder—I'm thinking—My mind is racing—He looks severely retarded. Oh God—This is so terrible! I feel so sorry for him. His tiny face—blonde hair—so blonde it is actually white. His skin is as white as a sheet—His eyes are open! They're really strange. Brown and gold slits. They aren't round enough. This is so sad. This poor child is beyond any help I can give it. This isn't my child. I'm leaving the room. (I-30)

I'm walking out of the room now. I'm going back to my room to where my baby is. I'm calling the doctor into my room. I never actually have to speak. My emotions and thoughts are somehow getting through to him. He enters the room. Now, I speak to him: "I DEMAND that you examine me!" Yes. That was what the woman said to me. She said, "If you really had a baby you can find out by having them examine you. They are supposed to take care of you afterwards." I repeated myself, "I DEMAND that you examine me! I'll prove to you that I am not the mother of this baby!" He is just staring at me as though I'm a child or something! I'm very angry now. "If I have just given birth to this baby then you better take care of me! I could get sick without the proper care!" I feel much better now. They probably just don't understand how the human body works. That ought to get a reaction out of him—He is just staring at me with that empty look on his face. "Okay," I tell him, "come over here and look at this baby." He is actually responding to me. He's walking toward the baby and me. "Look at these growths on its face. I think you should have them all removed immediately. It's hard enough for a child to have to grow up in our world without looking like that."

Suddenly, I feel ashamed. I feel vain and embarrassed. The Doctor is now looking at me as though—it's almost as if he is disappointed in me and slightly perturbed. I've offended him. I feel terrible. I should have behaved differently. I should be thankful that the baby is normal and healthy. But none of this is normal! The doctor is walking out of the room. He's disappointed and frustrated with me.

I had an appointment for a regressive hypnosis session with Dr. Overlade the day after this experience. Dr. Overlade was very interested in determining what it was I saw when trying to practice self-hypnosis at home earlier that week. I had a quick visual impression of an unusual looking instrument. (I-59) I told him a little about the experience that occurred the night before and showed him a drawing I made of the instrument I saw. We decided to try to look into what this unusual instrument was. However, after the hypnosis session began, my mind went straight to the memory of what had occurred the night before.

During the session I relayed what I remembered from the night before.[7] There was no new information until we came to the point when the doctor was trying to convince me the baby was mine:

> "Can you describe the voice?" Dr. Overlade asked.
> "There is no voice. I just know. They must have told me earlier. I believe them. They make me believe them."
> "How do they make you believe?"
> "They're in my mind. They're very strong." I said.
> "So, it isn't by argument or persuasion. Somehow you're impelled to believe it?"
> "Yes"
> "Did you know how it became in their possession?"
> "I don't—I don't care. I think it's theirs and I think they're lying to me. They want me...they want me to think it's mine, but it's not. They said it was ours...Erik's and mine...my baby."
> "Do you have some sensing of why they're trying to persuade you that this is so?"
> "They want me to care for it."
> "Specifically, what care do they want you to take of the baby?"
> "To see how I react to it. They're studying me." I said.
> "And their purpose in studying you?"
> "To help the babies live."

The questioning continued about the baby. Dr. Overlade wanted me to describe its physical characteristics. I got a good look at the baby and had just come to the conclusion that the baby could not possibly be Erik's and mine. It just wasn't logical.[8]

> "Now, it's after you decide, if I'm understanding you correctly, it's after you decide that this is not your baby that you look at another one. Is that correct?"
> "Yeah, I leave."
> "You leave?" He asked disbelieving.
> "Yeah. I go into this other room, and there's a lady lying on the bed..."

> (I described the woman. She appeared to me to be another abductee and we were there for the same reasons.)

> "She has a baby. He has blonde hair. This must be ours...but he's too old."
> "It's too old?" Dr. Overlade asked.

"It's too old. He's about four or five years old. He's in a glass box too. He's real white. I see his chest. He's really sick. That must be why she's so sad. Pick him up...(Somebody must have told me to pick him up) I pick him up, and then I see how big he is, and then I put him back down. This isn't my baby because he's too big. He's moving funny, like jelly.

"Say that last again." Dr. Overlade requested.

"He's like Jell-O; jelly, or something. He doesn't move right. He's real weak and real skinny. He's like a five year old that's the size of a one year old. Or, he looks far away, but I touch him. I'm leaving—his eyes are weird.

"His eyes are what?" Dr. Overlade asked curiously.

"They're strange. They're real small. Gold-yellow..."

The doctor in this experience was very humanoid looking, but he was not human. He was the same doctor who was explaining how the incinerators worked in my experience with the blue-skinned female baby and the blue-skinned Being. He has short, dark hair, and is about five feet, five inches, or maybe a little taller. He always seems to wear a white lab coat over some other type of clothing that I cannot recall. The clipboard type thing he was holding seemed to be more of a machine than something to keep notes on or in. I never saw him write anything, but he would look at it when I would talk to him. I almost think it may have been some type of translator device or monitoring device. He seemed to be looking at it as if he were reading information. I believe this clipboard, or thin panel, was a monitoring device that aided him when trying to deal with what he seemed to think was my unusual behavior. Although he seemed generally unaffected by my emotional state, he did exhibit signs of confusion and frustration at my reasons for not wanting to accept the baby as my own. I cannot say that he was unemotional, however, because he was irritated, and yet, at the same time he seemed somewhat amused with me.

The idea I had that hospitals are losing or misplacing babies all of the time is somewhat unusual, and I wonder where I would have received this information. Certainly not from any experiences in my ordinary reality. I wonder not so much if they have a problem keeping track of babies, but how often I may have seen this occur during my experiences with them. It did not seem unusual for me to walk down the hallway and look in a total stranger's room for my baby. It's almost as if it doesn't matter to them which human female and baby they pair up, so long as they manage to get two of them in a room together in order to achieve whatever their goal is at the time.

At times the Beings seem to know and understand how to use the most complex behavioral nuances to their advantage, only to turn around during the next encounter and not realize it would be genetically highly unlikely for two white parents to produce a black child, as well as two black parents to produce a white child. What I was left believing after this experience was: if this really was my child, they had somehow managed to take an egg from me and fertilize it with sperm from a black male. Had they told me this, I would have accepted the baby as mine, and I would have responded very differently. However, they chose not to. If this was not my baby, then they exhibited illogical or even ignorant behavior. Since I have remembered many experiences that have led me to believe they are at least as intelligent as we are, I am left with the belief that in this case they were being totally illogical. They made the deliberate decision to keep the truth from me, and by doing this, my behavior had no positive effect on this baby.

The hypnotic regression continued with me reliving the argument I had with the doctor. Some new information was revealed about the number of abductions I had experienced until that time.[9] We then decided to look into the experience from May 10 of the same year. As you will recall, this was the night Erik was out of town, and I telephoned Mary because I believed the aliens were coming for me.

> "Describe to me what you're experiencing." Dr. Overlade prompted.
> "Somebody's here."
> "Inside your head?"
> "No. Here, next to the bed."
> "Is this next to your bed at home?"
> "Yeah."
> "How many?"
> "I see one, two, three, maybe. I don't know." I said, while reaching for my neck.
> "No matter. It's not happening right now. You're safe. You just reached for your neck. Can you tell me what that was?"
> "I just keep seeing this needle about this long." (Motioning with my hands.)
> "What are they doing with it?"
> "That was the night I woke up with blood on the sheet. I think they stuck it in my neck, right here." (Motioning with my hand.)

I went on to explain that I thought I saw a tan-looking alien holding a syringe. The session ended there because that was all I could remember. There wasn't much new information from the experience that left behind a large drop of blood on the sheets and two puncture wounds in my neck. All I knew was there was an alien holding a syringe. It had a bald head, large, dark eyes, and light tan skin. It was a male, and he was about three to four feet tall.

Besides the blood on the sheets and the puncture wound in my neck, the third most unusual occurrence connected to this experience was the fact that Erik tried to telephone me several times during the night. He said he was very worried because the phone would ring and ring, and I never answered the phone. He was going to call the police but decided to call my parents first. The same thing happened. The phone would ring and ring, but no one ever answered. He then called the operator and he was told that some of the phone lines were out in one particular area: ours. My parents lived a couple of miles away from us at the time.

I had another appointment for September 8, and another regressive hypnosis was performed. This time we looked into the missing time experience from July 23, 1988.

We determined that I did in fact have a period of four hours where I was not in my home. I also left my bed in the middle of the night for purposes other than going to the bathroom. It was difficult to obtain any new information about the experience. What we did learn was while I was on their huge ship, I saw about seven "little people" standing around in a semicircle.

> "As you saw a bunch of little people standing around, what's your posture?"
> "I'm above them." I replied.
> "Are you seated, or standing, or—"
> "Just above them."
> "And how many little people would you suppose?"
> "About seven or eight." I said.
> "Um-hm—describe them some more."
> "They all look alike. I think they have their eyes closed...They are just standing next to each other in a little semicircle."
> "Facing you?" Dr. Overlade asked.
> "No. I'm over them."

The direction of the questioning changed.[10] Dr. Overlade wanted to understand the purpose of my contacts.

> "Tell me what you recall."
> "Babies."
> "Babies?" He questioned.
> "That's all I know."
> "And your conscious conjecture is that somehow these little people (in the semicircle) were your children? Isn't that correct?"
> "No. They're just little."
> "That they're just little? There's a distress reaction just now. What was that feeling about?"
> "They just seem helpless."
> "*They* seem helpless? Is that what you said?"
> "Yeah...Weak." I added.
> "What is it you are to do? What is your role?"
> "I don't know...I'm supposed to help them."

"You're somehow to make them feel less helpless?"
"I guess so."
"Do you have any sense of how you are to accomplish this?"
"Take care of them, I guess. But I don't know how. I just feel sad for them."
"What is it about them that suggests the helplessness?"
"I don't think they take care of them. The others don't take care of them."
"The others?"
"The ones in charge."
"Do you have any understanding of why the ones in charge don't take care of them?" Dr. Overlade asked.
"No. They just don't seem to care...I think they're just really different. They don't feel."
"The ones in charge don't feel or the little ones?"
"The ones in charge. They must not, I just feel that." I said.
"They seem not to feel?"
"Yeah, like I do."
"And, the way you feel is?"
"Sad."
"Sad, and a feeling that somehow you're supposed to help these little people?"
"Um-hm."
"Then we're talking about something that comes very close to compassion."
"Yeah, that's the word. That's a good word." I said.
"I wonder how we can reconcile the fact that the ones in charge lack compassion and yet present the little Beings to you with the implication that you were somehow to help. I can think of a way, but I don't want to suggest it. I'm wondering what you think. How could you reconcile a lack of compassion with a behavior that implies compassion. By presenting these Beings to you for help and assistance, that would imply a caring, would it not? About something?"
"Maybe they're just learning from me."
"See if you can figure out how they're learning from you."
"I don't know. I guess...I guess they want me to touch and hold these babies, but I don't."
"You don't?"
"No. I'm not very good with babies. I feel so much...I care for them...without touching them."

During the week that followed, I had a dream that really bothered me. It involved an unusual looking male humanoid with blonde hair. This is what I remembered:

> *I'm standing in front of a glass door, and I don't have any clothes on. There is a blonde male that is peculiar looking. It's as if he isn't totally human. He is standing on the other side of this glass door. I'm smiling at him because he is naked. He's entering into the room and is walking toward me. I'm lying on my back on some type of table. He is leaving...he said he would be back.*
>
> *A little time has passed and he is back in the room with me. I feel as though we are being watched by several Beings from behind a one-way, see through wall. He's reaching out to me...he has taken my left hand. He's holding my left hand, gently. Then he reaches out and touches my left breast and I instantly have an orgasm. I don't remember the physical act of sexual intercourse...he just touched me.*
>
> *I'm feeling terrible now. I feel so guilty and ashamed.*

I awakened in the middle of the night feeling devastated. I suddenly remembered that this encounter had occurred about a month earlier, and I didn't record it because I had been suppressing it. I felt as though I had betrayed Erik, and it was a terrible feeling. This unusual looking male appeared to be partially human, but he was definitely *not* a human being. I began to refer to him as The Blonde. (I-13)

9-17-88

> *I'm sitting outside in what looks like Germany. I'm eating German food with my mother. It's as though we are back in 1967 visiting the farm we stayed at that summer. We're having fun and we're eating outdoors. There are others around too, but the only one I really know is my mother.*
>
> *Suddenly, I'm inside a building. Everyone is wearing white except the "patients." I feel as if I'm still in Germany, although everything around me feels different. It's as if I'm in a psychiatric ward or a nursing home as opposed to a hospital. I think I see Erik. He is dressed in white too. Somehow, I know I have to go inside a big box and be tied down. I'm feeling absolute dread over this. Erik seems insensitive—He is telling me what to do—so unlike himself—He is telling me I have to lie down in this box under restraints. I'm angry.*
>
> *I'm walking around. I'm going to go to the bathroom because I know I'm going to be tied down in this box for a long time. Just before I have to go into the box, I ask him, "Why do I have to be tied down? I hate it!" He replies, "Because it will be good for you, you'll see. It will calm you down." I'm standing over the black box now. I'm looking down*

into it. It is about four feet wide and six feet long. It is metallic. I'm really angry. "I don't want to be tied down! I hate it!" He is looking at me as though he finds my behavior amusing. I'm looking down at it. I know I have no other choice. I have to lie down in it, and let them tie me down. I know they will leave me in it alone. I'm thinking about a blonde, alien looking male.

I overslept that morning. I recorded this a little later that day because I felt so bad. After I got up, I walked into the kitchen, looked at Erik and began to cry. At the end of this journal entry I wrote: "I feel like hell today. I have a migraine headache and severe pain from my right nostril to my right tear duct. It hurts the entire side of my face."

This pain lingered for a day and a half, and I had the distinct feeling that something had been removed from me. I felt certain the Beings knew what I was doing, and they did not want me to tell anyone about my experiences, especially Vicki Lyons, Don Ware and MUFON. It seemed the aliens knew everything Vicki, Don and MUFON were attempting to do. To make matters worse, after this encounter Dr. Overlade believed the Beings put something inside my nostril, while I believed they removed something from my nostril. In any event, the one thing I was certain of was my nose was extremely sore for a day and a half.

Dr. Overlade felt this was so important he asked me if I would make an appointment with an ear, eye, nose, and throat specialist. He knew of a doctor who was sympathetic to MUFON's objectives. I went to see this doctor and he conducted a physical examination of my nose and my ears. I then made an appointment for a CAT scan, because Dr. Overlade believed that would be the next logical step. Unfortunately, it would be another month before I could have the CAT scan performed, and much was to transpire over the next thirty days.

It is my belief that the first paragraph of this journal entry is a memory of a real event from my childhood, a trip to Germany when I was seven years old. However, I was not simply dreaming about it or remembering it. I believe, very strongly, that the aliens probed my mind, took this memory from my mind, and therefore, mentally set the stage for the "nursing home" event. For me to feel as though I am in a familiar, yet foreign country, is similar to what it feels like for me to be on one of their crafts. I know I am not in my country or on Earth anymore, but I do have some sense of familiarity with my surroundings, having been there before. It was probably orchestrated like this: I am abducted and taken to their craft. They know I realize what is happening to me and they probe my mind and use my own memories of being in another country, and having visited my father-in-law in a nursing home regularly to create a type of smoke screen. I can still see through the smoke, so to speak, but the image is somewhat distorted. This is another example of a screen memory.

Erik was not really there forcing me to get into the black box. This is an excellent example of the camouflage technique I spoke about earlier. I did not feel as though Erik's behavior or his speech was normal for him. Indeed, I thought it was "so unlike him to be treating me like this and talking to me like this." I sensed a great amount of deception and believe this was really an alien, somehow superimposing Erik's image over his own. As I stated, he too was wearing white. The distinction between "patients" and all of the other people dressed in white leads me to suspect that I was not the only "patient" or abductee, they had in that place.

When I looked into the black box, I was looking down at floor level, and the box was almost level with the floor. It was almost as if it was "docked" next to a ramp, or it may be that the floor ended and there was a drop-off. The box was large enough for two adult humans to fit inside, but it was empty when I looked into it. I did not see any distinguishing features inside the box, but somehow I knew I would be inside it for a long time. That is why I wanted to go to the bathroom first. I sensed, probably from a previous experience inside the black box, that I would feel extremely alone while inside it. I believed I would be isolated from all exterior stimuli and it would be terribly lonely. It was almost as if I were going into isolation.

This was not a pleasant experience, both in an emotional sense and in a physical sense. The pain I had the following morning was almost unbearable but it did eventually subside. I did not find any blood on my sheets or in my nostril, which I found unusual in view of the amount of pain I was experiencing. I also remember the two days following this experience being very unproductive days for me.

In mid-September of this year, I enrolled in school again. I became so intrigued with what I was remembering that I wanted to learn everything I could about the human mind, so I began studying psychology. I ended up maintaining a 4.0 GPA in my psychology course work and had plans to obtain my Ph.D. However, I have recently come to the conclusion that even with a Ph.D. in psychology, I will probably not find the answers to this abduction mystery that I am searching for. My studies taught me a lot about myself, and about how the mental health community views subjects such as alien abductions.

As is often the case, when an abductee or experiencer begins exploring his or her lost or partial memories through hypnosis, spontaneous memories begin to surface. These memories may surface in dreams or while a person is going about his or her everyday activities. Even the most benign stimulus may trigger hours or even years of memories that have been forgotten. A spontaneous memory from my childhood surfaced during the same week as an actual visitation and a hypnosis session. Many abductees can attest to the drain that a week such as this can have on you. I would like to reiterate how vivid these memories are. These are not fantasies or wishful thinking. These memories are as real as my computer is sitting here in front of me while my fingers tap away at the keyboard. How can I remember these encounters or the spontaneous memories as well as, or even better than, my own wedding day? My wedding day was one of the happiest days of my life!

The following is a spontaneous memory, and I have no doubt whatsoever that this event occurred in my childhood when I was between the ages of seven and nine years old.

9-24-88

I see a wide open space outside. It is daytime, and there is nothing here except sand and dirt. There are no trees, shrubs, or flowers of any kind. Just a light orange sand for as far as I can see. Everything is flat here.

Now I'm seeing a stone structure off in the distance—

Oh! Now I'm suddenly much closer to it and there are about ten to fifteen people standing around this place with me. There are no vehicles—I'm looking down at the ground at some old bricks or stones. Something was once here. We are being told it was ancient plumbing of some kind. People are looking at this spot on the ground as they walk by it.

I'm now looking up at a man's face. He has ugly glasses on, and his hair is real messy. I feel uneasy with him. I don't trust him. Somehow I know he is deceptive. He is speaking to me but I'm mentally tuning him out because I don't want to hear what he has to say. I don't want to hear deception. I'm blocking him out of my mind...I am very small compared to him. I'm just a kid. I'm not going to trust him. I don't know any of these other people that are with me. They are mostly adults—I'm walking toward that structure—

Suddenly, I'm inside the structure. That seemed sudden—I'm walking around inside now and I need to find a bathroom. The inside of this thing is stone. I'm looking at the walls—the steps—everything around me is made out of stone. BIG stones. The stones are bigger than I am, and they are very close together. They are so close that I can barely see the lines that separate them from one another. The walls are slanted inward toward me. It looks just like I imagined the inside of a pyramid would look. I must be inside a pyramid. I've never been inside a pyramid before. That is what this looks like to me. I'm walking around a corner. I have to find a bathroom.

I see another slanted wall, and there's a mother and child coming out of a small room. I never would have known it was there if I hadn't seen them exiting. The walls are so uniform I can't tell where the doors are. There aren't really doors here. I'm inside this little room now, and I'm looking at an unusual looking toilet. It is white and the water is constantly flowing up from the ground and out over the bowl and toward the back where the tank should be, but there isn't a tank. This is strange. How am I going to use this? It's too pretty and clean to use as a toilet. Oh, now what am I going to do?

Suddenly, the wall to my left is gone! Oh! There are people in white lab coats watching me! I have to get out of here. I don't have to go to the bathroom anymore. I'm leaving.

I'm traveling in some kind of vehicle. God! There is that Being—it's The Doctor. It's at night. I'm looking around. We're arriving—I'm back home. I'm at my house. I think we have stopped under the carport, but our car isn't here and it should be. This is weird. This isn't right. It's the middle of the night and where is our car? I want out of this vehicle very bad. I want to get out. I'm sitting, no—I'm not really sitting. I don't have a seat. My seat consists of a metal floor with black straps to tie me in. There are four straps, but they are not tied around me anymore. Two for my arms and two for my legs. This isn't fair. The Doctor has a seat, and he is seated slightly above me. He is driving this thing—I'm looking at him now. He is responsible for me and he doesn't like it at all. He really looks nervous about being here with me. Someone else was supposed to bring me home, but for some reason, he got stuck with me. He looks very nervous. I want out of this "thing." I just want out.

I'm feeling something from him. I sense something, as if he wants to do something I think is wrong. He expects me to do something. I think I'm supposed to kiss him—I'm feeling really terrible about this. I feel dirty, as if we just had sex or something—He is moving me toward him somehow—now he is kissing me and it hurts. My whole face hurts. "Not again," I'm thinking. I've done something with him before. I feel as if I'm dead inside. As if I'm a machine.

I will not deny that the second half of this memory has peculiar overtones. It was quite disturbing to me. This was the doctor that was on the ship explaining how the incinerators worked. He was the same doctor that was attempting to make me accept the black infant as my own child. I see him the same each time, and although he appears very human looking, he is not human.

My feelings and interpretation about the first part of this memory were that I was probably in the middle of a desert somewhere, either on this planet or some other planet. The pyramid could have been real, and if so, it would lead me to infer that I was still on Earth. My being inside the pyramid in just the blink of an eye indicates some possible missing time, or being physically moved from one location to another in the matter of a second or two.

Since I have stated several times that I have seen the Beings in white or wearing white lab coats, I must be viewing them sometimes as scientists who are studying me. Could they really have been interested in whether or not I would use this exceptionally clean and attractive toilet? It may seem unimportant to focus on this issue, but it is noteworthy. The moment I decided not to use it, the wall to my left disappeared. It was almost as if the experiment was terminated and it no longer mattered whether I saw them or not. Whether the Beings were performing urinary tract or bladder experiments, I cannot say. I have never had any urological procedures performed on me, other than leaving a urine sample once a year for a yearly checkup. Certainly at the age of seven or nine years old, I hadn't even done that.

The ride in the "car" with The Doctor appeared to be the return trip home. It was not a car, however, as the description of my missing seat and the straps would indicate. It also did not roll. I felt as though we were moving above the ground because I had to look down to see my front yard as we moved across it. It is interesting how uncomfortable The Doctor was at having to be with me. He seemed afraid of being seen with me. I cannot imagine having sex with him at such a young age, but the possibility cannot be overlooked in light of similar information that is being reported by abductees.

I do not have a complete memory of the sexual encounter, so I truly do not know if it was good or bad, violent or gentle. There is also the possibility that this feeling, or belief that The Doctor had sex with me, was implanted in my memory. What better way to prevent a child from talking about their abduction experiences than to tell them what they did was "bad" or "dirty." Since I don't have enough information to go on, and until I know for certain, I can't come to any definite conclusions.

CHAPTER 6

Visions of the Future?

There have been many messages and warnings given to abductees over the years. Usually these involve a cataclysmic event that is supposed to happen in the future. I have been given visions and have been told of specific situations that would happen to me at some unknown time in the future. Some of these visions have come true, some have not come true, and some of them can be interpreted as events occurring in the present day. Interestingly, it seems the more specific and personal the information is, the more likely it is that it will come true. I had a very unusual occurrence in early October of 1988. It will probably sound familiar to some of you, but to others, it will clearly have "end of the world" overtones. Nevertheless, this is a part of the apparent scenario many abductees end up going through. I have been curious about this since it happened and I have two different interpretations of it.

10-4-88

> *I'm standing outside with Erik and what I perceive is a friend of his and two other males. I never really see their faces, but I sense that there are definitely four males with me. It is dark and as we are looking out into the distance, and across the horizon we see a war. Suddenly there is a huge red explosion and the sky turns a bright orange color. We all gasp in surprise and I am immediately very sad.*
>
> *Suddenly, I'm in an underground structure. I don't know how I got here. The walls are white and there are two hallways, one to my left and one to my right. They are curved away from me and seem to lead to other areas or rooms that are also underground. I'm looking at hundreds of "people." I'm not sure if they are all human but they appear to be humanoid. All of the people on my right are wearing thick, gray, rubber-like body suits. The suits cover every part of their body except for their faces. The body suits are very tight-fitting and leave the eyes, nose and mouths still visible. I'm looking at rows and rows of uniformed people. On my left side I see rows and rows of people dressed in civilian attire. They all seem to have a distant stare in their eyes. Something in my mind tells me these are civilians. They are standing in rows just as the uniformed people are except they are wearing regular street clothes.*

I am face to face with a man wearing a dark gray body suit. His eyes are piercing into my mind. He is just staring at me. His eyes are an incredible blue color. Now I'm looking into the eyes of a young woman. She too is staring into my mind. Her eyes are also a piercing blue color.

Suddenly I receive a powerful message. Even though the civilians are not wearing body suits, I know they will soon. They are as much a part of this as the people wearing the gray body suits. Suddenly, I am overwhelmed with a feeling that I should stay down here and fight with them and help them. I want to fight with them. This is incredible. I had no idea this was going on down here. I am overwhelmed with the thought of staying with them. I "have" to fight with them. I am still looking into the young woman's eyes. They are so beautiful and her intensity is astonishing.

Suddenly, I'm not sure how, but I am above ground again. I think I'm in an old abandoned house. There are "others" with me but I can't see their faces. I am holding a young boy about thirteen years old. He is crying because he doesn't want to be in this war. I know it is inevitable. I hold him and try to comfort him. He is not wearing any clothes, only a blanket. This is strange. I know what I just saw is real. It's going to happen.

Although it may sound ridiculous, my first thought was that I saw the future, and in the future there is going to be a terrible war. I am not the type of person to dwell on the end of the world prophecies, so I immediately tried to come up with some type of explanation for this incredible event. Were they showing me the future or was it just a holograph? Because I could not get this "vision" out of my mind, I came up with an even more unusual thought. What if the "people" in the gray body suits weren't human? What if this is really going on and it represented a message of some sort? This experience left me with the suspicion that the civilians represented abductees and other people involved in the abduction phenomenon. Did the "people" in the body suits represent the aliens? I began to wonder if I wasn't being psychologically conditioned to fight a common enemy. I asked myself, "Who is a common adversary of the aliens and the abductees?" This experience made me begin to think about a subject I always resisted contemplating. The only groups of people I knew of who had been accused of lying and keeping the truth about this phenomenon from the general population were elite groups of powerful people who have the ability to gather, control, and use information to their own advantage.

As of the date of this vision, my reading on the subject of UFOs had been limited to *Intruders: The Incredible Visitations at Copley Woods* and the article in my local paper about the Pascagoula abduction. Although I wondered why I had never heard of UFOs from my government or my church, I was not preoccupied with this thought at that time. However, *after* this event, I was left with the belief that the aliens were trying to give me a message and I wondered if I was capable of correctly interpreting what it was they were trying to say to me.

I began to try to look at other possibilities. I didn't like the thought of having to fight my own government one day in this gloomy future they had shown me. I tried to change the picture in my mind, in order to make it an easier "pill" to swallow. I thought perhaps they had shown me a holographic picture instead of a vision. They put me in the situation simply to measure what my response to war might be. Then I realized there was something wrong with this. That is not what my reaction to war would be. Yes, I would be sad, but I did not believe I would fight with humanoid looking Beings wearing dark gray body suits. I simply didn't believe I could fight. Killing is wrong. I would eventually decide that they put me through this to instill deep emotional responses within me, that only *they* knew the reasons for.

My hypnosis sessions, as well as the visitations, continued. I was remembering much more and I wasn't as afraid as I was during the first few months of my investigation. That is not to say I had no fear because I certainly did. It had just subsided more a little each time as I realized that even though they were still taking me, I was always returned unharmed, relatively speaking. The day after this vision I had another appointment with Dr. Overlade.

We discussed the two most recent experiences and I gave him a written copy of my journal entries from my journal. He glanced at the picture I had drawn of the uniformed Beings and people, and then at what I had written and told me he would read it later when he had a little more time. We would end up looking into the experience when I received the two puncture wounds in my neck. After Dr. Overlade gave me the usual induction procedure, the questioning began. Because I was so apprehensive, a distancing technique was employed. This involved having me view myself in the scene as if I were in a theater watching a movie. I remembered lying on a table and looking at an alien who had something in his hands.

"You say you saw something in his hands."
"Something in a container. The container is short and wide. It's something like a rod. Small, skinny, glass. Like a glass rod or spear."
"Can you take a close look at his hands?"
"No."
"Can't or choose not to?"

> "I just see his face and I see him holding this beaker-like container. I'm just looking at his face."

I was frightened because I knew the alien was going to do something to me with this clear rod-like instrument. He seemed to be reassuring me that I would be okay, but I didn't trust him. The next memory I had was of walking around on a huge spacecraft. There were Beings with me but they would not allow me to see them. It seemed they were more likely to allow me to see them when I was interacting with babies or children, as opposed to walking around on their craft.

> "Who is it they won't let you see?" Dr. Overlade asked.
> "The [Beings] in control."
> "They let you see the babies again, but they won't let you see who is in control? Unless you are in a clinical circumstance? Am I understanding you correctly?"
> "Yes—And under restraints." I added.
> "Under physical restraint?"
> "I think it's mental control."
> "Well, from what I understood you to say, under those circumstances you have sometimes been permitted to see them, or thought you had. Unconscious, was there such a clinical circumstance in this dream, abduction, or whatever? (YES) So she does get to see them in this circumstance? (YES) Would it be all right for her to remember and describe them? (NO) Uh, is the opposition to remembering and describing, fear? (YES)"

After a few more questions, Dr. Overlade brought me out of the trance.[11] At times, I still found myself somewhat skeptical of hypnosis, especially when it involved *my* memories. I suppose I was being overly cautious with its use. I couldn't help but feel more comfortable with what I remembered immediately after an experience, or with my spontaneous memories, than what I remembered during hypnosis.

Erik had an interest in UFOs as an adolescent, and he did a science project on the subject. It was not until 1988, when the two of us were cleaning out a closet together in the house we recently moved into, (the same house he grew up in) that Erik remembered the event that took place. He was at a science fair where he was displaying his science project titled, "UFOs: Fact or Fantasy?" His memory came riveting back to him when he found his ribbon for his project. We sat on the carpet together looking at the pictures and the ribbon. It was an uncanny feeling for both of us. This is Erik's account of what happened.

> *In 1969, at age 16, I participated in my high school science fair with a project about UFOs. My primary research was a Project Blue Book*

document supplied by the U.S. Air Force and other materials published and available through my local library. Almost all of the information gathered indicated the phenomenon was fantasy, but I wanted to remain open and objective. In designing the project, I decided what was really needed were photographs of a UFO. After arming myself with a 126 camera I began to sky watch. My effort was futile and I realized something needed to happen very quickly if I were to make my deadline.

I gathered an old plastic garbage can lid, a fishing pole, and some clear fishing line and headed down to the waterfront. There, I assembled my UFO and proceeded to suspend it over the water with one hand, while photographing it with the other. The photos were remarkable and much more realistic than I hoped. Just what I needed to complete my project.

The project won a blue ribbon at my high school and the opportunity to present it at the regional competition. That competition was held at a Jesuit college in a nearby town the following month. When I arrived that Saturday to set up my project I felt a little overwhelmed by the other true science projects that exhibited things in bottles and chemical odors I could have done without.

As an exhibitor, I was required to stand next to my project and explain my hypothesis. In mid-morning, I believe, a uniformed Air Force man came up to me and immediately started asking questions about my photographs. This was a great thrill for me to have someone from the Air Force review my project. He asked me where the photos came from. I told him I took them over the water near my home. He was very interested and wanted to know everything about them and me. He said thank you and left. I was thrilled. Someone from the Air Force had been interested in my project and me.

A short time later, perhaps after lunch, a Jesuit priest stopped by and said the Air Force officer would like to see me again. I went with him to a room off the main hall where the same officer and another man wearing a suit were waiting. The Priest left. They began to ask me more questions about UFOs. They asked if I had ever seen or believed in UFOs. They wanted to know if they could have copies of the pictures. As happy as I was to be talking with representatives of our government, I was beginning to get frightened. Their questions were coming faster than I could answer. I finally told him I faked the photos and showed him some other pictures that showed the pole, line, and lid. I gave him some of the photos and went back to my project. I didn't remember this experience until I found a ribbon from the fair some 20 years later.

As I stated, an uncanny feeling came over Erik and me. We talked about the project and wondered why an Air Force officer would be in uniform on the campus of a Jesuit College. We also wondered why the Priest would allow an Air Force officer and a plain-clothed man to take a sixteen year old boy into a room by himself, without another adult for supervision. Erik and I continued to talk about it for a little while longer, and then I suddenly remembered a term paper I wrote for an English class when I was the same age. It was titled *Dreams*. Erik and I both felt perhaps something that happened to us in our childhood or adolescence may have had an effect on our "waking reality," so to speak, without our being consciously aware of it until years later. It was an interesting thing to remember. But, we could not place too much emphasis on these events. They would have to be reviewed and stored with all of the other data we were accumulating. Four days after my hypnosis session with Dr. Overlade, I had another visitation.

10-9-88

> *I'm walking down a road near our house and I'm looking down at my feet—I'm wearing socks. It is the middle of the night and I'm carrying a box filled with clothes. It's a little heavy so I'm taking some of them out. I'm throwing them on the ground as I am walking. I'll come back for these later—Suddenly my legs feel like lead. I can barely lift them but I have to keep trying—I'm struggling to walk—it's really difficult. I'm walking past the gas station and convenience store.*
>
> *I'm heading for my house. How did I get out here? I'm really having a hard time walking—I don't think I'm going to make it home—A cat—I see a cat—it's getting ready to cross the street—I have to save it—make sure it doesn't get hurt—I'm heading toward her—now my entire body feels like lead. This is impossible—I can hardly breathe now—I'm looking at the cat. It's pink and turquoise with speckles. Her fur looks like Monet painted it—she's really beautiful—I'm not worried anymore.*
>
> *I'm looking up at my mother. She just got back from the "lady doctor." Somehow I "know" she is pregnant and I want her to tell me. I really want her to tell me. I'm furious now. She isn't telling me. She mutters under her breath, "First I'm pregnant, and then there's nothing there!" I'm so angry.*

I awakened in the middle of the night feeling very confused and drained. The road I was walking down that night had a Salvation Army clothes drop box very near where I was walking. I don't remember taking the clothes but I somehow felt that I had. I believe I was supposed to take them to their ship. Somehow, it made sense to me that they needed human clothing and they had chosen me to get it to them.

The memory concerning my mother is complicated indeed. My mother had two miscarriages between the birth of my sister and myself. One seemed to have occurred spontaneously. After it occurred, my mother called her next door neighbor, who was a nurse, and she came over. They agreed that her body had spontaneously aborted the fetus. Shortly afterwards, she became pregnant again and after having it confirmed by her doctor, the usual follow-up appointment was scheduled. At some time during the first trimester she went back for a follow-up appointment and her doctor told her that the fetus had disappeared! The only explanation her doctor had for her was that her body had *absorbed the baby*, even though there had been no indication that anything was ever wrong with the baby. She went back to living her normal everyday life, until again, a short time later, feeling that she may be pregnant, she went back to the doctor. He told her she was now pregnant again! Upon hearing this news she became extremely upset and she told her doctor that the baby would never be normal, if it survived at all. She never believed her doctor when he told her everything was okay. She was extremely upset and she believed that even if the baby lived, then something would be terribly wrong with it. The baby was born normal, and that baby was me.

I finally got my mother to talk about this experience with me when I was twenty-eight years old. I had been undergoing regressive hypnosis sessions and I so much wanted to talk to my family about my experiences. I began by telling my mother, "You know, I've been thinking there might be something to that story about those two men in Pascagoula, Mississippi, who claimed to have been taken on board a UFO. It appears that some other people are relaying similar stories." She was very quiet so I continued by telling her that, "I think these Beings, whoever they are, seem to be interested in how we reproduce." Then, for some unknown reason, she blurted out, "Well, your father was probably an alien!" I was absolutely floored by this statement. Never in my life had I heard my mother use the term "alien," even when describing foreigners. I didn't even use that term with her because I thought it sounded so science fiction-like. My mother was a foreigner, and foreigners were simply foreigners to her, but aliens? It was as if I was hearing someone else speaking. Both of us were silent for a moment and I had the feeling she was wondering why she would have said something like that.

"Why did you use the term *alien* when you said that?" I questioned.

"Because Katharina, you have always been so different from your brother or sister, or anyone else in our family. You just...turned out so differently."

It was at this time my mother finally decided to talk about the two miscarriages. The amount of time that transpired from the time my mother became pregnant with the baby that was "absorbed" until I was born, was twelve months.

I still wonder if the aliens showed me my mother prior to my own birth or if this "unusual pregnancy" situation didn't occur to her again, later on when I was a child. I seemed to know that she had been pregnant and I wanted her to tell me what was happening. When she didn't, I became angry. My mother eventually had a hysterectomy performed because she didn't want any more children and because the doctors told her she had an unusual amount of scarring in her "female organs" (her choice of words). The doctor told her she wasn't having problems now, but he felt she would in the future.

The following night (after my mother explained the unusual pregnancy situation to me) I got up to go to the bathroom in the middle of the night after having a terrible nightmare. I felt something or someone was in the house and I became very scared. I got back into bed and pulled the covers over my head and waited. I believe I was then taken to a ship where I was told about my children.

10-10-88

I'm in a dark room and there is a dark blue-gray mist all around me. It is a very large room and I feel I'm in an open area. "Where are my children?" I ask. A male Being is unfolding a rather strange material—animal skin—no—some kind of thick rubber material like those uniforms I saw when I was in the underground structure. He is unfolding this material onto a thin table about four feet long. This is personal—I'm looking at it—it is very important—I'm feeling very strongly now that this is personal. There is another Being to my left and the three of us are looking down at this—Telepathy—They are telling me about my child! "First, with your son—he is fourteen."

When I found myself back in my bed, my first thought was, "I was fourteen when he was born!" My next thought was somehow I knew I had several children who were living with these Beings. I sat thinking about them, about all *seven* of them. Something told me *seven*. I eventually fell back to sleep and had an extremely peculiar experience. It was as if some of the information I was receiving from the Beings was for learning purposes and I began to think of these types of experiences as "teaching dreams" and often referred to them as such when explaining my experiences to Erik, Vicki, and Dr. Overlade.

During the following segment of this experience, my first thought was that I was going to die by being struck by lightning. Then, I would be involved in an earthquake in a different city than the city I would have the lightning incident in. I would eventually have an extremely close call with lightning in August of 1989. The Beings would warn me about it prior to it happening. Their warning coupled with this teaching dream would, in my opinion, save my life. It was not until I heard Debbie Jordan (Kathie Davis) speak in Biloxi, Mississippi, at the Broadwater Beach Hotel on November 10, 1990, did I realize she felt she was also having experiences she called teaching dreams. As I listened to her describe one involving a butterfly, I was touched and reassured. I was just another face in the audience that day, but mentally and emotionally, I had a type of experience reaffirmed. It is almost impossible to describe the level of intensity that an experience such as this can have on an abductee; to know in their heart that someone truly understands, because they've been there.

10-10-88 (The same night, after being told about my children)

I'm in a city during the daytime walking down a sidewalk with a man who, although he seems familiar to me, I do not seem to remember knowing. There is a white structure behind me and a small tree near me and to my left—we are walking together at a quick pace when he suddenly tells me to stay where I am and to wait. He walks, very quickly, away from me. When he reaches the end of the block he turns around and looks at me. It's as if he wants to get a safe distance from me. I feel as though there is something behind me, perhaps that white structure I thought I saw, but before I can turn around, I hear a very loud snap and crackle sound of lightning. I jump out of fear, and think to myself, "God, I'm going to be killed by this if I don't get down!" I'm getting down on the ground as fast as I can and another snap and crackle unleashes itself very close to me. I'm still lying face down on the sidewalk. I have my car keys in my right hand and my right hand is underneath my stomach supporting my back. My left arm is stretched out above my head. I'm waiting to be hit by this lightning. I'm waiting to die. I'm terrified!

Suddenly, the ground begins to rumble and move, and although I have never felt an earthquake I immediately know what this is. I'm telling myself, "I'm not going to die by lightning, I'm going to die in an earthquake!" Somehow, I know this is to be my fate. I'm waiting in this face down position and I'm feeling that natural disasters are happening all over the world. I'm waiting to die.

I believe it is important to make a distinction between what I call a teaching dream and being given a vision. My interpretation is that I actively participate in a teaching dream. I am a character in the events they choose to have me participate in. When I believe they have given me a vision, the events are *shown* to me: I look, observe, and usually react on some emotional level. When I go to a movie, I am aware that I have traveled to a movie theater, that my physical body is inside the theater and I am really watching a movie. However, I am also aware that the movie is just that, a movie. Just as a vision can be similar to watching a movie, when I experience a teaching dream, I become an actor in the movie. In both types of experiences, however, it would appear the aliens' main interest is conveying information to me. Even during an event I call a vision, there is often telepathic communication and information relating to the vision. It must be emphasized again that these are not just foggy or illusive memories I can easily write off as simple dreams. These are extremely strong *memories* of what I believe to be *real events*. The term "teaching dream" does not simply mean the experience was a dream. Experiencing the teaching dream is, in itself, a *real* event.

After this teaching dream, I awakened with one of the strongest spontaneous memories I had ever had. I felt as though this had happened to me many times before and it was as if the Beings had just told me, "We want you to remember this now—"

> *I'm standing in the front yard of our house in Pensacola. The sky is crystal clear and midnight blue in color. I can see many stars. I'm looking up at them and I'm enjoying their beauty as I've done so many times before.*
>
> *Now I'm looking at a circular pattern of moving lights. A ring of white lights—They are all coming from a central location in the sky, and they are spiraling outward as if they are coming through a doorway in the sky. They have "entered." I am watching them as they move across the sky—*
>
> *Suddenly, I'm in another place! I think I'm up at college! I'm looking up into the sky here—It's happening all over again. The sky here has a thin layer of wispy clouds but they are thin enough to see through. There is the circle of white lights coming in from a central location in the sky. There are people all around me and we are watching this together. Everyone is so surprised and excited by what they are seeing, but I have seen this many, many times so I am watching the group of people watch the circle of lights. I'm turning around—*
>
> *I'm in yet another geographic location. The lights are appearing here also. They are coming in through a "door" in the sky. They are coming into our world. I believe everyone will be seeing them soon.*

When I recorded this I described how I felt about what I had suddenly remembered: "This is indescribable. Awesome! Beautiful! My feelings and my emotions tell me this is a part of my normal memory process. It is as real as my fondest childhood memories. It is a part of my life and it is so familiar to me."

I can see myself standing on the hill in the front yard of our house in Pensacola, looking up at this incredible ring of lights. I felt as though I was a teenager. I saw them again when I was up at school and was studying music, and I felt as though I was older when observing the ring of white lights in this second location. I saw them again in a third geographic location. Did I really see a ring of white lights enter into our world in three different geographic locations at three different times during my life? My memory certainly tells me I did because it is that strong. It is *that* convincing. However, the skeptic inside me wonders if this was really a vision. Was it their way of telling me that one day soon, they *would* come into our world through a door in the sky, and we would see them in many different geographic regions? I think the question has to be asked even though my memory pathways read this as a very real event. A ring of lights did eventually appear in Gulf Breeze, Florida, and it seems as though the Beings may have given me some reliable information again.

10-12-88

I'm driving my Mazda and it's nighttime—

Suddenly, I am inside a structure of some sort! It is silver and metallic. I was driving my car a minute ago, but I must have gotten out of it because the angle I was driving at a minute ago was so steep. I didn't think my car could make it upwards at an angle like that—I'm walking around inside this structure. Everything here is silver—It looks like a fabric of some kind—I'm bending down—no, it's a hard surface. I just touched it and it's not a soft material. It's definitely a hard surface. The ground beneath my feet is hard and solid but it has waves in it. This is really strange. This stuff looks as if someone took a material like fiberglass and shaped the floor into something that resembles little waves. These waves in the ground are about six inches high and they are not uniform. I'm looking around—This appears to be a spiral-shaped structure I am in. I'm still walking around—

I'm spiraling downwards now—but I must have walked down here—I must be at the bottom. Oh! There is a kitten sleeping next to its mother—they are so precious—There is a father cat too—he is waking up—now he is standing up. I must have awakened him. Oh my God! A bright energy beam of light is coming out of the father cat and it's moving upwards! The cat is transforming into a humanoid! A tall blonde male has formed out of the white light that came out of the cat. The cat has disappeared. I'm looking at The Blonde now. He has very unusual looking hair. It's very messy. His hair isn't long but it is standing straight out and it's really messy looking.

For some reason I'm grabbing him around his neck with my left hand—I'm going to kill him, I think. I'm pushing him into the wall behind him really hard—I'm thinking about the mother cat and the kitten—I'm yelling at him—"If you even think about hurting them, I will kill you!"

He is totally surprised by my actions. He is looking at me with a surprised and shocked look on his face. I'm not sure if he knows what I'm talking about. He looks totally confused.

Now I'm in a hospital. I'm in a room with shades of light blue and white. There is a nurse, a doctor, and The Blonde. I think I'm pregnant, or maybe I've just had a baby. I can't remember—The Blonde—he has come over to help me. Suddenly I'm feeling ashamed. I feel as though I've done something terrible—telepathy—The Blonde is reading my thoughts—he understands how I feel. He is going to help me. He is going to keep me from having to do something—I must be reading his thoughts as well—

I'm lying on my back on a bed or table—The Blonde is doing something to me internally. He has some type of instrument inside me. I can feel it near my stomach. It is scraping against my insides—I think he is checking me—He was supposed to let the nurse and the doctor do this to me, but instead, he is taking care of me—

The Blonde is now taking me away from the hospital. He doesn't want anyone to know he is doing this—The nurse and the doctor—they have just seen us and they look totally shocked by The Blonde's actions. They are coming toward us—The Blonde is transferring me from the table I was on into a box of some kind. It must have wheels on it because now I'm inside a box and we're moving. He's taking me away from the hospital—We are outside now. This is strange, when I came in it was dark and now it is daylight. I feel so helpless, even though I know The Blonde is protecting me.

This was an incredible event to say the least. From what I remembered, it would seem as though I was out at night and was driving in my car. Something then made either my car or my body move upward at a very steep angle. Suddenly, I found myself inside a structure. I am clearly missing some time since I do not remember entering the structure.

Here was another Being I recognized and was not afraid of. There were now two humanoid looking Beings, but they were clearly not human: The

Doctor and The Blonde. How could a white energy beam come out of a cat and transform into a blonde, male Being? I never recalled seeing anything like this before. This encounter led me to believe The Blonde could transform his shape whenever he needed to.

It is interesting to consider whether or not The Blonde needs a physical body in the first place. He may choose to assume a physical form in order to make it possible to interact with me. My gut feeling about him is that he is able to alter his physical appearance at his discretion, because I would see him alter his appearance again. My feelings for him are very strong. The Blonde is a kind and loving Being. He appears to be working with the aliens for *my* benefit, and he appears to be in a subordinate position to the other Beings, especially The Doctor.

10-17-88

I'm in a building with some type of large lift in it. It's like an elevator but it's not really an elevator. I'm on this elevator and I'm moving upwards. I'm looking directly in front of me. The wall of this elevator is glass. I can see through it.

There's an alien! A small Grey—He seemed to appear out of nowhere. Now he's gone. I'm wondering—was I moving on this elevator or was he moving? I've just realized that I'm in a room and this alien is on the other side of this glass wall I'm looking through—I can see him again! There he is. I'm actually looking at an alien and I "know" what I'm seeing is really there. I'm totally conscious of it. This is so exciting! I can really look at him without any memory loss! I've got to tell those men—

I'm running toward a room to my right. I know there are military men in this room because I saw them earlier. Humans—They are wearing military uniforms—Navy Dress Blues—They are sitting around a large oval table and they appear to be having a serious meeting. I'm interrupting them. I'm telling them what I just saw. They're ignoring me! I know they heard me. They don't seem interested at all. I guess seeing an alien is like an everyday occurrence for them. They must think I'm really stupid for getting so excited over seeing an alien— They know about this already—These guys look pretty busy with their meeting. I'm going back over to where I saw the Grey.

I'm back in the room with the big glass wall—There's the alien again! Oh, now he has stepped out of my field of vision again. Oh! There he is again! This is so funny. I think he is playing with me. I'm saying silently, over and over to myself—"Not human—not from here—not human—not from here—" Every time the little alien appears he lifts

> his arms as if to say "boo." It's really funny. I'm laughing. This is really fun. I'm so happy I'm getting to see him. This must be some kind of game. He must know how excited I am.

It was as if I was being entertained by this Grey while these men were conducting their important meeting in the adjacent room. I gather it would be appropriate, if not expected, for me to explain the humans wearing military uniforms. Actually, I have no concrete explanation. Although I'm sure there are individuals in our government who know about the abduction phenomenon, at that time, I had a difficult time accepting the fact that my own government would abduct me and hand me over to the Greys. As unusual as this may sound, I was not surprised to see the military men in that room. I knew there were four to five men in the room and that they were human. One of them had gray hair and appeared to be in his late fifties to early sixties, and none of them cared that I had seen a gray-skinned alien. These military men knew about the aliens and I knew the military was involved, on some level. There was nothing unusual about it. As it was occurring it was as if it were something I accepted a long time ago: A very elite group of people in our government are aware of the alien presence here and are interacting with them. The men looked at me but did not speak to me. I felt as if I should have known better than to interrupt them. I was not, however, reprimanded for doing so. The looks on their faces spoke volumes to me. I knew better than to interrupt them.

I can only describe these events as I see, feel, hear, and remember them having occurred. Is it equally as probable the aliens themselves set up this entire scene in order to make me believe they are interacting with our government? I suppose they could have used holographic imagery or given me a vision of these four or five military men, sitting around an oval conference table conducting a meeting. A question I have learned to ask myself is: Was I in an alien environment? Here is a description of what I saw:

The room was large and square. There were a few metal chairs in the room but other than that I would have to say it was empty. As I was facing the glass wall that the alien appeared behind, I remember windows to my left and the meeting room to my right. The lighting in the room was of a yellowish tint and the room was well lit. The meeting room was also square and it was not nearly as large as the main room I stood in while looking at the alien. The meeting room was approximately one-fourth to one-third the size of the large room. The oval table was made out of wood. The men sitting around this table were wearing dark blue, military uniforms. I knew they were high ranking military men but I cannot say they were *all* in the military. One of them may have been with the government or simply out of uniform, but he too had on a dark suit. They were there for an explicit purpose and my presence did not seem to surprise them. It was apparent they already knew who I was and that I was there. I realized the importance of their meeting, and I knew they were already aware of the alien's presence. So again, was I in an alien environment? I would say no, because other than the small Grey, there was nothing unusual about my surroundings and the military men who were there.

If all of this were not enough, an anomaly occurred with this abduction. It transpired one month to the night of the abduction after which I experienced the severe pain in my right nostril (9-17-88). In addition, my appointment for the CAT scan of my sinus cavity was scheduled just two days after this latest abduction involving the military men and the Grey. These events may have been coincidental. In any event, nothing unusual was detected on the CAT scan.

10-20-88

> *I'm lying on my back with my legs spread out slightly. The Blonde is standing in front of me. Someone has told me we are to have sex—I'm not aroused but I am relaxed. It's simply something I "have" to do—*
>
> *I'm screaming—Something went inside me—The pain is unbearable—I'm screaming at The Blonde, "Can't you ever do it without hurting me!" I'm on my left side—then my stomach—I'm trying to get away. My arms are extended outward and above me—I'm trying to get away—The Blonde is looking at me with a look of sheer surprise on his face. It is as if he didn't think I would feel anything or that it might even feel good.*

The next morning and throughout the day I had cramping and light vaginal bleeding that was not associated with menstrual cramps. About one week later I told Vicki what had happened and she very nearly went through the roof when I told her I didn't go to the doctor afterwards. Vicki told me, "For health reasons and for documentation purposes, the next time anything such as this happens you are to go to a doctor immediately!"

She was extremely frustrated with me. I knew she was right, but even to this day, a doctor is the last person I want to see after an experience such as this.

10-23-88

> *I'm in a large room with very bright lights. There are others here but I'm not sure what they are. There is something in front of me that appears to be similar to a deep freeze. It is some type of large freezing device. It is about waist high and it is long. I think the top is open because I can see something that looks like ice or frost and there is a cold smoky looking fog coming out of it. It looks very cold. I feel that this structure is camouflaged somehow—*

I'm standing in this huge, brightly lit room and there is a Being on either side of me. They are responsible for me and they are in control. They are taking care of me. I am not allowed to remember what they look like even though I am looking directly at their faces. They are real, but their image—I'm not allowed to retain their image in my mind.

Something is wrong with my ears. "What is wrong with my ears?" I ask them. I'm holding two objects like Q-tips but they are much larger than normal Q-tips. They are covered with blood. "Is this okay? Is this supposed to happen?" I'm asking them again. They reply telepathically, "Yes, you will be fine." I'm still cleaning my ears out because I can still feel the blood oozing out of them—It's not as bad as it was before. I don't feel any pain—One of these Beings is handing me a tampon, "Put it in." I am—I'm looking around but nobody is paying me any attention. It's as if this is an everyday occurrence. I should be embarrassed but I'm not. These two Beings appear to be very eager to be finished with me. They seem to have something else important they need to do—

Suddenly, I'm in a car with a man that looks like Erik except he is much younger. We have arrived at a strange looking trailer—maybe a building. He looks so young—I think he is going to a bar. "What kind of place is this?" I ask. There is no reply. I don't want to go inside. A woman is walking toward us. Her skin is spotted and bruised and it looks old, but otherwise she is a normal human. She is about seven months pregnant. I "know" this woman. She is a friend of Erik's. He is going to be godfather to her little girl after she is born. I'm going to tell her that she will have a little girl and what her name will be—Then I receive a telepathic message, "No, do not say anything to her—that would be interference." Oh God. I must have gone back in time or something! They don't want me to say anything. I'm scared—

Now I think I'm inside that building. I tell Erik, "We must have gone through some kind of time warp or something—" There are two unusual looking females sitting across from me. I remember their hair. They are the same two Beings who were with me near the deep freeze. I'm not with Erik anymore— "It is 1957—" Telepathy. They just told me—Oh my God! I'm standing up—I'm really losing it. "I have to get out of here! Do you realize that I haven't even been born yet!" I'm yelling at these two females—they are looking at me as though they are amused. I'm so upset. I'm trying to subtract the years in my head but I'm so upset I can't. I can't even think straight. I'm trying to figure out how far back before my birth I have gone—"We will find you a calculator." Telepathy again. I can't believe this—This is crazy. I'm thinking about Dr. Overlade—He was alive in 1957. He is the only person alive now that I can talk to about this. I tell these two females, "I have a friend who will help me—I'll call him." They reply, "He is not here yet, he can't help you." Oh God! Get me out of here! I'm running into another room to look for a phone.

This is a small room. There are controls and panels everywhere. I'm grabbing a device—I think it is a phone. (I-41) *It doesn't look anything like a phone though. It has many wires with small panels attached to the ends of them. These panels have little buttons with symbols on them. I'm trying to dial his office number with these buttons. There's no seven button!!!* (Dr. Overlade's office number had four sevens in it) *For some reason I try my own phone number—My body is suddenly jerked backwards with a very powerful force. I feel as though I'm almost thrown into my bed. I'm awake! How in the hell did I get back here?*

I awakened in the early morning hours feeling nauseous and sweating profusely. I then got up and put my robe on. I went out into the backyard and stood by the water. I looked around for some sign of the aliens, but I didn't see anything. I tried to ground myself back to this reality. It was three-thirty in the morning and I was exhausted.

I saw Erik as a younger man. It was as if I went back in time, and as ludicrous as it may sound, that is exactly what I believe happened. I was terrified because I thought they were going to leave me there. It was an unbearable thought. The woman who was seven months pregnant was a real person. She really did have a little girl and Erik became her godfather. Erik's age seemed right. This occurred some ten years before I met him. Everyone's physical appearance was how it would have seemed they would have looked ten years earlier. It was uncanny.

I doubt very seriously that this was a trailer or a small bar. My suspicions tell me it was probably one of their crafts and it was sitting on the ground. These two female Beings were the same two that were standing with me in front of the deep freeze object. All I remembered was their strange black hair, piled high on top of their heads in a very unnatural, ridiculous looking way. I am extremely confident that these are the same two female Beings. I am also confident that they were deceiving the hell out of me. I felt as though they were aliens, but I was not allowed to retain a complete image of them in my memory.

My near state of hysteria upon being told it was now 1957 was amusing to them. I haven't been this upset too many times in my life. It was terrifying to me to know I had gone back to 1957, a date before my birth. I can only speculate and say they were somehow interested in what my reaction would be. The "phone" was a communication device and I have had at least one other abductee confirm this from their own experience with the same device. It had small panels about two inches wide and attached to these panels were little buttons with symbols and numbers on them. I remember the small room I went in when I retrieved the "phone." The interior walls of this little room were covered with electronic equipment of some type. The walls were covered with gadgets and wires. The room was about four feet wide and eight feet long. The whole "trailer" was quite small and elongated. I still do not believe this was really a trailer. It just didn't feel right. Something wasn't quite right about it, sitting there in the darkness of the woods.

Do the aliens time travel or was I astral projecting? Could this have been an abduction carried out by the use of astral projection? Those questions still consume me when contemplating this experience. I feel silly stating this, but I believe I may have actually time traveled.

During this month (October 1988), one night several people reported seeing UFOs over the bay. I went outside to see what I could see and it was most unusual. I watched a peculiar looking craft fly over our house that night and the following night. This craft flew quite high and made absolutely no sound at all. It was boomerang-shaped and had about five faint lights underneath it. It flew in an unusually slow, loop pattern, similar to a bumblebee in a cartoon. It moved slowly and was totally silent. I watched this craft through binoculars for twenty-five minutes the first night and for about forty-five minutes the following night. (I-43)

On October 25, two nights after the latest abduction encounter, I awakened with a memory of holding my baby. The following day I had a session with Dr. Overlade. I knew I wanted to find out more about the experience that occurred on 10-20-88, but I didn't know what else I had to connect with it.

During the session on 10-26-88, I learned that the aliens removed something from my body. The pain was both uterine and vaginal.[12] I didn't know what was really going on, but after they were finished they brought me a baby to hold.

> "He's so pretty though—He showed me a little boy and he's so pretty."
> "He's the one the aliens took from you?"
> "I don't know—This is another one. I've just got to hold him."
> "Are you holding him now? Describe him to me."
> "White hair and real white skin—looks like his dad."
> "Is he clothed?"
> "I just see white. I see his chest—Yes, I think so—I think they just took him away. He looks a little like my nephew except he's smaller. Looks more like me I guess. Big eyes—Big blue eyes."

I can hardly believe the statement I made, "...looks like his dad." After I finally read through my transcripts over a year later, I realized this was a very obvious unasked question. It would seem that I had seen the father of this child. Why this statement was not pursued, I will never know.

I do not believe a fetus was taken from me, or should I say, I do not want to believe a fetus was taken from me. I had no indication that I was pregnant. However, I did have cramping and light bleeding the following day so something was done to me internally. Again, I could not bring myself to go to a doctor.

My feelings are that the aliens removed something from me and I may have to remain open to the idea that it could have been a very young fetus. After they completed the physical examination or procedure, they let me hold a small baby boy with very white skin and hair. It was almost as if they were showing me what they were going to do with what it was they removed from me. I felt that what they took from me was going to become a baby, and they had done this to me before. I also felt as though the baby they let me hold was mine.

After this session I needed some time to ground myself back to this reality. I had quite a bit of shopping to do for Erik's and my wedding. I visited with my abductee buddy, Mary, and then went shopping. I headed home at about 7:45 p.m. Here is a description, from my journal, as to what happened next:

> I was thinking about how relaxed I felt and I was glad the session was behind me. I wanted to forget about it, and I managed to do a pretty good job. Just as I was thinking I couldn't care less if I ever saw the aliens or a UFO again, I saw a large and very bright white light out of my peripheral vision. I was driving on the interstate at about 65 miles per hour with my windows rolled up and my radio off. I watched as it headed toward me increasing in size and intensity quite rapidly, for approximately five to ten seconds. As quickly as I could glance to the road and back to this light, it was approaching my car. I slowed down to 45 miles per hour and instead of seeing one light, I saw six lights in a "T" formation. The size was comparable to a 747 that might have been coming in for a landing just on the other side of the interstate, but the shape was not. All six lights were extremely bright, of equal intensity, and appeared to be exactly the same size. I saw no flashing lights or strobe effect. I would say with confidence that even though I only had four or five seconds to view the six lights in the "T" formation, I got a good, clear view of them. There was no detectable structure in between the lights. I perceived the lights to be moving rather fast even though they were quite large. There wasn't any traffic near me when these lights passed over my car. I could see cars approaching from the eastbound lane off in the distance and I could see cars very far ahead of me on my side of the interstate, but that is all. As they passed over me I felt a presence. I pulled off the road and almost came to a complete stop. A few minutes later I started back on my route home thinking,

"That's so funny that they would try to disguise themselves as an airplane. Don't they realize I know who they are?" Something peculiar happened as I continued to drive. I can only describe it as an afterthought or an afterimage. I received a strong mental impression of a faint orange light and a stronger blue light. The blue light seemed very pretty and both were constant, that is to say, they were not flashing. I want to call it an afterthought because it was after I looked out of my front windshield that I received a mental picture of the orange and blue light. Something told me these other two colors must have been present, but now as I try to remember where they were in relation to the six white lights, I cannot.

Today when I think back to this sighting, I feel the aliens might have been thinking something similar to, "Yes, it's okay if you see us since you already know we exist, but we're really going to mess up your memory."

I had no missing time associated with this sighting, and I ended up stopping at the nearest telephone to call Erik so I could tell him about it because my excitement wouldn't allow me to wait until I got home.

Erik and I had been planning our wedding for several months now. We had been together for four years and our wedding was right around the corner. It was a time of great anticipation and excitement. We recently moved into the house he grew up in and decided to do some major renovations on it. Even though it was more work than we ever dreamed of and the contractors were still working the day before our wedding, we were so happy and so much in love. Everything worked out beautifully in the end.

On October 28, I had a spontaneous memory surface in the afternoon while I was studying psychology:

> *There were three aliens with me and we floated through the front wall of the house. The three aliens and I ended up out in the front yard and stood together among the construction. The Beings wanted me to tell them what we were doing and what all of the construction was for. I sensed they already knew the answer to this and were actually trying to find out something else. I remember thinking that we had just sealed up the two front windows in order to add a three car garage onto the front of the house.*

A strange feeling came over me when I remembered this. It was during the middle of the day while I was going about my daily ritual of studying. I stopped what I was doing and recorded the memory. I realized it couldn't have occurred too long ago because I remembered when the builders sealed in the two front windows to make room for the garage. I let out a long sigh. October had been one hell of a month for me, and I wasn't sure what to expect next.

11-1-88

I'm sitting across from The Doctor—I'm asking him, "How is it we seem to know each other so well?" Telepathically, he replies, "I have been visiting you off and on since 1965." I'm taking a deep breath—I'm thinking to myself—"But I was only five years old—" Telepathically, he is giving me an "affirmative."

I'm in a very dark place now—I don't know where I am—it's very dark and it seems dirty, but I'm not sure—I can't see too well. I feel as though my life is in danger for being here. I'm only here because—I'm following my parents! We are all bent over as though we are hiding from someone. We are on something—something silver. It's not very wide—It must be a conveyor belt of some type—Some kind of moving walkway. I know I shouldn't be here—but I'm just following my parents. It can't be wrong to follow them. To my left—I think I see children—They are all dirty and dressed in gray. They seem dangerous. They seem strong and powerful somehow—as if they are more intelligent than we are. I'm afraid of them. It's strange that we're all bent over like this and we're moving along—almost like we're floating—

I am climbing down an incredibly huge, round, metallic object with a ladder on the outside of it. I'm escaping—I'm getting away—I don't remember—is someone waiting for me at the bottom? I think someone is waiting for me—

The following morning Erik asked me if we made love last night because he was really sore. I chuckled and told him that of course we hadn't because he would have remembered if we had. I got out of bed and suddenly realized that I could barely stand on my left leg. I began to limp into the kitchen. I looked at my leg, specifically the outside of my left knee where it hurt the most, but I didn't see anything unusual. My vision in my left eye was also badly distorted and remained that way throughout the day. I remember I took two aspirins and went back into our bedroom to talk to Erik about what I remembered.

Portions of this most recent experience were clear to me: The Doctor appeared normal and his usual self as I have come to know him, and for a change it seemed as though he was interested in giving me some information. The earliest memory I have of The Doctor was when I was between the ages of seven and nine years old. I felt his statement was true, although it was fantastic he was interested in communicating with me, and that he allowed me to remember the brief conversation. He appears to be very sure of himself when he interacts with me, especially when he speaks to me (by way of telepathy). He has emotions, and he comes across pompous and somewhat sarcastic at times. I do feel a sense of "relation" with him, as though we are somehow connected. I believe he is a hybrid Being, perhaps a second or third generation cross between a human and a Tan or a Grey. The Tan Beings are similar in appearance to the Greys, but there are some differences and a picture is included for reference purposes. I saw a tan-skinned alien during a hypnotic regression (when The Doctor was trying to convince me the black infant was my baby). When I saw the Tan's face, I described it as a face that I had seen before and I didn't want to continue the session.

Here was a statement that led me to believe The Doctor, and possibly other alien Beings had been visiting me periodically for twenty-three years! What could an alien Being find so interesting about me that he would continue to visit me for such a long time? If I analyze this in non-human terms, perhaps twenty-three years isn't such a long time for these Beings. Perhaps comparing our life cycle to their life cycle is like comparing a dog's or cat's to a human's. Maybe it isn't taking them such a long time to do what they came here to do after all. Imagine what the lab rat would say to the scientist when you consider that the average life span for a rat is three years!

When I was following my parents through the place I described as dark and dangerous, I thought it was very unusual that we would be moving along as if we were bent over and floating, or moving along a conveyor belt. I recall not mentioning this to anyone because I felt I would certainly not be believed and it couldn't possibly be relevant since I had never heard anything like this before. At that time I never heard of such descriptions from any investigators or read anything like this in the published literature, even though my reading was extremely limited. I would, however, eventually read an account of a similar experience having occurred to Betty Andreasson, and later I would hear of other accounts from other abductees. Sometimes an abductee will say they feel as though they were moving in single file, following the aliens or someone they know, and they feel as though they were floating.

I would like to give a small piece of advice to abductees. If you have had an experience and it doesn't fit in with anything you've heard or read, please do not withhold this information from your journals, your discussions in support groups, at symposiums, or with researchers and mental health care professionals. No matter how insignificant or even ridiculous your experience may seem to you, remember this: The book, so to speak, is still being written. There is no one set scenario in these encounters. Certainly, research has shown that there are many similar events occurring to many people, and many times they occur in a certain order, but this is not the case in every encounter. There is so much we still do not know. It is imperative for anyone looking into these experiences, abductee and investigator alike, not to overlook a single detail, no matter how insignificant it may seem. It may happen many years down the road that these details could be the difference between finding the truth to the aliens' agenda and the abduction phenomenon, as opposed to finding one's own truth. It all depends on what we want. In the end, I believe the two will be *very* different.

Until the following abduction occurred, Erik and I felt that he was only indirectly involved in these encounters I was having. Usually after I would have a visitation he would say he felt drugged the next morning and would have an extremely difficult time getting out of bed. Since we don't take drugs other than those prescribed by our doctors, this was becoming more than a coincidence to us, and we were beginning to believe his feeling this way was a direct result of the Beings having visited me.

11-2-88

> *I'm lying in bed and Erik is next to me. I'm straining to get up but all I can move is my head and neck. I'm straining to move—I'm looking at Erik—He is lying on his back—I can see his chest. The sheet is not over him and he appears to be floating a few inches above the bed. Something must be wrong with him—he looks as though he is in pain. Something—I think something is happening to him down at his groin. His arms are by his side and otherwise he is perfectly still—but something is happening to him.*

That was the last thing I remembered and I recorded this memory the next day along with the fact that a bruise was beginning to appear on the outside of my left knee. This corresponded to the area of my knee I had the pain in after the encounter that occurred the night before.

A very interesting scenario was taking place which will be more evident as this story progresses, however, for now it seemed as though the Beings were becoming more interested in Erik. Interestingly, Erik had a vasectomy one year prior when we became engaged. We were both comfortably adamant about not having children. It was a decision we both felt at the time, and still feel to this day, was very right for us, and we have no regrets whatsoever.

As is the case with many abductees who are aware of what is going on in their lives, Erik and I were becoming more aware of our feelings and behaviors prior to an encounter. We were beginning to realize that these Beings had the ability to control certain things we did before we went to bed at night in order to make the abduction "easier," so to speak. One of their favorite tactics with us was to make me really edgy. For a totally, unexplainable reason, I would suddenly get in a bad mood and go to bed early and sleep in the back bedroom. We always slept together except on these occasions. Two nights after I saw Erik floating above our bed and experienced the paralysis this is exactly what happened. I got up in the middle of the night because I heard the dogs in our neighborhood howling and crying.

11-4-88

> *I'm walking down the hallway—it's about 2:00 a.m. I was asleep in our back bedroom. I'm walking toward our bedroom where Erik is sleeping. I'm terrified to go in. Somehow, I know I shouldn't go into the bedroom—not yet. Oh, he's not back yet.*
>
> *All of the dogs in the neighborhood are barking and crying. It's a sad sound. I have to see what's outside. I look out the window but I don't see anything. I want to go back into our bedroom but I'm so afraid. I'm thinking to myself, "Take me but don't hurt Erik"—*
>
> *I'm looking into our bedroom—*
>
> *I just saw him floating—He's floating through the wall—the antique washstand—the ironing board I forgot to put up—*
>
> *I'm looking at Erik now—he's asleep in our bed. "When did that happen?" I'm wondering. I'm shivering with fear. I want to go outside to see what is wrong but I'm afraid I might come across a prowler or a rapist—I'm getting into our bed.*

As I reflect back to what I saw in our house that night, it seems impossible for something such as this to have occurred. As soon as I saw Erik floating through our wall and furniture, I knew I wasn't supposed to be seeing this. That is why I wasn't supposed to look into the bedroom yet. However, I did look, and I did see him. I believe the Beings realized that I was watching because as soon as he passed through the ironing board and the foot board of our bed, they altered my perception. I did not see him as they floated or placed him back under the covers and back into the bed. It was after he was back in his normal sleeping position that I got into bed myself, feeling extremely shaky and wanting nothing more than to go to sleep.

On November 6, 1988, I awakened from my night's sleep with a migraine headache. I had some errands I had to run and afterwards I came back home to try to deal with the pain. Erik taught me self-hypnosis several years prior and I often used this technique, sometimes in conjunction with my medication, to alleviate the pain. This particular afternoon I decided to write off the day and deal with my headache. I lay down on the bed and began relaxing. It was almost immediate:

> *I'm seeing two pale, greenish-white, chalky looking pellets. They are about the size of a half a grain of rice. Somehow, they are attached to*

the end of a long, skinny, bony, finger. It looks like a pinkie finger, but it is much longer—and skinnier. Now someone is rubbing their finger inside the right side of my mouth where my lips come together. Whoever is here seems to have been successful in getting these two objects into my mouth. They went in quite easily—

Suddenly, now—I'm floating upwards—I'm floating up and out of my bed—I'm looking around my room for whoever is here doing this—I'm following them—we are going somewhere—

The next thing I remembered was sitting up in my bed and coughing rather severely. I remember thinking to myself, "Someone was just here!" and then not being able to control my coughing. I had no memory of what the Being looked like. I was positive a Being drugged me because I saw its finger and the pellets. It was not a human's finger. Unfortunately, I did not check the time.

The following entry represents an example of one of those unusual memories I talked about earlier. I hesitated about including it, but on the off chance that someone else has had a similar experience I have decided to include the entry.

11-22-88

I'm outside and I'm standing in our courtyard. It is at night—There is a small child with me. He is naked and appears to be about two years old. He has very white skin, straight, and very thin brown hair. He has a round face. A small nose and innocent little eyes. We are facing the courtyard wall and I am kneeling down next to him. I'm receiving a telepathic message telling me he is in pain because he is unable to urinate properly. I am supposed to help him—I, very gently, pull and squeeze his penis and he immediately begins urinating. The little boy seems relieved that he can go to the bathroom now. I am relieved that his pain seems to be gone—I'm glad he is feeling better now.

There was no other memory except that this experience felt just like all of my other encounters. The child appeared to be a hybrid but only slightly. He really looked more human than alien. I felt as though I was helping him and I felt what I did was a maternal instinct, something I *knew* was correct to do in that situation. In reality, however, I do not know if my behavior would have helped a male child urinate or not.

My regressive hypnosis sessions ended in November 1988. Yet, I was to have encounters that seemed even more incredible than the encounters I had explored with Dr. Overlade. I had been working hard at getting rid of the intense fear I associated with my abduction encounters and I felt I was making much progress. There was still fear associated with the anticipation of the aliens' visits, but it was not nearly as intense as it had been before. I was beginning to feel as though I had regained some control in my life again and it was a wonderful feeling. Little did I realize how long my experiences would continue.

CHAPTER 7

Theatrics and Hints of The Government

Sometimes I feel the need to preface some of my encounters by saying that the aliens either have a sense of humor or they enjoy going to the theater where I am one of the performers. Erik was beginning to remember more of his encounters and this was the beginning of a new chapter in both of our lives. We had just returned from a wonderful honeymoon in the Pacific Northwest and we were extremely happy.

I was to begin a series of encounters where it appeared that teaching dreams and theatrics were becoming central to the aliens' study of me. The following experience reminds me of the scene in the movie *Communion*,[13] where Whitley Strieber, portrayed by Christopher Walken, was involved in a type of theatrical representation. He was watching himself play a magician while his wife stood by as the magician's assistant. I have heard more than a few investigators say this scene didn't make sense to them. However, for me, it was like watching one of my own abductions being played out on the screen. Whitely Strieber described a specific event as a Chinese box—a box, within a box, within a box, and then he just shook his head and chuckled out of frustration. I have to admit that I never read the book, but I did see the movie much later when it came out on video. I found the movie to be representative of some of the experiences I have gone through. The book was published (and the movie was released) during the time when I was not supposed to be reading anything on the subject of UFOs and abductions, (as requested by Vicki and Dr. Overlade). Even as of the date in the following journal entry, I still had not read anything other than *Intruders*.

1-13-89

> *I'm in a huge multilayered "house." It's like a house, within a house, within a house. It is more of a "maze" for humans—Yes, I must be in a human maze. Sometimes I think Erik is with me—sometimes it is a small alien. There is some purpose for my being here—I'm following Erik right now—We are going to the top of this "maze"—Oh! This isn't Erik! It's two big glowing eyes! I'm leaving the room—I'm leaving these eyes—I feel a presence associated with them and I don't like it—*

I'm in another room now. It's happening again—the eyes are here—I don't like this—I'm calling out for Erik. I'm scared, but I'm concentrating on controlling my fear. This Being can see me and it is following me. It is very dark here—I don't know how I can defend myself against something like this. This short Being next to me—I thought I saw him earlier—he is different from the one with the eyes. This Being has a device in his hands. I hope it is some type of stunning mechanism. Maybe he is going to catch this little Being with the scary eyes. I'm waiting.

I'm totally out matched by these eyes! I'm running down some type of stairs—It's difficult to run—These stairs—I don't think these are normal stairs. They are inconsistent in depth and length. Maybe I'm not supposed to be using them. Where are the ramps I came up on? I remember I came inside this place in an unusual manner. I think I came inside by way of ramps.

There are the eyes again! They seem to be everywhere! I'm at the bottom now. I see Erik, but this is very strange. He's sitting at a table eating a bowl of cereal! I can't believe this! I'm telling Erik, "I found this thing—this entity—" but he can't hear me. He doesn't even look at me. I'm going to go look for the short Being who was with me a little while ago—I remember now, he was looking for this thing with the eyes and he has some type of weapon, I think—this must be some kind of game.

Now I am outside with a group of people. I'm not getting a clear view of them, but they are digging something up. It is being presented to me. I have a familiar feeling, as though something like this has been done before. At first it appears to be my yellow aluminum lawn chair—but, oh my God—I'm looking at a bone with tendons attached to it. Whatever this is—whatever this is—it's still alive—My heart is pounding and I'm screaming inside, but on the outside I'm trying to stay very calm and aloof. I don't want them to know how upset I am—I can't let them know how terrible this is for me to look at. There is a group of "others" standing around me. They are waiting for me to tell them what they should do with this Being—I'm beginning to panic. The Being is moving again—I must be trying to block this horrible image I'm looking at. I wish it were just my lawn chair they are interested in—How can this Being still be alive? It's still moving, slowly—I'm feeling so much inner compassion and pain I can barely stand it any longer. Finally, I say to them, "My God, it's still alive after all of this time. We have to help it. Can we help it?" I'm watching it move very slowly—its joints—I can see them—The hip or waist area—it's moving up and down slightly. It looks to be in extreme pain.

It is so thin and so emaciated. I don't understand how it can still be alive. I'm seeing the yellow straps of my lawn chair again. Is this a Being or my lawn chair? Am I camouflaging this Being by mentally superimposing my yellow lawn chair over its image? Are they trying to fool me? This is the third time I have seen something like this. I'm remembering—this has been done to me using two other animals and I have to stand helplessly by—watching—the inner pain I am feeling is beyond words.

Now I am standing in the middle of a road with one-way traffic—There are double lanes—Traffic is heading away from me, but there is one car approaching me. It must be going down the wrong side of the road!

Suddenly there are a lot of cars. They are now swerving out of the way from that other car—This car is heading toward me. Oh! Someone has let a dog out of this car! They slowed down and let a dog out of the car. One of the cars almost hit it! Oh no! Now there are two other dogs—I think they are beagles—Suddenly another car swerves and just misses hitting these two dogs too. My nerves are shot to hell. I'm running toward the animals to save them. I'm tired of this—I'm so angry—I'm so frustrated.

It's over now. Oh—this part is finally over. I'm walking toward the car that almost hit the dogs. Now there are campers conveniently parked off to the side of this road I was standing in. This is strange—Everyone has been observing me. Just standing there and observing me—to see how I would react. I'm looking inside the car that almost hit the animals. I'm looking for a bottle of liquor or something. I'm thinking that this idiot must be drunk to have done something like that—I see someone, "You must be drunk—I'm going to report you to the authorities!"

Now I am standing under one of the canvases from one of the campers that are all lined up on the side of the street. Someone is handing me a drink—it is a warm liquid. Oh—now it's over, finally—I'm walking away holding this warm drink up to my nose and I'm inhaling the steam and aroma—I receive a telepathic message, "It has apples and chicken broth in it. Drink it, it's good for you." I want to drink it because I'm tired and very hungry, but I am extremely angry now. They gave me something with chicken in it and they know that I don't eat animals. I feel as though they are trying to test me. I think back to him, "How dare you tell me it has an animal product in it. You don't eat animals." I'm taking a sip, yes, it does have chicken in it. I'm pouring it out. I'm not going to drink this. I am now receiving a telepathic impression that this male Being is smiling or is pleased with my decision. I'm looking at him and I know that "now" it is finally over.

My feelings about this encounter are very strong. I believe I was undergoing a type of testing procedure regarding animals and my being a vegetarian. Erik and I began cutting out red meat in our diets in 1985, and by 1986 we had stopped eating chicken. By 1989 we were not eating any animal products except for milk and occasionally cheese, and we eventually stopped eating dairy products until we moved to Portland.

Animals were always a large part of my life and a love of my life. However, it now appeared they were becoming a part of my encounters with the aliens also. The Being I saw who appeared to be dying was part of some type of training or testing procedure they were interested in. I strongly believe this was an alien and not my yellow lawn chair. I remembered being shown sickly or dying animals twice before they showed me the alien. This alien they showed me was extremely thin and had light tan skin. I saw a bone and tendons as if the skin had been cut away, but there was absolutely no blood. The condition this Being was in was beyond any help I could have given it. I'm not even sure if a medical doctor could have done anything for it. It appeared to be dying. The emotional pain I felt was intense. It is possible I might have tried to superimpose another image in my mind because I could not deal with what I was seeing. Importantly, I was aware of this possibility as it was happening. The helplessness I felt about the death of this alien is almost beyond description. I can say with certainty that I was being trained or conditioned for something. The only emotion or feeling I received from the "others," and I call them that because I cannot clearly remember their faces, was *curiosity*. It was pure *curiosity*.

Later, I was put in a situation where I could have been harmed, but not being concerned with the fact that I might have been hit by a car, I chose to save the dogs. I am emotionally drained, physically tired and in need of a break from all of this. Do they give it to me? No. I am tested yet again. I'm hungry and thirsty and they give me something they know I will not eat in my normal reality, but I believe they wanted to know if I would divert from my decision not to eat another animal under extenuating circumstances. After all, I was physically weak from hunger and thirst, and the aliens knew this.

The most fascinating events were yet to happen relating to this encounter. I found myself in situations where I was in a position to help animals. These occurrences happened over and over again. I found myself putting my life between animals and humans. Whether it was a turtle crossing the road or a dog, it seemed as though it would never end. I eventually got to the point where I became nervous when I had to drive somewhere. I began to notice that a pattern was developing. I would have to go to school or to an appointment, and for some reason I would feel a sudden sense of urgency. Invariably, I would end up being in the right place at the right time to prevent the death of an animal. I ended up saving so many that I lost count. It was gratifying in one respect, but emotionally draining in another.

Another abduction occurred just three days later, which again involves a test concerning my positive feelings toward animals. First, however, something more typical (in the abduction phenomenon) took place.

1-16-89

I'm in a very small room. It's about eight feet long by eight feet wide. I see a table, two cats, and The Blonde. He seems to be in control. I'm on my back and I'm having an examination done—Telepathically—"Not yet. You're not ready yet," he says to me. He's leaving the room. Some time goes by.

I'm not on the table anymore but I'm still in this small room with the cats. I know these cats have spent their entire lives in this small room. I don't know how I know this—I just do. I am certain of it. They look healthy and appear to be just under a year old. I feel as though I'm responsible for them.

I'm a little worried now. For some reason I'm feeling extremely anxious about being in this little room. I feel as though I've been in here for a long time.

Now I feel as though I've been in here forever! For my entire life. Oh! This is a terrible feeling, to spend one's life in a little room like this. It's a terrible feeling—I have to get out of here—I'm looking at the cats—I wonder who will take care of them when I am gone? I'm feeling very strong emotions—I'm mentally weighing whether it is more important for me to stay here and take care of them or if my own well-being is more important.

I can't stay here—My own need to get out is stronger than my desire to stay and help them—Self preservation—This feeling overwhelms me.

I'm out now. I'm back in my house now. I'm standing in my kitchen with The Blonde. I'm looking at him and I'm telling him, "I'm sorry, but I can't continue like this—I have to leave." He seems to understand, but he wants to come with me. Yes, he wants to come with me very badly—I can feel this from him—but he is also apprehensive about coming with me. I want him to come with me also, and I feel very sad because I don't think he can.

Suddenly, I feel as though I'm out in our garage. The Blonde is still with me. I'm being given a vision of something that will happen in my future: I'm walking down the sidewalk in our courtyard toward our front door. To my left I see workmen repairing our courtyard wall. Something has happened to the wall—In the middle and again near the gate. Now—a very loud noise. It seems as though the wall has been destroyed. I'm saying something to the men repairing the wall and one of them replies, "We were told it was unsatisfactory so we're doing it over." I say to him, "I knew you were going to do this."

I have a memory of someone just telling me that something is supposed to happen from 1990 to 1992—Something extremely important is going to happen.

This visitation was very special in many ways. It was not the first time I had felt extremely positive feelings for The Blonde, but this visitation made it more than obvious to me that we both had strong feelings for one another. I felt love from him. This Being cared for me and he wanted to be with me. Indeed, he wanted to stay with me and I wanted him to. I had the distinct feeling that I was doing something for him, something that I had made a conscious decision to do and wanted to do.

In eight months I was to learn that this visitation had a dual purpose. It is obvious I underwent some type of examination and it also seemed they were testing me with the two cats. I have no doubt these were cats. They were not aliens using camouflage, although that is done quite often. These were normal cats in every way. Their appearance, their movements, everything about them was right. I sensed no deception. I also believe they are intensely curious about my love for animals. I believe they are trying to determine just how far I am willing to go in order to save animals, and care for them. It is also possible the Beings are interested in whether this type of behavior transfers over to human, or even non-human babies.

This still wasn't the most important purpose of this visitation. In eight months it would be plainly evident that the vision I received during this encounter and the encounter on October 10, 1988, were instrumental in saving my life.

Just eleven days later I experienced another abduction. Again, before I went to bed that night I became very edgy and started bickering with Erik for no apparent reason. I went to sleep in the back bedroom again, for reasons I would not understand until the next morning.

1-27-89

I'm sitting up on the edge of the bed facing the wall and the closet. There is a young male Being standing just to the left of me—he is facing me. I am very close to him—about two feet away. I'm looking down at his feet—his legs—groin—oh, I shouldn't look there. I'm looking higher now—his chest, shoulders—now his face. He is looking down at the floor. He seems so helpless. It's almost as though he is sad—he is very frail-looking. His shoulders and collar bone—I can see them because he is so thin and his skin is so—so thin and light gray. I'm not afraid—I feel as though I have just done something and they are pleased with me—I have just done something right—something good. Everything is okay now—it's over. Not this young alien—it's something else, but it's over now. He is somehow involved in all of this.

I'm looking up at his face now. He looks Oriental because his hair is so dark and so straight. He is moving his face up so I can see him better. It's as though someone told him to do this so I could see his face better. He seems to be afraid of me. I feel sorry for him. I don't want him to be afraid of me. I'm looking at him—His skin is very pale and his eyes are huge and round. His eyes look exactly like the little blue-skinned alien female I was with in September of 1987. I don't see any pupils—just gray. Maybe his eyes are closed too. It looks as if the eyelids are closed over his eyes. He must have his eyes closed. He looks so submissive and young. He is about five feet tall. His head is very round and his eyes are extremely large—his neck is thin—thinner than I have ever seen before. His shoulders, chest, and arms are also very thin. I don't see any other body hair on him—I'm only two feet away from him.
(I-36)

My feelings about this experience were and still are extremely profound. I felt as though he was a part of me. I felt as though they had just done something to me and now they were showing me what the results would be. I also felt as though he was a gift. It was as if they were allowing me to see one of my children because I had been cooperative. It was their way of saying *thank you*.

The following morning, while showering, I avoided washing my stomach and naval area and I told myself, "No, not today, it will be too sore." Oddly, I didn't give it another thought. The following morning I had a discharge with a little blood in it, coming from my naval. It took three days to heal. When I looked closely at it I noticed a small scrape and a small puncture wound. I have had pain associated with ovulation each month for most of my life. Sometimes it is severe enough for me to have to take a couple of aspirins. Fortunately, this only lasts for eight to twelve hours. After this visitation I did not have the pain I associate with ovulation and because of this, and my feelings about the entire experience, I suspect the aliens removed an egg from me that night.

Erik and I were now realizing there was a definite relationship between our sudden feelings of tension and edginess, followed by my sleeping part of the night in the back bedroom. Prior to the next abduction I began to sense their presence either in the house, or very close by, and I began to resist the feeling that I should go to sleep alone in the back bedroom.

On February 3, I was lying in bed studying psychology and I had the distinct feeling the Beings were watching me or monitoring me somehow. I kept getting up, fully expecting to see them in our house, but I never did. Erik was attending a business dinner and I knew he would be home soon. Then I was suddenly overcome with drowsiness. It was as if someone took a big blanket and put it over my head and everything became dark. I felt I was losing consciousness and I fell asleep. An hour later I woke up when Erik came to bed and we both went to sleep.

2-3-89

> *I'm with my gray cat. Somehow he has been surgically altered because he is about half his normal size. I'm holding him and I'm thinking, "Wow, he's so small, but otherwise he looks exactly the same and I still love him so much." I'm holding him and I'm stroking him—he feels so good in my arms.*
>
> *Now—I'm looking at a tiny embryo. I'm picking it up. It's dark here— The place I picked it up from—is dark. Oh—I'm feeling a profound sense of concern and love for this tiny thing. I know I have to take care of it. I'm holding it in both of my hands, not because it is big, but because I love it so much and I have to be extremely careful with it. It is a milky white color and it is an embryo, not a fetus. I can just barely make out where the appendages are. It has tiny protrusions that will be arms and legs one day. I'm carrying it around with me and I'm loving it. I'm showing it affection. I want it to know how much I love it—I'm putting it down now.*
>
> *Some time has passed? I'm very worried for the little embryo—I'm looking for it. I'm picking it up again. I'm cuddling it and I want to take care of it. My feelings of love are so profound I can hardly contain them.*

At some time during the night I looked at Erik. He was lying on his back with his eyes open and he was staring up at the ceiling with a distant stare in his eyes. Somehow, I knew he was angry. I awakened the following morning feeling extremely drugged. Erik's first words to me were, "Not again—"

Erik and I decided we would begin to try to find a way to catch a glimpse of the aliens before they visited us again. On February 14, Erik set the alarm clock for 4:00 a.m. He had gotten in the peculiar habit of setting the dishwasher to come on at 3:15 a.m. Since we felt the aliens were abducting us about that time, we made a conscious effort to start setting the dishwasher at an earlier time because we felt the sound of the dishwasher might be interfering with something that was associated with the Beings, and it might be important for us to hear it, or at least sense it. Here is Erik's memory from a visitation on the fourteenth.

2-14-89

> *I had the alarm set for four o'clock in the morning to see if we could spot them. At 3:30 a.m. I opened my eyes and saw a figure. It shocked me at first because they weren't supposed to be here until four o'clock. I told myself I was dreaming and went back to sleep. Several minutes later, I opened my eyes again and they were still there. Two of them were to my left and one was behind and above me. I thought they were in my mind because the one looking down at me would have had to be floating and partially in the wall. The one overhead seemed older and more green than gray in color. His face was also longer than normal. I told myself to go back to sleep, and I did. At 4:00 a.m. the alarm went off and we got up. I thought to myself, they weren't here now because they had been here earlier.*

I was somewhat frustrated with Erik for not waking me up and telling me they were standing right next to us! I couldn't believe it. Clearly, something more happened than Erik was remembering because the next day when I got into my car to go to school my radio was playing!

My car radio was never wired properly to begin with. My ex-husband put the radio in the car when we first purchased it back in 1983 and he didn't connect it properly. This meant the radio would have to be manually turned off even if the ignition was off. It wasn't a big deal and it was something I was used to doing. The radio is still operating like this today. What was unusual about my radio being on was the sound was up rather loud and there is no way I could have gotten out of my car the afternoon before and left my radio on because I would have heard it. In addition, by this time I had been turning my radio off each time I got out of my car for six years!

When I got into my car that day I felt very uncomfortable. I was almost afraid. I had an extremely eerie feeling. If I had left my radio on, it would have been playing ever since I returned from my psychology class the previous day. I feared my car wouldn't start since it had been on for at least twenty-four hours, or so I thought. I was relieved when the engine started and I was thankful that I wouldn't have to miss my class. After my classes I got into my car and suddenly realized how low on gas I was. I quickly drove to my favorite gas station. When I pulled up a young man asked me if I knew that my headlights were on and, of course, I said no because I didn't turn them on. Why would I turn my lights on in broad daylight? Again, I felt an uncomfortable feeling set in. The young man then asked me if he could check the oil and I said, "No thank you," since Erik always takes care of my car and I usually check my own oil.

Then the strangest feeling came over me. I thought about my radio playing all night, and then my headlights coming on. I know I hadn't touched the switch except to turn them off. I am also fanatical about keeping my doors locked at *all* times even while I'm in the car. I told the young man I had a feeling it might be a good idea for him to check the oil after all. By this time I was curious as to what I would find out next. The gas station attendant said, "Your car seems to be totally out of oil, Miss. I can't believe your light didn't come on. Apparently there's enough in the engine but there's nothing on the dipstick." I walked over and looked at the dipstick for myself. It was clean. I inserted the dipstick and pulled it out again and looked at it. It was still clean. I asked the attendant to put a couple of quarts of oil in for me, but they never registered on the dipstick. I hoped it was enough to get me home and I nervously drove straight home. Erik and I added several more quarts of oil over the next two days.

I drove home wondering what could possibly be happening? All of this seemed so crazy to me. It seemed as though someone did something to my car, but it just didn't make any sense. I began thinking, "What is going to happen next?" It only took five days to find out. As amazing as this sounds, I think someone came back to repair my car!

2-20-89

Erik and I are driving along a highway (a road we travel on daily)—traffic has stopped. There is a woman in a white car—now I'm looking up and I can see five alien crafts! They are flying in a sideways "V" formation, in the direction of the wide part of the "V"—A delta formation? (<) **(I-53)**

I'm out of our car looking for a camera. The woman in the white car—I'm opening her car door because she has a camera on her seat. "I'm going to borrow your camera, is that okay?" I'm taking her camera—I have to get a picture of this! The woman is so stunned—she is staring up at the crafts with a distant stare in her eyes. She responds with a drugged sounding voice, "Um-hm." I'm clicking off pictures of these incredible crafts. Picture after picture, as they move across the sky.

Suddenly, Erik and I are in a very large city with very tall buildings—this looks as if it could be New York city, but I'm not sure where we are. We are looking up at practically fifty to a hundred crafts! They're everywhere! It's like watching traffic on an invisible interstate in the sky. Wow—the feeling I have is so positive—it's as if I'm finally "home." This feeling is almost indescribable. I feel as I did when I was a child and I would be lost for what seemed like hours, and suddenly I would find my way back home somehow. I would be so happy—I'm feeling as though I have been away from my "family" all of my life—since the day I was born—and now I am back home again—where I belong. I no longer think this is New York city—could this be one of "their" cities? I'm so happy, so at ease. Nothing I have ever experienced on Earth can touch this feeling I have right now. Visual and emotional beauty surrounds me. I'm looking down on this city from a very high place. It is so full of activity and electricity! I'm looking up too—And I'm seeing all kinds of different crafts above me. (I-46) (I-47)

Now I'm alone in a large, white room. The government has just taken my car and my camera away from me. The camera I more or less stole from that lady in the white car. I'm worried—"Do not worry"—A telepathic message—It's "Them"—I feel at ease now. The aliens are working with the government and everything is okay. They just told me that everything is okay and I will get my car back. Something was wrong with it and they are going to repair it. I'm feeling relaxed now—I trust them completely.

Now I'm in another room. This place is very big and dark down here. It looks like a huge warehouse or hangar. There are humans and aliens working side by side here. My car is being studied. They have all kinds of devices hooked up to it. There are many wires attached to different parts of the engine, and these are in turn connected to a large machine of theirs. There is a large, silver metallic cylinder in the middle of the interior of my car. It's about eight inches wide and two feet high. It is between the two front seats where the gear shift should be. I don't trust these government people—the humans, but I do trust the aliens. I know when the aliens tell me they are going to do something they mean what they say and they do it. I never know what to expect with these government people.

Now I'm back in the room I was in earlier—The large white room. Telepathy—Someone has just told me everything will be okay and I will have my things back in a short while. I feel happy. I know the aliens are capable of doing everything they say.

I remember trying to describe my feelings of being home to Erik. I struggled with the words but there were none in our language to describe the intensely wonderful feelings I had at being home again. It was very frustrating to even try.

    I mentioned there were government personnel working with the aliens. I am not implying conspiracy, I am just reporting what I remember. I find it strange that I would trust an alien race before I would trust my own government, but that is indeed what I felt and I do not know why I felt that way. Once again, I did not feel in any way that it was wrong or unusual for our government to be working with these Beings.

All of the humans I saw were males. They were wearing blue shirts with dark blue slacks and were busy working on one sort of task or another. These men did not appear drugged or dazed, nor did they behave as though they had been forced into this situation. They were simply doing their job.

I am highly suspicious about my car. I believe I may have been taken six days earlier while in my car on 2-14-89. Although I do not have any memory of this event, it is possible it could have occurred. This was the night Erik saw the aliens standing around our bed. At the very least, it is possible the aliens did something to my car while it was parked in the driveway. That may account for the radio being on the following morning, the missing oil, and the headlights turning on by themselves. I am curious, however, as to why it would take the aliens six days to get back to my car or me.

I believe the implications for this next visit are even more incredible. Although it should have been somewhat disturbing to me, it did not make me feel the way I would have imagined it would if I had heard this from another abductee.

3-1-89

> *I'm on another planet. No one has been here before or so they are trying to lead me to believe. There is an "omnipresent" city on the horizon. All of the buildings are either domed-shaped or triangular-shaped. The triangular-shaped buildings are extremely tall and they look like gigantic crystals. They are all located in a cluster and are closer to me than the domed-shaped buildings. The crystal-shaped structures are far away from the rest of the city. The domes are illuminated from within. They glow with a soft white color and the sides of these domes are silver-gray. The city goes on along the horizon for as far as I can see. (I-22)*

> *Now I remember. A little while ago I was in the air. I saw these gigantic crystal-shaped objects from a position above them. I flew over them in some type of craft. They were beautiful. Now I'm looking at them from my position on the ground—wherever I am.*

> *Some time has passed—I am now engaged in some type of warfare. The city is still off in the distance. I think I'm being trained for some type of guerrilla warfare—I'm wearing a body suit—I can see other people in body suits. Yes—we are engaged in some type of training. I'm engaged in combat. I'm firing a strange weapon. It is long, like a machine gun but it is very light and there is no jerking motion associated with it when it is fired. I've never seen a weapon such as this*

before—I'm surprised I know how to use it, but I do. I've learned to do this and we are practicing for something. Someone is coaching me. I think I just messed up. Someone has just told me I have been hit. I think they are a little disappointed in me because I wasn't paying attention to what I was doing. I don't know if I really believe in what I'm doing here. This doesn't seem right—to learn how to kill.

This planet I was on was somewhat desolate looking but the dome-shaped buildings and the huge triangular-shaped objects were aesthetically pleasing to me. There were no trees, shrubs or grass that I could see even when I was flying over the crystal objects. These crystal structures may have been buildings of some sort, but I suppose they could, in fact, have been large crystals. It does seem impossible for crystals to be as large as a fifty to one-hundred-story building. I am left with the idea that they were probably buildings or artificial structures of some sort. The sky was always dark while I was here. I noticed it when I was viewing the city from above, probably from inside a craft because I remember looking through windows and downwards, while moving through the sky and observing the city.

I was told something during this experience that I included in the original journal entry of this event. However, I did not want to include it in this text until now. I feel all of the information I am given has the potential to be important in some way, even though some of it may be difficult for some people (including myself) to accept. I ended up using this information in my journal by titling the journal entry after the information I had been given. The information I was told was: "You are on the dark side of the moon. No one has ever been here before." I thought they meant no one like me, that is, an abductee. It would appear there were other people, or other Beings, living there because of the city. I also fired a weapon at two other figures wearing body suits. Somehow I knew these people were not abductees, but were there to help in my training. I am not sure what I feel the result of this training is, but I have a strong feeling that I am being prepared to fight in a war. If you are keeping count, this is the second experience that involves the idea of a possible war.

When I use the term "dark side of the moon," in my mind it refers to the side of the moon that never faces the Earth. It has nothing to do with where the sun does and does not shine. I have no way of knowing which meaning the Beings who told me this were implying. Do I really believe I was on the dark side of the moon? The answer is yes, if I was in fact on a moon. However, I do not believe I was on the dark side of our moon. If I was on our moon, then this base has to exist in another dimension. If it exists in our dimension, then why would the astronauts and cosmonauts have withheld this information from the rest of the world?

The memory of this next experience is fragmented at best, but this may prove to be relevant one day. This was a teaching dream and I will include all of my memories like this on the off chance that someone else out there might have the pieces of the puzzle to which my pieces fit.

3-24-89

> *I'm looking through a pair of binoculars or something similar to binoculars. They are very large and long. Someone is watching me—someone is with me—it is my sister. I'm looking directly into space with these binoculars. It's like looking through a telescope because they are so powerful. I'm looking at four, maybe five different nebulae, or possibly even galaxies. I see hues of blue and green from them. Each time I find one I'm really excited—I'm handing these binoculars to my sister so she can look too.*

The next thing I remember is having a terrible nightmare about the slaughter of many different animals. I was in a maze that was also a zoo and I remember seeing seals. My sister was in this nightmare and I was led to believe, very successfully I might add, that she and the rest of my family were contributing to the slaughter of these seals. I was put in a position where I had to choose between the animals and my own family. I decided to forsake my family. I could not, and would not, accept what they were doing to these animals. It was a very powerful experience and it still bothers me to this day. I was so upset the following day that I could only record an outline. I could not bring myself to write down the details of this experience and I didn't like what this teaching dream was showing me. I felt the Beings were trying to manipulate my feelings for my family by putting this experience into my memory.

3-28-89

> *I'm driving my car on the west side of town. I'm not exactly sure where I am, but I am definitely on the west side of town. This feels so familiar and I feel as though I was just out this way not too long ago. I know exactly where I am going—I'm turning right onto another road—Oh! It's not a road after all! My car is driving in something that is all blue and wavy. I must be on a platform of some type. I'm looking out of my window and there is a drop off of at least fifteen feet! I can see a young couple in a car in front of me—I don't like driving on this—*
>
> *Now none of us are in our cars, but we are still in this blue wavy looking—stuff. I can't maneuver on this! I'm scared! I'm falling! I'm falling!*
>
> *Someone is putting something up my nose. It's cool—It's cold and wet. I'm floating now. I'm putting my arms up in the air—I'm lying on my*

back with my arms up in the air—I'm trying to get my balance. I'm trying to figure out which way is up. I'm falling asleep—I'm falling asleep—I'm going to go to sleep for a long, long time—

I'm awake now. Wow, I'm feeling extremely dizzy, almost delirious. I'm trying to stand but I'm having a difficult time—I'm trying to walk now—I must have slept the entire night through. I'm really having a difficult time standing—where am I? I have to get home. Erik will be so worried about me because I've been gone for such a long time. I have to go and find Erik.

I'm looking at John and another man. (John was a friend of mine in high school.) *They are both dead. They both committed suicide some years ago in separate incidences. What are they doing here? Am I where dead people go? Am I on "the other side"? Someone is handing me a phone—This isn't a phone—I'm trying to dial out on it, but I can't figure out what this is or how to use it. This is the same "phone" they gave me when they took me back in time. I'm looking at a central point where all of the wires are connected. At the ends of the wires are little panels about one and a half by two inches. They are flat and about a quarter of an inch thick—there are little rectangular buttons on these panels and they have little symbols or numbers on them. I've just pushed three buttons and I've already reached someone—I'm trying again and before I can push seven numbers, I can hear someone talking again. Am I calling these people? How does this thing work?—I hear someone telling me something that only I myself could know—I can barely stand up—I'm having a difficult time standing up—I'm putting this "phone" down—I must be passing out—I feel so delirious—*

Suddenly, I'm in another place! I must have passed out and now they have brought me to another place. I see cages with birds—the cages are about eight feet square—This is like a zoo, except they only have birds—I see two of my cats! They look frightened and unhealthy. I don't like this. I'm wondering—are the rest of my cats okay?

Now I am talking to the other dead man. Something about him is strangely familiar. It's not the dead friend I knew—it's "THEM." Okay, this Being is in charge—He's telling me something—he's telling me I'm on the other side! I died and I'm where you go after you die—I died when my car fell off the blue wavy road! I remember the fall—I'm sighing—breathing heavily—God, I feel as though I'm in another dimension!—I'm not on Earth anymore—I'm dead, but somehow I am still alive—somehow.

Apparently they did not finish whatever it was they were doing with me because the following night they came back.

3-29-89

> *I'm on the west side of town again—I'm driving again. I'm out of my car and I'm walking up to an old structure that has been built into the side of a hill. The only part that is visible is the roof. The remainder of the structure is underground.*
>
> *I'm inside now talking to a family: a mother, father and two daughters. Now I am underground in a very dark place. It is musty down here. I'm looking at musty caverns and there are cobwebs everywhere. I'm walking through this maze-like place. It is very large. I'm with the two daughters. I only get a good look at one of them. She is small and thin and like a tomboy. They are taking me through every single one of these little rooms. We are at another room—each time we pause and I look into the little cavern, and they observe my reaction to the room. Nothing here is impressive and nothing is scary. It's just a big, dark, dirty maze of small earthen rooms. It looks as though a hundred people could live down here together—I'm tired now—Oh, it's over. I think we're through looking. We are exiting the caverns into a parking lot. I'm back at the house looking for my car. This side of the structure is above ground. I must have exited on the opposite side from where I left my car. I'm asking them, "Which way should I turn up here"? Someone replies, "Right." I'm walking toward my car.*

I feel as though I got into my car on both nights (3-28-89 & 3-29-89) as well as the night my radio was left on (2-14-89). I then drove to some (consciously at least) unknown destination where these strange experiences occurred. The question I have to ask myself is this: Did something go wrong on the night of the twenty-eighth? From what I remember seeing and feeling, it would seem that my car was lifted off the ground by a blue beam of light while I was driving. I saw what being inside this blue light looked like. It was as if I was surrounded by a blue light and I could see some kind of distortion that appeared as waves inside it. Sometimes it appeared as a cross between a royal blue color and a sea green color. Another analogy would be to say it was as if I were in water containing a blue dye, with many bright lights, but no one particular light source. Did something go wrong when I began falling back down in the direction from which I was lifted off the ground? Did I really die and go to the "other side"? I knew that I would go to sleep for a long, long time, and even felt as though I had been asleep for a long time when I began coming back to consciousness. I do not remember ever feeling as delirious as I did in this particular experience. Was I drugged, or dying? Could it have been their intention to deceive me into believing that I was really dead in order to study what my reaction would be?

They definitely used several tactics, if not to confuse me, then to elicit strong emotional reactions from me. Here again was the unusual communication device I called a phone. I was put in another emotional situation and then given this device to try to communicate to the "outside" with. As you will recall, this phone was given to me once before when I was extremely upset after having been told they had taken me back to 1957. I received personal information through this phone that only I could have known about.

Perhaps something did go wrong. Could I have had a near death experience and really crossed over to the "other side"? Did they go with me, possibly to where my soul was, and continue on with their work and later revive me? Or could I have been physically taken to this "other side"? Perhaps whatever was put into my nose, whatever it was that felt cold and wet, was a drug that was used to induce this altered state of consciousness. Did they believe I would simply accept what they told me? That I had died when my car didn't make it and I was, in fact, on the "other side"?

After carefully examining these events I am left with the belief that they took me out of my car by the use of a blue energy beam and immediately drugged me. I slept for a very long time, possibly even days, because when I was revived I was in an extreme delirious state and could hardly stand up. As I was losing consciousness, I knew that I would sleep for a very long time and as I was awakening, I again knew that I had been asleep for a very long time. The place they took me had an inter-dimensional quality to it, but I feel I was there in a physical state. I guess what I'm trying to describe, as unusual as it sounds, is I believe I might have traveled through time and out of the ordinary three dimensional world. Seeing the two men who had committed suicide some years earlier was purely emotional and somewhat confusing to me. Many other things could have happened, but I have to believe there was a purpose in my seeing this. Both experiences created strong emotional responses from me about two very different things. The quality of state between this experience and the experience where I was told I went back in time were identical. I don't have any proof but I strongly believe I traveled through time and that time only exists in our three dimensional world here, on this planet.

While I was underground in the earthen caverns during the experience the following night, I thought to myself, "A hundred people could live down here." I believed people could and people might have to live down there one day in the future. This could be a real event (in our future) or it could be an unconscious fear related to a set of events the aliens seem interested in having me concentrate on. Perhaps there will be a war in the future and I will have to fight or defend myself in this war.

The small tomboyish female who was observing my reactions while viewing the empty caverns looked very similar to The Doctor. They are not the same Being, but rather the same type of Being. I believe they are both hybrid Beings. She too appeared very human looking and had vertical pupils and no noticeable ears. The facial expressions and emotional qualities of the two Beings are very similar. This is evident in my illustrations of them. (I-4) (I-5) I would see The Female and The Doctor again, but I have never seen them working together, as I have seen The Blonde and The Doctor.

It was about a month later when the next encounter occurred. This is only a fragmented memory but I believe it is important.

4-26-89

> *I'm wearing my pink nightgown—the same one I went to sleep in—someone is handing me a rubber alien head to hold. I think it is a toy. It is inflated. I'm holding it now and I'm beginning to push the air out of it—I'm squeezing the air out of it—Now it is deflated. The people around me find my actions amusing and I think they are laughing. Another head is being handed to me and now I'm pressing the air out of this one too. This happens yet again with another toy alien head. I feel as if I should be pleased by their "gift," but all I feel like doing is deflating them because it is fun and everyone is laughing. I feel like a child who has been given a new toy to play with. Am I with children I wonder? I thought I heard them laughing. I'm holding a deflated alien head. I'm amazed at how close it resembles the real thing.*

I almost believe I may have been in a nursery or waiting area and was supposed to be baby-sitting. This rubber alien head was obviously a blow up toy. It seems unlikely in one way, but it probably isn't any more unusual than our toys. In my opinion this would be an excellent way to condition young children to become accustomed to the visual qualities of an alien race. You could give them a harmless toy in the shape of the unpleasant (or at least unusual) stimulus, and allow them a sufficient amount of time to cultivate happy and harmless memories around the stimulus by playing with it. This would lessen the possibility of the child being afraid the next time they see it attached to a body, that is, an alien body in their bedroom at night.

Is there a possibility these aliens are wearing rubber masks? This particular alien head looked extremely real. It had light tan skin and huge, upswept eyes. A triangular-shaped head with a thin pointed chin. It had very thin lips and no ears. The one unusual aspect were the eyes. They were the same color as the mask, and it would seem that in order to make it appear more real, one could color in the eyes with a black marker or insert black eye pieces similar to our sunglass lenses. Otherwise, it was a perfect representation of a Tan alien's face.

So, to answer the question, is there a possibility these aliens are wearing masks made out of rubber or some similar substance? I think anything is possible at this point, since the only thing we *are* sure of is that the aliens are extremely good at deceiving us.

Back in 1988, Erik and I were talking about their eyes and something about them didn't make sense to him. He told me he believed the shiny, black eyes many people were describing may be artificial coverings to protect their real eyes. Since I had seen differently shaped eyes and different types of Beings from the beginning, I thought he might be correct. We would eventually talk to other abductees who were seeing other types of Beings with differently shaped eyes. However, it was not until the 1992 MUFON symposium in Albuquerque, New Mexico, that I heard of an actual investigation being conducted by Linda Moulton Howe involving the Tan Beings.

5-1-89

I'm standing on the shore behind our house. Erik is handing me a paddle and is instructing me on how to use the paddle and a very small boat. I'm looking at the boat and it is white and very, very small. I am extremely anxious about traveling across the water without him. This boat looks like a dinghy—it is about two and a half feet wide by five feet long. I'm getting inside of the little boat—I'm paddling—two strokes to the left—two strokes to the right—the distance between me and Erik is growing—I'm looking back at him—I'm closing my eyes because I'm feeling a sense of dread—

I'm opening my eyes and I can see that I am on the other side now.

Suddenly, I'm out of the boat and I'm walking along the shore. My feet are wet. It's very shallow here and there is a very strange looking crab following me. It's making me a little nervous and I want to try to out run it. I know I am faster than he is, but I also know he won't bite me—I'm amazed at all of the little life forms here—little crustaceans everywhere.

Now I am looking down at my breasts—I'm lactating. I don't have any clothes on either. Someone is either hooking up a device to me or I am breast feeding. I don't know which. Someone is standing next to me—they want this done. That is all.

It is difficult to say what really occurred here. This memory followed four nights of Erik and me having dream memories of tall cats that walked upright inside our house and crossing over the water behind our house. We were remembering the same general scenario, but we did not appear to have any other details. We used our binoculars and later went out on our canoe to look at a spot in the high grasses next to the water, where a small area of tall grass had been flattened down. This was the same location that we both remembered seeing a four to five foot tall cat standing in.

I felt as though I traveled across the water in something very small and white. I reached the other side, which was quite a distance away, although I don't remember the entire trip. I then saw a lot of little crabs and other crustaceans, i.e., "life forms." One crab in particular made me nervous by following me but I somehow knew he would not hurt me. I also do not believe he was really a crab.

Female abductees remembering that they were lactating or breast feeding infants during an encounter was published by David Jacobs in *Secret Life* in 1992. It was, however, quite disturbing to me when this happened to me and I did not want to tell anyone about it. It is my belief that this is a very fragmented memory of an abduction. An abduction that disturbed me greatly.

My next visitation occurred a short time after this but still in the month of May. I was so flabbergasted when I recorded it, I forgot to date it.

5-?-89

> *I'm in a rather small, clinical-looking room. It is like a hospital or laboratory. There is a humanoid male doctor, a humanoid female doctor, and a nurse. The male doctor is tall with brown hair, but his hair doesn't look real. It looks very artificial, as though he is wearing a wig. His skin is very tan and it also looks artificial. It is almost unnaturally tan. His skin looks old, but he does not have wrinkles. This doctor's forehead is very large and protruding, not like a human's at all. (I-7) Not like the Being I call The Doctor. I'm looking up at him while he is working on me. He is bending over me and I'm getting a really good look at him. I'm lying on my back—I can see the top of his head now—His hair is thinning on the top of his head—his skin here is also very tan and shiny. The room I'm in is small and rectangular. It's about twelve feet long and not very wide. I see purple—on the floor— The floor must be purple or there is a purple rug on the floor. The doctors and nurses are wearing white. They all seem to be of equal status. I think I trust this male a little more than the others. I'm lying on my back on top of a small platform or table. The male is to my left and the two females are to my right. I'm naked. The doctor is inserting a device into my naval that, because of the severe pain, I am fighting against. I'm looking down at this device. It is metal. It looks to be about four or five inches long and a half inch wide with a long needle protruding from one end of it. (I-58) I'm moaning because of the pain—The doctor is handing this device to the nurse or the other female doctor. He wants her to take over for him. She is trying to calm*

me down. She is speaking to me, but I don't know what she is saying. I think she just told me to put my hand on this device. She wants me to try this procedure myself. I think I want to understand how this instrument works and I also want to get this over with as soon as possible. I'm trying it myself—I'm trying to get whatever is on the end of this thing through my skin. The skin is difficult to penetrate and it is extremely painful—

I'm really tired now—must be from the pain—I'm reaching out to the doctor with my left hand and I'm touching his arm—and now his hand—I'm squeezing his hand now, really hard, because the pain is so intense. He is extremely surprised by this—I can see the expression on his face—he is looking down at me. Something tells me to breathe deeply and to concentrate on relaxing. I know I can go into a self-induced hypnotic state to block the pain as I do with my migraines sometimes. Somehow, this seems to coincide with my touching the doctor's arm and hand—I'm feeling lightheaded now—I feel as though I'm floating—The pain is gone now.

The procedure is over now and I'm sitting up on the table. I can see a wall for one-way viewing in front of me. I know there are "others" watching through this wall. There are three humanoids standing next to me—it's the doctors and the nurse still—The doctor is taking pieces of my hair and he's cutting it—He's cutting it in the same place on both sides so it will not be noticed. He is working very quickly—I think he wants to finish before I get angry with him. I don't like it when he cuts my hair! "One more thing—quickly—" I hear him—He is using a metal object and is scraping my skin just above my temple at my hairline. I think he is getting skin cells or something—I feel like a cat at the vet. He seems eager to get this over with. I think he knows I'm running out of patience with him.

I think this is some kind of setup. The doctor has just made some type of racial slur. This is so strange. This is so out of character for him to do this. I thought I heard the word "nigger" in my mind. I'm feeling much emotion from his remark—That is a bad word—it isn't proper for him to say what he said.

Suddenly, I'm in a room by myself. How did I get here? I see purple around me. I'm looking at the floor and the walls—there is a mirror across from me. This is the same place—I'm in the same place. The mirror is so they can observe me. For a moment I thought it was a two-way mirror, but I can't see myself in it. Someone is opening the door. A black couple is walking in. The woman is looking at me and the man is telling her that he loves her, their relationship is beautiful, and he doesn't want to be away from her. I'm putting on my bra out of embarrassment. Now she is saying something loving and romantic to him. He is walking away from the door and I am trying to get my clothes on. "This is all so corny and stupid" I'm thinking to myself. The black female is looking at me and she speaks to me using her mouth and vocal chords, "Look at you—you're all dressed!" She seems a little put out with me. I must not have responded properly. I didn't respond to her at all. Did she somehow hear what I was thinking? Somehow, the doctor's racial slur and this "scene" are related.

I have my clothes on again and I'm walking through what looks like a waiting room. There are other humans around. I feel conspicuous and I'm looking for a place to sit. There is a chair away from everyone else—I'll sit there—I'm sitting down now. There is something that looks like a big block on the floor. It looks like a table and there is a pillar just to the left and in front of me. The architectural materials are dark, smooth, and shiny in texture. The pillar seems to be made out of a rust-colored marble, or something that looks like marble. I see a pen—it is on the table in front of me. I'm picking it up. It is made out of burled wood and it's very pretty. There is an inscription on it— "Clark Air Force Base." Suddenly I feel as though I'm not supposed to know where I am—I'm not supposed to be remembering this! I'm still looking at the pen and the writing is slowly changing to read, "Clark Office Supplies." This is really strange. I don't think I'm supposed to remember where I am. I'm looking to my right at a counter with two or three females working behind it. This looks like some type of waiting room, but the decor reminds me of a military base office. I've been to enough of them, and this really looks like a military base office. I'm seeing the two doctors and the nurse walking into this room now.

Suddenly, I'm in the hallway—a hospital hallway—and I'm waiting for an elevator. There is an older man about sixty years old with gray hair. He looks totally human. He is about six feet tall and slightly heavy set, but not fat by any means. He is a normal human man. He is wearing a white lab coat. I'm studying him. He is looking at me and is smiling at me. "He's one of them." I'm thinking this to myself. I'm supposed to believe he is a normal man, but the fact that he is here working with "them" makes me distrust him. I think he knows what I am thinking, but it's not telepathy, just common sense on his part. My expression probably gave my thoughts away. The elevator is here, thank God. I have to get on before he does so I can choose a floor and get away from him. I'm on the elevator looking for the controls—Oh, he's on the elevator now and he has already chosen the floor. We're moving—he knows I recognize him. I know who he is!

Wow! The elevator! The elevator just tried to "get" me! It just suddenly plunged toward me. This man jerked me out of the way and closer to him. The elevator is now much smaller. It's as if part of the elevator went in another direction to pick up someone else. I'm standing in this small elevator with this man. I feel creepy being with him. Even though he prevented me from getting hurt I still don't feel any better about being with him. I'm shocked. I've never seen an elevator do anything like that before.

This procedure involved an enormous amount of physical pain. I don't think I will ever forget the intensity of the pain when the needle was going through the skin in my naval. It seemed as though I was helping them at one point because I really just wanted to get it over with and felt I might be able to somehow get this device through my skin better than they could, since they seemed to be having such a difficult time.

It is difficult for me not to believe that I was in some type of government installation. Perhaps it was Clark Air Force Base, but in all respects, it would be highly unlikely that someone could be careless enough to leave a pen with the name of the base lying around for an abductee to find, pick up, and read. Nevertheless, could this have been what really happened? This experience has haunted me for a long, long time. I have mentally gone through every possible scenario I could think of to account for this pen. It was made out of burled wood so it could have been part of a desk set that might indicate that it belonged to a high ranking officer. All the pens I ever saw, from Milton's flight school, Pensacola's naval air station, New River's air station, Camp LeJeune, and Cherry Point were black pens with black ink, and were always a ball point. They have "SKILCRAFT—U.S. GOVERNMENT" printed on them in white paint. If I was not on Clark Air Base, is it possible the pen belonged to someone who at one time was stationed on that base? Perhaps it was part of someone's private collection of desk items. They may, or may not have remained in the (military) service. My feelings and memories about this incident are very vivid even after all of this time.

I remembered the older man I accidentally encountered while waiting for the elevator. As I stated, he had gray hair, but it was not a white-gray, it was more of a silver-gray. He was at least six feet tall and was wearing a white lab coat, which to me indicated he was in a medical or possibly other scientific profession. I probably didn't *accidentally* encounter him either. It is likely he was waiting for me and was to be my escort. My feelings about him were that he was a doctor, and he seemed to know why I was there. When he looked at me there was a look of familiarity and recognition on his face and I can understand why. He was the same man I saw in the meeting room sitting around the oval conference table with the other military men. He was the same man who ignored me when I tried to tell him I had just seen a small Grey alien behind the glass wall.

After this experience I found myself wondering again if an elite few individuals in our military and a secret (government) agency were working with some of these Beings after all. One thing was becoming clear to me. Either I was right, and I didn't want to be right on this issue, or these alien Beings have a reason for wanting me to believe our government is deeply involved in the abduction of its own citizens. Other encounters were to occur and they would force me to seriously consider this possibility again.

CHAPTER 8

They Repaired My Heart

As I related earlier, on January 16, 1989, I was visited by The Blonde and was given a vision. That vision involved seeing our courtyard wall being repaired by workmen. It also involved my being told that 1990 to 1992 would be important years.

On August 7, we were having one of our usual late afternoon thunderstorms that are common for the Gulf Coast. I usually opened the garage door for Erik since I was the first one to arrive home. I didn't want him to get wet trying to park his car in the garage whenever we would have these hard rains. This particular storm was intense. There was much thunder and the sky was almost black.

I was at the front door and I opened it to go outside. Suddenly, I told myself, "You are going to get struck by lightning and be killed if you don't put on rubber-soled shoes—" I don't go around talking to myself, but this was a strong feeling I suddenly had. I could not ignore it. I remember chuckling to myself and saying something like, "Yeah, yeah—right—" as I put on the rubber soled shoes and started down the stairs. I walked under our covered walkway and toward the garage. After I entered the garage the thunder really started roaring. I opened the large, overhead garage door and saw a flash and heard a crackling sound from the lightning. I remember walking back toward the door that led from the garage to the courtyard. I stared out into the courtyard and suddenly became very frightened. I had a peculiar feeling I would never make it back into the house alive. I stood in the garage for what seemed like an eternity, while listening to the thunder and watching the flashes of lightning.

Several minutes later, it appeared the storm had broken so I decided to go back into the house. I opened the garage door and began walking down the covered walkway toward the front door of our house. When I reached the very same spot I was standing in when I was given the vision, I heard what sounded like a bomb explode. I felt something hit my head and the back of my neck. I then felt as if I floated up the six steps toward the front door. I remember saying, "God, don't let me die in Pensacola—" Then I saw my hand reaching for the door knob and the next thing I knew I was inside my house. My first thought was, "Why am I still here—I'm supposed to be dead!" I looked around me and realizing I was still here and was generally unharmed, I wondered who in the world would have dropped a bomb so near our house! I looked out the window and saw broken concrete everywhere. It was then I realized I was shaking uncontrollably, probably because my adrenaline level increased substantially in my "fight or flight" response to the sound of the explosion. When I looked out of the small windows in our front door, I saw all three of our box turtles walking around in the middle of the courtyard. Their little necks were outstretched and they were looking all around the courtyard. The turtles were surrounded by large chunks of concrete block from our courtyard wall. It was a miracle they were not hit and killed. I had to sit down at this point because I was so worried for them. I was thinking about what might have happened if a large chunk of concrete had hit them. Then I suddenly thought about my cats and ran down the stairs to check on them. Thankfully, no one had been harmed. I couldn't believe it. I was so relieved. When I came back upstairs, I realized I had glass and pieces of concrete block in my hair. I looked around for the broken window. It was the window that was above me when I heard the explosion. This happened at approximately seven o'clock in the evening. Erik came home about ten minutes later and he couldn't believe his eyes. We suddenly smelled smoke and immediately called the fire department. The lightning damaged several of our appliances and our two television sets. The insurance company estimated the lightning strike caused four thousand dollars worth of damage to the courtyard wall. It looked like a war zone.

    I felt unusual that night. I still couldn't believe I was alive. I kept wondering how I knew to put on the rubber-soled shoes. It would have made much more sense for me to have put on my wooden clogs because when we had these hard rains our courtyard would accumulate about two inches of water. The clogs allowed me to walk through the water without getting my feet wet. Why would I put on rubber-soled, *canvas* shoes?

    I do not read my journal regularly because reading it (and therefore reliving these experiences) makes me feel somewhat depressed. I record my memories in my journal only as an outlet, and to keep accurate documentation. I had not thought about the vision I was given since the night The Blonde came. I was busy with school and too worried about the next time the aliens might come. After the firemen left, Erik and I surveyed the damage to the house by the lightning. The courtyard wall was hit in five different places and the lightning grounded itself on two ends: the house and the cat's enclosure. I was so thankful none of our cats were touching the fence when the lightning hit.

    As I indicated, I had a strange sense of anger about being alive, and although I knew I should be happy that I didn't die, I wasn't feeling as relieved as I felt I should have been. The floating sensation I felt when I was reaching for the door knob was incredibly peaceful. For some reason, it left me with a yearning sensation. I also felt unusual in a physical sense. Something wasn't quite right. I assumed it was my proximity (eight feet away) from the bolt of lightning that hit the courtyard wall. Erik and I thought I would probably feel better in the morning if I went to bed and got some sleep. That night I was visited.

8-7-89

I'm lying on my back on a table. There is a gray, large-eyed Being on each side of me—I'm looking up at them—Oh God—The pain—I have a deep and excruciating pain in the middle of my chest—The pain is deep inside my chest—I'm looking up at them—"What are you doing to me?" I ask them. Suddenly, I'm out of my body—I'm above my body and I'm looking down at them and they're still working on me. The table is metallic. The aliens have a black square cut into my chest. It's about three to four inches square—there is some type of black mechanism attached to this square area, and there are two extensions leading off the center: one to the left, and one to the right of my body. I can't see what they're attached to— (I-17)

I'm in my body again—The pain—it is so intense—Telepathically, I receive a message from the aliens—"We are repairing your heart. You will be okay now—" I feel relieved.

Now I'm looking at a female alien. She has long, unnatural looking hair. It is very straight—I'm looking at her. She has very, very pale skin and her eyes are like slits that curve upward. I'm thinking, "Oriental—but not Oriental"—

Oh, it's like Halloween—she is wearing a disguise and she is spraying an entire can of hair spray on her hair—this is so strange.

The first thing I did when I got out of bed was to look for a scar or a square cut into my chest. I found *nothing*. No blood on my sheets and no scar. My chest was sore throughout the day, but it was not as sore as I would have expected it to feel after such a radical operation. I believe this machine they had over my heart was realigning the electrochemical impulses in my heart because they had been altered by the lightning. I realize this does not have any meaning in science or medicine, but this is what I "believed" was happening. Somehow I believed the aliens were repairing the damage the high voltage of the lightning had done to my heart. Since I had never heard of this occurring before, I then considered another possibility. Perhaps the aliens were repairing a small implanted device that is located very close to my heart.

(The idea of an implant in this location also came to me because I have had two cysts suddenly appear over my sternum or breast bone. The first occurred in 1983 and the second occurred in 1993. In each case I went to a doctor. Both physicians told me if the cyst didn't go away it should be biopsied. In each case, the cyst slowly subsided over a period of three months. Both cysts left behind a small point of scar tissue resembling a small bump).

Two days after this abduction I was still feeling unusual. My entire body just seemed to feel different. I couldn't describe it. I called my doctor and I told him I had almost been hit by lightning and I wasn't feeling very well. He obviously thought this was amusing because he laughed at me and told me if I didn't feel better in a *week*, to come in for an exam. Well, this was very reassuring. I did eventually feel normal again, but it took eight days. I was hoping he would give me an EKG or a chest x-ray, but I couldn't even get an appointment. I thought my doctor's behavior was very unusual for him. I was very disappointed.

It turned out to be several months before I read the January 16 journal entry. When I read it I couldn't believe my eyes. I realized I remembered enough about the experience to remind myself to put on the rubber-soled shoes. Whether they intended to or not, the aliens saved my life by giving me this information.

It was brought to my attention by Vicki that the aliens may have caused the lightning to strike in the first place as a type of experiment. After seriously considering this possibility, it is impossible for me to believe they arranged to have the lightning strike me. They simply have too much time and effort invested in me to simply "fry" me one evening in order to see if I'm going to remember a message they told me eight months earlier. In addition, the aliens may be capable of moving through time and, therefore, knew this incident would occur to me in the future. This was the third encounter that made me seriously consider whether or not they had the ability to manipulate time. I am very thankful for their warning and I believe it saved my life. I am very happy to be alive today.

A rather peculiar spontaneous memory surfaced the beginning of September 1989. Even though it was only a fragment, it was an extremely vivid memory. It would seem to indicate I witnessed much more than I was consciously remembering and I was not supposed to remember what I found. I was a child of approximately twelve years old. Today I wonder if remembering what I found might have radically altered my life. From my surroundings and my size, I believe this event occurred at the playground of the elementary school I attended. I played there sometimes after school.

1972

> *I'm standing on a hill. I'm looking at a group of lights moving across the sky. They are a very bright, yellowish color and they are coming out of the east and are heading northwest. It is still daylight but it is very late in the afternoon and the sun is about to set. There are six groups of lights—This must be six objects. There are six groups of four yellowish lights. Now they are changing—A larger light has appeared in the middle of the four lights, so now there are six groups of five lights. Now they are changing their angle of flight. They have turned a little—I think they are moving higher up into the sky—Now they are*

> *closer to me and are to my left. Oh! One of them has crashed I think. I'm running up a steep hill—I'm running up a steep hill to see what it is. I see something on the ground—it's not big—I'm picking it up and I'm looking at it—It is suddenly "transforming" into a yellow daisy. I'm now holding what appears to be a yellow daisy in a cracked Styrofoam cup! This is something from one of the crafts up in the air, but now I'm not supposed to see it. I can't see what it is, but I know it's something from one of the crafts, so I'm going to take it home. I have to hurry because I feel as if I have to take care of it. I feel responsible for it.*

This could very well have been a screen memory. I believe I saw six alien crafts flying in a rectangular formation while I was playing on the large school playground of the elementary school I used to attend. It is possible that instead of crashing, one of them may have landed and I was then abducted. The yellow daisy in a Styrofoam cup was probably a prop or something for me to focus my attention on as opposed to the experience that was transpiring. I am still curious, however, about my feeling responsible for something or someone.

In less than a week I had another abduction experience. It began with The Blonde trying to show me a possible explanation for my doubts about the aliens' ethics. It may be possible The Blonde was using my thoughts and emotions about his symbolic death to teach the other aliens about our belief in an eternal soul. It continues with my having to "be responsible" for something totally outside my control. Perhaps this is just more mental manipulation, or perhaps they are preparing me for something. The climax of this encounter occurs when I see the Tan Doctor from my experience on Clark Air Force Base. Only the aliens, my real doctor, (and anyone listening in on my phone conversations) could have known I was scheduled for a complete physical examination the following morning.

9-10-89

> *I'm standing with four Beings out over the water behind our house. There is The Blonde—He is extremely upset. Oh no! He is being controlled by the other three Beings. His body is half in the water and half out of the water. The water here is very deep so they must not need to swim—The Blonde is pleading with the other Beings. I'm watching all of this—a clear body-cast—like a part of his body, is rising from him. I think this is a part of him. It is separating itself from him—lifting up now—it's floating toward the other Beings. This "second" body looks exactly like he does except it is translucent. The Blonde is pleading with the other Beings—he is very emotional—he is saying, "Please bless him—that is the least you could do—he is departing—please pray for him." These other Beings are ignoring his*

request. They don't seem to believe in an afterlife. The concept of prayer does not seem real to the other Beings either. I can't believe what I am seeing. I am full of sympathy for The Blonde. I want to help him, but I know I can't. Somehow I know this is being done for "my" benefit. This is wrong—it is wrong to hurt The Blonde for my benefit. I'm watching his translucent "other self" float away from him. I feel so sad. I wonder, is this his soul?

Okay—now I'm somewhere else. Someone is handing me a gray tabby kitten with a patch of purple fur on its head. Telepathically, they say to me, "Take care of this—You are responsible for it." I'm taking the kitten. It's so cute. It has purple fur on its head. This is unusual—I'm so happy to be able to take care of it. I love animals. I'm petting and caressing the kitten. I love animals so much—

Ugh—(Sigh)—now there is an emaciated, gray-skinned, female Being standing next to me. She is about three to four feet tall and has straight, stringy brown hair and not very much of it. She's not very attractive at all. Another telepathic message, "Be responsible for her." She looks weak. I'm walking toward her thinking, "Great, this is all I need."

I don't like this. I have to help her get into this box-shaped craft. She is absolutely helpless. I'm going to have to do everything for her. I'm putting the kitten in this craft—Now I'm helping this small female Being. I'm lifting her up and into the craft. She isn't very heavy, but she isn't doing anything to help me get her into this craft—(Sigh)— I'm putting her back on the ground—I'm trying again.

Now, finally, she's inside, the kitten is inside, and I'm inside. Whew, I'm tired. I'm sitting down and I'm holding the kitten. Someone to my left is moaning—he's moving back and forth—I recognize the gait— Parkinson's disease. It must be Erik's father. I'm looking away from him. I'm so tired—I'm exhaling a deep breath—I'm really frustrated because I don't want to be here. I'm looking down at my body. I'm wearing my white and pink T-shirt, my pink running shorts, and my running shoes—I'm stretching my legs out in front of me. I'm sliding down the seat a little. I'm relaxing and mentally preparing myself for a long trip. I don't particularly want to make this trip but I've done it so many times before—I'll just do it—get it over with—I know what to expect.

I'm trying to relax—I'm staring across the inside of this craft—There's my doctor—He's probing my mind—Oh, it's not my Earth doctor— I'm trying not to let him know how stressed I've been lately. I have an *appointment for a stress test in the morning—I'm sitting up straight now. I don't want him to know. A creepy looking smile is forming on his lips—he knows everything I was just thinking—why in the hell can't I conceal my thoughts? I begin communicating with him telepathically: "You even tried to make yourself look like him for a minute, didn't you?" He's staring at me with that weird grin on his face. He doesn't give a damn about what I have to say to him even though he "heard" every word. Telepathy works both ways. The craft is moving now and I'm getting up. I'm bending over a little and I'm looking out a window. We are flying over a mountain range covered with snow. I'm amazed at what I'm seeing—I must be out west somewhere.*

We have landed. I'm looking out of the window—Now I'm outside walking around—The ground is like hard dirt here. There are some shrubs but not much greenery other than that. There is no grass here. This looks like some kind of camp or base. I'm looking for someone who works inside a small building that is supposed to be a "pet shop." They are taking the kitten from me. Suddenly, a strong feeling—I don't think she will be safe with them—I shouldn't have given them the kitten—oh, I had to. They have one of my cats and I can't have my cat back until I give them this little kitten with the purple fur on its head. They are handing my cat to me—She is emaciated and sick! They have almost killed her! I'm so angry and upset. They didn't take care of her and I'm so happy to have her back! I'm reaching for her—this—this—cat doesn't really look like my cat—what have they done to this poor cat?

This was obviously not the first time I had seen this doctor who was in the craft with me. I recognized him from before. It was the same doctor who performed the laparoscopy procedure on me when I thought I was at Clark Air Force Base. It is important to distinguish him from the Being I call The Doctor. They are two separate Beings, both humanoid-looking. The Doctor has more human looking skin, no ears, dark brown eyes with vertical pupils, and black hair. This doctor has extremely shiny, tan skin and a large, protruding forehead. Both are human-appearing in a way, but they are definitely not human. This tan-skinned doctor likes to make me think he is my real doctor. I guess he enjoys the deception; however, he's not very good at it.

The day after this encounter with this tan-skinned doctor, I was to have a yearly work-up and a stress test performed by my real doctor. I had been having chest pains and was continuing to have migraine headaches occasionally. My doctor wanted to rule out any possible abnormalities that might be effecting my cardiovascular system. My stress test showed no abnormalities; however, my doctor did detect my heart flutter that I have had since I was a small child.

I don't remember seeing the little alien female again after we boarded the craft. It is very disturbing to me that I gave them the tabby kitten with the patch of purple fur on its head. Especially since the cat they handed me in exchange for it looked abused and as if it had been experimented on. I still feel considerable emotional pain over this incident.

When I stood up and bent over to look out of the window, I saw a snow covered mountain range. I felt as though I was in the western United States and these were the Rocky Mountains. The only two times I had ever been west of New Orleans was when I was twenty-seven and Erik and I flew to Hollywood, California, to visit a friend. The other time was when we flew to the Pacific Northwest during our honeymoon. However, the craft I was flying in during this abduction encounter was flying extremely close to the snow covered mountain range. This is another interesting thing to remember because I believe every piece of information such as this might someday help me and other abductees discover where it is they are taking us. During this encounter, I believe I was taken out west to a base and remained on this planet.

My doubts about the well-being of The Blonde were put to rest a couple of days later when he visited me again. I got up in the middle of the night because I was awakened by a noise. I wanted to walk through the house to investigate, but for some strange reason I fell back to sleep.

9-12-89

> *I'm standing out on our deck with Erik and The Blonde. The automatic flood lights didn't come on as they were supposed to. I'm hugging Erik. I love him and hugging him makes me feel warm and loved. I have my arms around his waist—I'm turning toward The Blonde. Okay—Now I'm hugging The Blonde. I have very special feelings for him and I feel love when I hold him.*

> *I've just noticed that all I am wearing is my long pink nightgown. Erik has on his bathrobe—I don't think The Blonde—I'm not sure what he's wearing—*

> *I'm hugging Erik again—I'm giving him a hug. Now I'm hugging The Blonde—Oh—this is so strong—the feelings I had a minute ago have suddenly been multiplied ten times. The love and warmth I am feeling are much, much stronger than they were a few minutes ago. I'm feeling a strong yearning sensation. I will miss The Blonde very much. I'm wondering if he loves me and cares for me—I feel a great amount of love for Erik and The Blonde Being.*

Now we are downstairs, outside in our cat's enclosure. My gray cat is extremely excited! He is so excited that he's running the length of the enclosure and back and he is meowing. He is very hyperactive tonight. Oh, it's because I've brought The Blonde in to see my cats. I think there is someone else in here with us—maybe it's Erik.

The emotions I had from this experience were very strong and positive. I felt as though The Blonde was in love with me and was learning how to reciprocate these feelings by sensing what I was feeling for Erik and then returning the sensation to me. He seemed to either be learning how to experience the emotion of love, or he was trying to make me feel more love from him than from my husband. It was a powerful experience. The next day I remember thinking how much emotion The Blonde had and how different he was from some of the Greys. This experience proved to me, undoubtedly, that he was not only capable of experiencing emotions, he was also capable of acting like a conduit for emotions.

9-26-89

I'm outside at night and I've just finished something—A very familiar feeling—It's over. This has happened before—I've done this before—I'm walking with a small child. Its head is soft and I'm rubbing my fingers back and forth across his head as we are walking. The child's hair is very short and fuzzy and soft—I think it is a little boy. I'm rubbing his head and I'm gently guiding him to walk with me by the light rubs on top of his head. He can't walk very well yet and I want him to know I'm near him and to walk with me without having to hold his hand. We have reached a road and it is very dark here.

Suddenly we are looking at three—no, four—deer. Three adult deer with a very small baby deer on one of the adults' backs. This is strange—They are afraid of us and are running to the other side of the road. I'm picking up the child so he can get a better look at them, and I say to him, "Look at the beautiful deer. You are so lucky to see them at such a young age. You must remember them. Aren't they beautiful?" The child is looking at them, but I'm wondering, does he understand what he sees? The deer have come back into the road, and there is a red Camaro approaching them with its lights off. I have to go out into the road to protect the deer—I'm scaring the deer back to the other side of the road so they won't be hit. Good—They have crossed the street again and the car is gone.

The little boy and I are walking on the grass along this road. It is so dark out here—there aren't any street lights. Another car is approaching—this one has its lights off too. Oh—I'm worried for the deer again. I'm looking back over my shoulder to see if they are back in the road—Something—What's that? I'm picking the child up—I just realized there are woods very near us—I'm hearing a loud rumbling sound—I think I'm hearing a train coming through the woods—it's very close now—I can feel the wind from it—Oh! An enormous amount of wind now—I'm looking up—Oh God—There's something huge flying over us. I'm afraid—there's something I'm supposed to remember—I'm looking up at a "ship!" That's where we were coming from! It's leaving now! It's huge! I can't even see the sky it's so huge! I'm looking at the underside of this ship—It's one of their crafts and it's dark—there is only one light on the underside of it. The sound and the wind coming from this huge craft are so strange—so powerful—I'm in awe—

Suddenly, we are in a house. My God. This is my grandmother's apartment. What are we doing here? She hasn't lived here in well over ten years. I can't believe this. I'm peeking around the corner—I'm telling the child, "You know where you are now, don't you? The furniture looks familiar doesn't it?" He doesn't really seem to know what I'm talking about—Jesus Christ! This is my two year old nephew I've been with! There's my mother. She's smiling, but I do not think she can see us. I can't believe we're here.

This experience was absolutely fascinating. Today, when I think about seeing the deer in the middle of this dark road, they are clearly tan-skinned aliens with big black eyes. That is why I was wondering if my nephew understood what he was seeing. It seemed at some level close to consciousness I even knew what I was seeing was special and not a family of deer. Again, I believe they were testing me to see if I would try to save them from the red Camaro. I put myself between them and the "car." I've done it so many times with them and in my everyday reality with animals it is practically second nature to me. I no longer think about the possible consequences of my actions if the car does not, or cannot stop.

Going back to my grandmother's apartment is something I have to look at with much skepticism. Since it appears that I have "time traveled" with them before and have been taken to "the other side," it would seem to indicate that we were somehow placed back in time. I felt as though I was an adult, looking back at my family when I was about eight years old! Of course, my little nephew didn't recognize anyone. We were seeing something that happened twenty-one years ago!

I have spent a lot of energy trying to figure out what really happened during this encounter. I believe they somehow took this image from my memory, and very accurately so. All of the furniture was as it should have appeared and in its appropriate place. My mother had on a 1960's dress and the colors in the apartment were real and vivid. *Everything* seemed right!

Again, besides the theory of time travel, the only other explanation I have is that they stimulated my brain, took this memory out, and somehow put it in a holographic form for us to see.

The following is another example of camouflage, theatrics, and deception. It amazed me that with just a telepathic message from their mind to my mind they could easily make me believe them.

10-4-89

> There are large cats inside and outside our house. There is a lion in a cage next to our refrigerator and a bluish-gray bobcat. It stands upright and it is also "in charge." There was another cat, but now she appears to be a female humanoid with dark curly hair. She is outside with a Bengal tiger who is walking around the house trying to figure out how to get inside.
>
> The lion is out of the cage now! I have to save my cats!! I'm putting our old cat that lives upstairs with us into the bedroom—He's safe now. My other cats are in their enclosure and I think everything is okay now.
>
> I'm watching the lion transform into a very large, male humanoid. He's well over six feet tall, and the area from his shoulders and across his chest looks as though it is about two or three feet wide. This Being is huge. He is massive and abnormal looking. The female who was outside a few minutes ago is now inside the house. The others have somehow convinced me she is a dangerous cat, but to me she looks like a humanoid. This blue-gray bobcat is still in charge—He is handing me a pair of scissors—They were in my hand a second ago—now they are sticking into the female humanoid's back!—I am told all I have to do is push them in—It was a telepathic command.
>
> I do—It's terrible! I had no other choice! She was acting strange and wild, and they wanted me to do it. The Bengal tiger has just walked right by me. He almost touched me! I'm breathing heavily now—If he had wanted to kill me he could have—I know this—I'm surprised he didn't. All I can think about right now is how to protect my cats. I'm terrified.
>
> "What is that?" I ask, as I stare into the eyes of the blue-gray bobcat. I'm very close to his face—Telepathically, I am told, "A bobcat—" Oh. That is why I believe it is a bobcat, and that is why I believe everything else—Because they told me. (I-24)

It seemed as though all of that "helping behavior" and "protecting behavior" the aliens were so interested in for so long was out the window now. I do not believe for one minute there were wild cats in my house that night, nor do I believe I killed a human or an alien. It was all theatrics and a test of some kind. I would not respond this way in my everyday reality, of course. When they want to make a point, they are capable of making you see and believe whatever they want you to. I am amazed at the power they had over my mind during this encounter. The scissors they handed me were my own, silver scissors with a black handle. They had been sitting out on the coffee table very near the location this was taking place. The message I received from this experience was very clear in my mind: If they wanted to kill me, they would have surely done it by now.

Although there is a lot of time missing from the following encounter, what I did remember was riveting. I felt as if I was totally conscious while it was occurring, but that is the way I always feel during these encounters.

10-5-89

> *I'm in the cellar, and I'm walking down the steps—I think I'm going to float—I think they are going to float me now—Yes! I'm floating! I think I must be having a flying dream—Oh! I almost fell—They are definitely floating me—I'm floating across the cellar—I'm passing the shelves—This is fun!*
>
> *I think I'm going back now—I'm floating up the stairs toward the door—There is Erik—he's at the top of the stairs. He looks mad—*
> *"What's all the noise?" He's asking me.*
> *"Look at me! I'm floating!"*
> *I'm so excited. Erik looks rather perturbed with me. He replies,*
> *"It only takes one of them to control you."*
> *I just saw a bright white light to my right. I'm feeling a little uneasy now.*
> *I'm walking through the doorway from the cellar back into the house. I'm looking up at Erik and I'm asking him,*
> *"Is it wrong to let them control me?"*
>
> *Erik and I are walking back to our bedroom now—I think we're going to go back to sleep. I didn't mean to wake him up.*

I felt a little guilty for having such a good time floating around the cellar after Erik got angry with me. For a time, I knew they were floating me around, and I found it enjoyable. It appears as though there is much unaccounted for time because I remember going and coming and the bright white light, but that is *all* I remember. This was a fun experience for me. Interestingly, it is possible I may be remembering having had such a good time because I have no memory of what was actually done to me.

The following encounter left me with no other choice but to believe it was real and that it had occurred exactly when I remembered it—sometime during the middle of the night.

10-15-89

I'm walking through a parking lot at night. I think I'm walking toward a truck. I'm very tired—I'm so tired—I feel so drugged. I just fell down. I'm lying on the ground face down—I'm lying on top of white shells. I just want to stay here. I just want to give up and stay here, face down on the ground. There is a post to my left. I'm receiving a telepathic message from The Doctor, "If you try, you can get up and walk." He knows I can walk. He's not very sympathetic to my state of exhaustion. I'm getting up and I'm trying to walk. I'm stumbling toward a vehicle.

I'm lying on my back and I think I'm being given a series of injections—I think I'm in a Bronco truck out in the woods somewhere—I don't know why I haven't felt anything yet.

I'm looking at The Doctor—he is to my left. I think Erik is on my right—No, it's The Blonde. The Doctor has a huge syringe—I've never seen anything like it before in my life—The Blonde is taking the syringe now and he is sticking it into an old boot. He's trying to show me what he is going to do to me—he is going to have to stick it into my leg. I think The Blonde is explaining what they intend to do with me. He looks as though he is sorry for what he is about to do. He feels bad about what they are going to have to do to me.

The Doctor is angry now. He's angry with The Blonde for telling me this. He is looking at The Blonde as if he is inept. Telepathically he angrily tells The Blonde, "It's going to be hard for her to get the injection when her leg isn't even in the boot!" The Blonde is looking at me apologetically and it's as if he doesn't want to be here doing this to me.

I'm scared. I've just had a close look at this syringe! It's about a quarter of an inch thick—The Doctor has it in his hand again. There are also two other smaller syringes shaped exactly like the large syringe. They are metallic, smooth and silver.

PAIN—Oh, the pain is so intense—My left leg—it is intensifying. I feel a fluid being injected into my leg—I can feel it moving up my leg toward my knee—I think they are putting the two smaller silver objects into the big syringe, and they are injecting me with something. They are emptying the entire contents of these two smaller syringes into the big syringe while it is in my leg. My entire body is shaking now. It must be from the intense pain. I'm moaning, "It's hurting me—"

I awakened at six o'clock in the morning in excruciating pain. I got out of bed and fell to the floor. Slowly, I got up off the floor and limped out into the kitchen where I took two aspirins. Still dazed from this experience, I got back into bed and when I did, I saw a large drop of blood on the sheet where my legs had been while I was sleeping. I noticed the pain was coming from an old small scoop scar on my shin, but it wasn't bleeding and there wasn't even any redness associated with it. I was dumbfounded. There was blood on my sheets and my leg hurt for the next two days.

It was almost as if everything were being done so I wouldn't have any other choice but to believe this was a real event. There was The Doctor and The Blonde working together. It was clear The Blonde really did care for me. This experience left me feeling that The Blonde probably didn't like what was going on too much more than I liked it. It appeared as though he was subordinate to The Doctor. Both of these Beings had emotions and were clearly demonstrating certain aspects of their personalities by arguing! I am glad to know The Doctor doesn't have any more patience with The Blonde than he has with me.

I described the device they inserted into my leg as syringes, but they really didn't look like normal syringes. (I-61) They were silver and appeared to be made out of a metallic material that had a brushed or dulled finish on them. The end of the large syringe went into my leg so far that it felt as though it were actually in my shin bone. Initially, I thought they were emptying the contents of the other two smaller syringes into the large syringe. I further assumed they were injecting me with something because I became dizzy and eventually lost consciousness. I often wonder if they took a blood sample or possibly even a bone marrow sample from me after I lost consciousness. I could have become delirious from the pain or from the injection. Ever since this encounter, I have felt compelled to have my bone marrow screened. It's almost as if someone told me I could help someone by doing this, or I was helping by giving this sample.

Originally, the idea that I had been drugged and taken across a shell covered parking lot and into the back of a parked Bronco truck disturbed me greatly. I automatically assumed I must have been remembering a screen memory (the Bronco truck) instead of being taken on board their craft. Since I've had several years to think about this encounter, I have come to the conclusion that this probably was a Bronco truck, a *terrestrial* automobile.

11-3-89

Erik and I are in a hallway standing in front of an elevator. Suddenly, he is not permitted to come onto the elevator with me. I am face to face with a small, tan-skinned female Being. She has very dark hair. A mirror has appeared in the elevator and she is mentally drilling me. She is somehow telling me things about me she could not possibly know. I think she is reading my mind. This is strange.

Now I'm in another room looking at a very, very strange female Being. She has rainbow colored spots all over her and she is floating in the air just above my head. I'm looking up at her. She has the strangest looking gold glasses on that I have ever seen—they swoop upwards—Oooh—I have to tell her about the Monet cat I saw in my neighborhood that night—"Once I saw a cat that looked just like you, only smaller."
"I know," she replies. Something—Telepathy—She has just told me she is the Monet cat. It is the same Being.

I'm standing outside our house with Erik. We are on the grass next to the patio. A spacecraft is coming out of the water! It's white and it's round! It's turning over, and while it's turning it is also ascending into the air!
"Whoa! What's—where did that come from!" Erik is really surprised.
"It's a UFO." I reply.
"No it isn't!" Erik says.
Now the craft has changed its appearance and it looks a little more like an ultra-light with water skis on the bottom of it.
"I guess you're right" I tell him. Oh! There's another craft coming out of the water—This one is orange—It's shaped kind of like a Coast Guard helicopter—but not—really. (I-48) (I-49)

I had no explanation for what I was remembering. I never imagined that these peculiar looking crafts could possibly come out of the water! It was crazy! What was even more unusual was there was not any water dripping from these crafts as they came out of the water. Somehow I knew they were alien crafts, but they seemed to transform before our eyes as if they did not want us to remember what they looked like. I don't understand why they would allow us to see them and then not want us to remember their true appearance.

I believe our witnessing these two crafts rising out of the water marked the end of this encounter. We were probably told ahead of time by the aliens that we would remember their crafts as conventional aircraft. They had no sound to them and they moved extremely quickly.

The female Being in the elevator was clearly reading my mind and for some reason she wanted me to know it, perhaps to study my reaction, although it seems they know what my reaction to telepathy would be by now. I was left believing that I am having experiences with different Beings who do not share their information with one another. Perhaps some of these Beings are as alien to one another as they are to us.

Nine days later, on November 12, I had another spontaneous memory surface. It was as if a dam were breaking thereby causing the memories to flow out very quickly. It was almost more than I could deal with. I wrote so frantically in my journal that I could barely read what I had written a few days later when I entered it into my computer. Judging by my hairstyle, the arrangement of our home and yard, and the way I appeared when I saw my reflection, I was able to place the experience sometime in 1972. I was twelve years old.

> *I'm approaching the side entrance to our house and I'm fumbling for my key so I can unlock the door. It is dark and I'm—God—I'm seeing five white lights flying in a sideways "V" formation (>). They are in the sky to my left. I'm still fumbling for my keys—I'm getting dizzy now—I'm so dizzy.*
>
> *I'm looking back at the five crafts. I can't believe what I just saw. Yes—they are still there—I'm watching them fly across the sky in a sideways "V" formation.*
>
> *I'm standing in my backyard now. I must have walked back here. There is my father. We are facing one another. We're standing in the backyard together. It's dark out here.*
> *"Daddy, I just saw five crafts flying through the sky."*
> *Suddenly, I'm seeing an intense bright light approaching us. It's coming into the backyard. This isn't what I just saw—these things aren't real.*
>
> *I'm looking up into the sky and this light is coming right over us. IT IS REAL—It looks like a giant glowing, luminescent barrel with lights on each end. It's hovering over us—now it is retracing its path back toward the direction it came from. It looks as though it is surveying our backyard—Now it has stopped and it is landing in our backyard. It just "blinked" out! I can't really see it anymore. I can only see some strange type of electric current or static that is flowing around the craft. (I-45) It is sporadically emitting electricity, and as it does, it follows the contour of the craft so I can just make out the outline—Oh—I "know" them! I know who this is in this craft! I can feel their presence and I know them! Immediately now—telepathically—I'm in mental contact with the Beings in the craft and we are communicating*

greeting messages to one another simultaneously. My father is overwhelmed with fear and is running away from them—I was just going to tell him to stop, and that he could never get away, but a blue beam of light has just paralyzed him—he has disappeared now. This communication is unbelievably strong and positive: "I am not afraid—Do not be afraid—We are peaceful Beings—I'm not going to hurt you—Come to visit—I am here—" This message is from me to them and from them to me all at the same time. This is incredibly familiar to me.

There are several adults in the backyard with me now. They are afraid. I think my parents were having a cocktail party or something and they have all come outside. They all appear to be terrified—Oh, now I think they are all paralyzed. They have a distant stare, filled with fear, in their eyes. Almost everyone is still holding their drinks in their hands. They look as though they have been frozen in one place. I'm still in telepathic contact with the Beings from the ship. I feel heavy and somewhat drugged, but I am somewhat aware of what is going on around me. I'm not afraid—why are all of these grown-ups afraid?

I've just been given a "flash" message—Someone is standing in front of me but I'm not allowed to remember what they look like. Telepathically, "Your mother is not at home right now?" I answer, "No." They seem to think she is out of town, but I know that "out of town" means she is on their spaceship.

I think I see large cats that are standing upright. I'm in our house? No, they want me to think it is my house, but I can tell it isn't. It is a very familiar place, however. I have been here many times before. I'm sitting on the edge of a small bed in a small cluttered room. This room is very familiar to me. A female is sitting next to me. She wants me to believe she is my mother, but my mother is really somewhere else right now. I know this. This female is showing me a picture of a dark-haired woman. She is holding the picture in front of me and I'm receiving a telepathic command: "This is a wonderful human being—she is strong and beautiful—you will admire her." This command is being repeated over and over again. It is inside my mind. I am listening very dutifully.

Someone is walking by me and they have something—a cart or something. It is made out of a shiny silver metal. I just caught a glimpse of my own reflection. My hair is longish and I have bangs.

I am sure that I was twelve years old when this occurred. I was probably coming back from baby-sitting when I saw the UFOs in the sky. It was quite a dramatic encounter and remembering it helped me to release whatever remaining fears I had associated with my anticipating their visits. I wrote in my journal in March of 1990: "Do not get me wrong, but I've actually reached the point where I want them to come visit me sometimes. I'm not afraid anymore. It's like seeing an old friend or your family after years and years of being away from them and knowing you only have an hour or so for a visit."

As the white light approached my father and me, I suddenly realized this was not what I had seen while standing in the driveway. I believe this was actually a one or two "man" probe and it seemed to be reconnoitering the backyard out, along with the two of us, before it landed. My father was overwhelmed with fear and I knew ahead of time that he would never be able to run away from them. The blue beam of light somehow paralyzed him and took him up to one of their larger ships. Interestingly, this blue beam of light came from a position above us while this smaller, probe-like craft was cloaked and sitting on the ground. This would indicate there was at least one other craft over us, and it was more than likely one of the crafts I saw flying in the delta formation while I was standing in my driveway.

The other adults appeared to be at our house for a social gathering and were "turned off" by the aliens. It was clear by the look of fear and shock on their faces that they had come outside and had seen *something*. I believe both my parents and I were taken on board the larger craft which emitted the blue beam.

The image of the woman they were showing me and telling me to admire is peculiar. I have tried to figure out who this woman is for a long time. I have, for the time being, come to the conclusion that she must be a composite of many different, attractive brunette women. She appeared to look similar to a woman who was friends with my mother during that period of my life, but I cannot be certain. It may have been a random image of a brunette female they intended to teach me to trust at an early age, so they could use this same image when they wanted to deceive me as to their true appearance. Interestingly, it is very curious that the many times I have seen what I believe is a female alien in disguise or camouflage, the most vivid thing I will remember about her is her brunette hair. Then I immediately think back to this picture they were showing me. I firmly believe this was an attempt by the aliens to condition my mind to see (or remember) a much more human appearing alien Being during my abduction experiences.

CHAPTER 9

Teacher or Student?

It had been a little over four months since the Beings had taken either of us and that is assuming we were remembering every encounter, which I cannot be certain is the case. On March 21, we were visited again. I was lying in bed and I felt a sudden feeling of paralysis come over me. It was then I felt myself begin to fly. My ears were ringing and I felt myself losing perception of my senses. My hearing must have been the last sense I lost because the last thing I remembered was hearing an unusual ringing sound in my ears.

3-21-90

> *I'm looking at a light colored hill or wall. Someone is standing behind me, someone is standing in front of me, and someone else is floating above me near the top of the wall. I'm not allowed to see who is here with me. They are trying to encourage me to go up and over the wall to the other side. I know I'll be able to do it because I've done it before.*
>
> *I'm hearing something metal rocking back and forth. It is a hollow, empty sound. I can't figure out what it is—what is making this noise?*

I got up in the middle of the night and investigated the house to see if I could find out where this noise was coming from. I looked out of every window to see what could possibly be making this hollow, rocking sound. Since we didn't have windows in the front of the house anymore due to the added garage, I couldn't see what was in our front yard. I did not notice anything that would account for the hollow, rocking noise so I climbed back into bed.

The first thing Erik told me the next morning was that he had been outside last night. He said he was standing outside under the walkway in our courtyard. The next thing he knew he was standing in front of our house next to the right hand corner of the garage. While he was standing in that location, Erik observed a small white craft in our driveway shaped similar to a car. There was a white mist coming out from under the object and it appeared to have a bright, white light source. He then found himself facing two white humanoid Beings and one black humanoid Being. All three Beings were six and a half feet tall and were wearing body suits. Erik said he was very angry with them and he took a rock and threw it at the

Beings in order to make them go away and leave him alone. When the rock approached them one of the Beings took a porcelain staff he was holding and deflected the rock. When the rock hit the staff it created a spider web effect in the area of the staff that was hit. The rock did not break the staff. It then fell to the ground.

I told Erik about the noise I heard during the night and he said he recalled hearing a similar sound. At this point during our conversation our suspicions overwhelmed us and we quickly went outside, only to find four gray marks in our concrete driveway. They were in the same location the craft was in when Erik saw the three Beings during the night. There were marks where the craft had been parked, but none leading into or out of our driveway.

Erik and I took some paper towels and pressed them into the driveway. We were able to get some of the dark particles to adhere to the paper towels. I then put the paper towels into zip-lock bags, and for some reason I put the bags into the freezer. I must have forgotten them because it was a year later when I found the zip lock bags with the paper towels in them. By that time I didn't think the substance was worth having analyzed. I will be the first to admit how careless this was of me. However, I also do not believe this was a totally conscious decision for me. Sometimes I think abductees are made to feel as though the obvious, that is, evidence, is unimportant, perhaps as a posthypnotic suggestion by the aliens.

4-9-90

Someone has just told me to wait for someone or to expect something to happen in relation to the aliens.

God—I've traveled back in time again! I can't believe this! I really don't like this! It's 1973 and I'm in a small town. Someone has just told me this town is dependent upon manufacturing some type of mechanical device. I'm looking at a young girl—Somehow I know her family was successful and prominent all of their lives, but suddenly they are losing all that they have worked for.

No!!! I'm in another person's body!! This is so unbelievable!! I'm actually inside this woman's body! I am experiencing everything she is! The Blonde is with me—He is taking me through some kind of training session, I think. Oh God—I'm experiencing the loss of my job—my family's jobs—The entire community's welfare is at stake here. I think it is dependent upon manufacturing cars, but the imports have closed them down. These people's lives are wrecked. This is unbelievable. I've never thought about these people before. I never seriously considered what it must be like to have to deal with this. I am experiencing all of their emotions—Fear, anxiety, loss of employment,

> *emotional swings, loss of home, loss of food, having to care for a family—I'm looking at The Blonde and I ask him, "Is this really what happened?" He replies, "Yes." He is looking around at these people and now back at me. I must be back in my own body now. Yes, thank God. The Blonde is observing me. I feel crushed—in body, mind, and spirit. I'm thinking about everything I just experienced. I never knew what it was like to have something such as this happen to you, until now. I'm shocked.*

The Blonde is a very curious Being. After this encounter I wondered, was he, and possibly the other Beings as well, not only interested in studying my reactions to various stimuli, but interested in teaching me something as well? Was this another teaching dream? Were they trying to teach me to buy American? This idea seemed preposterous to me. However, shortly after this encounter I started buying more American-made products. Is this manipulation at its finest or were they interested in helping me feel empathy for my fellow human? It is fantastic to believe that I could have entered someone else's body, but my mind tells me that is exactly what I did. While it is difficult for my mind to accept the reality of what I experienced, I am left with no other choice but to believe it. The experience was so powerful. I *experienced* it. I cannot deny it.

As The Blonde looked around at the other people in this town and then back to me, I sensed sadness from him. It was as if he also felt empathy for these people. I have often wondered why he would be working with Beings like the Greys or even The Doctor. They sometimes appear incapable of understanding what I am feeling in certain situations. I began to ponder the idea that if The Blonde really is a subordinate, as I have noticed him to be when around the other Beings, maybe the aliens were using him, as well as me, for their own purposes. The question now was if The Blonde has the power to physically transform at will, why wouldn't he be able to remove himself from this situation? Is he an alien abductee, or has he elected to be involved with me for personal reasons?

Just two days after this encounter I was visited again. This time by a little girl. *My* little girl.

4-11-90

> *I'm sitting up in my bed and I'm facing the headboard—Now a force is pulling me toward our open bedroom door. There is a child floating in the hallway just outside the doorway to our bedroom. It is a small child—Oh, it is "my" child! She is talking to me in a tiny, high pitched, mechanical voice. Even though I can't understand what she is saying, her voice has a sweet sound to me. The air around her is gray and smoky, and there is a force that is drawing me toward her.*

I'm afraid—Still. I want to go with her but something is keeping me from going—Oh, it is Erik. He is holding onto my left wrist and is telling me not to go. He is squeezing my wrist very tightly. He doesn't want me to go with her. "No, don't go—just get back into bed—stay in bed." Suddenly, she's gone—she just vanished.

I'm waking Erik up. I'm angry with him. Why isn't he awake? He should have already been awake. I'm telling him about the little girl and I'm asking him why he wouldn't let me go. He's having trouble understanding what I'm talking about. He seems really tired. He's going back to sleep.

Suddenly, I'm in a large white, round room and there are a lot of people in here with me. Erik is here with me too. This is really quite wonderful! We all have our arms and hands up in the air, and we are touching these colorful swirls of light that are floating above us. There are all kinds of shapes and colors. This is incredible! I'm touching one now! It's shaped like a swirl or a spiral. It is pink, turquoise, and white. When I touch it, it sparkles and tingles. It is exhilarating! It must be emitting a mild electric current of some type. This is really fun! **(I-40)**

OOPS! My jewelry just popped off! I'm looking down on the ground for my wedding ring—there are my earrings—all I want to find right now is my wedding ring. Where is it? There is jewelry all over the floor. Oh—someone is handing me my wedding ring. I feel much better now—They are smiling at me. We're all having a wonderful time. I guess we're playing a light game of some kind.

Interestingly, I came to complete consciousness after the little girl disappeared in the hallway. I was still sitting up in bed just as I remembered from a moment earlier when she was out in the hallway. I tried to wake Erik, but he just wouldn't wake up. I was so angry because he held onto my hand and would not let me go with my little girl. She appeared to be floating in some type of gray smoke or fog-like substance. She had gray skin and appeared to be about three feet tall. She looked as if she was approximately three years old and she was not wearing any clothes. I did not see any hair and she did not appear to have the huge eyes so many of the other Beings have. Her voice had a high pitched, mechanical quality to it. I don't know how I knew she was my child, but I know I had asked to see her. I somehow remember asking someone if I could see her. I believe I went with her after all.

The next thing I remembered after seeing the little girl was being inside what I believe was an alien craft. We were in a large white, round room. This is where the "swirls of light" game occurred and there were other abductees with Erik and me. The game seemed like it was something we were doing for fun or to pass the time. The game may have had scientific significance to the Beings, but to us it was just fun. There was a certain level of physical satisfaction when touching the electrical swirls in the air and feeling the tingling sensation in our hands and arms. The swirls of light were also pleasing to look at. It is possible the Beings were interested in studying one or more of our senses by having us interact with these mild energies and lights. This part of the encounter was very pleasant.

Erik and I decided to drive to the Smoky Mountains the weekend of April 15. We thought some time away from the house and our routine would be good for us. We also thought it would be good for us to get away from the aliens. After much driving and sightseeing we began our drive back home. We tried our best to make it back in one day, but we ran into a bad storm about three hours away from Pensacola. Erik and I didn't feel it would be safe to try to drive the rest of the way home because we were so tired and the storm quickly became intense. Reluctantly, we decided to get a hotel room and we went to bed around midnight.

Erik fell asleep almost immediately but I tossed and turned for a while. It seemed that I was hearing every sound around me in such a way that the sounds seemed amplified—the rain outside, the air conditioner in our room, and the voices in the adjoining room. Eventually, I became so irritated I thought about calling the front desk. That was the last thing I remembered.

4-15-90

I'm on one of their ships again. Oh, it's huge! Something has just happened. I think I just finished something. I'm now walking across a large platform. I'm approaching a small craft. This is a shuttle. I must be going back home now. This small shuttle is white and round, and the top is open. Strange, there isn't a roof on this thing.

I'm inside now with some other people and we're getting all situated inside the small craft. A female humanoid is giving me a strange look—She has a sinister look and a sneaky grin on her face—This is that female—that Female Being I saw before—Ssssss-Zooooom! My God! Suddenly we're flying! I feel a strong centrifugal force against my body! The last thing I saw was a door shutting over us—now we're flying through the air! I feel as though I'm going to fall out! I hate it when they do this! They've done this before and I hate it! God, we could all fly out of this thing and be killed. That Female Being knows I hate to travel this way. That's why she was looking at me like that. She knew I would get really upset.

Uh—I think we're finished—This shuttle craft is heading out into darkness—into what looks like space—I'm—Uh—I must be in space.

I found the movements of this small shuttle craft very frightening. I had been in it, or a craft similar to it before, and I absolutely hated traveling in them. As far as I can determine, the craft seemed to spin at an extremely high rate of speed, thereby creating a force that held the occupants in place. Although this was how the craft moved through the air or space, it also had a peculiar effect on our bodies because it seemed to keep us in place. It is possible the movement itself created a special force field by spinning the way it did. In addition, there must have been some kind of balancing effect occurring simultaneously. I feel certain if we were really spinning that quickly we would have all become nauseous and ill together too.

Our trip Erik and I took to get away from it all did not serve its purpose. When we arrived back in Pensacola, I was so happy to be home with my cats and the stability they brought to my reality. Unfortunately, that stability turned out to be short-lived. One month later I found myself back on one of the alien's huge spacecrafts again.

5-17-90

Okay. I'm back at the "hospital." This is where Erik and I were shown the little black baby. I remember it well. I know my way around this craft. I'm walking down a huge, white hallway. These hallways are very wide and spacious. I'm sure this is what some people call a "Mother Ship." I like these large ships—I love big rooms with a lot of space around me. I feel very comfortable here.

I'm approaching a male technician. He is sitting at a small table out in the hallway where two of these large hallways intersect one another. My stomach feels full—maybe I've been eating too much lately— Telepathy—"Your pregnancy test is positive," the technician tells me. Oh, I'm really happy—but—Oh no! I just celebrated my birthday the other day and I drank three drinks! It will effect my baby! I'm frantic now—A telepathic message from the technician, "Do not worry, it won't hurt the baby—it's still in the spindle phase." Oh, thank God. I'm so relieved. I'm walking down the hallway to another room where I will find out more specific information about my baby.

I believe this type of ship is what many people call a mother ship. I've been on these large ones before, and I feel very comfortable while I am on them. I also seem to know my way around quite well and I am able to walk, somewhat freely, around these large ships. In order to describe the size of these huge ships in terms that everyone can understand, I would have to compare them to a three or four story shopping mall. The rooms are usually a white, cream, or pale bluish-gray color, with white being the most prominent color. The hallways are extremely wide and they are not always white and extremely well-lit like the rooms are. I would estimate the width of the hallways to be a minimum of twenty feet.

"Do not worry, it won't hurt the baby, it's still in the spindle phase." What was this statement supposed to mean? I immediately thought back to my biology class. I thought this was a stage in meiosis. Or was it mitosis? I searched through my old textbooks, realizing at one time in my life I had all this stuff memorized. Then finally, there it was, *the spindle phase*. It turns out that the *spindle phase* or *spindle apparatus* is formed during the *prophase* of both mitosis and meiosis. Both involve nuclear division of living cells with mitotic division occurring in somatic or body cells, and meiotic division occurring in sex cells, the ovum and sperm.

If my pregnancy test was positive and I didn't even realize I was pregnant, it would mean the aliens have a way of determining pregnancy, hours, or even minutes after fertilization. It was obvious—if the aliens could determine I was pregnant this early on, they could be taking fertilized eggs out of me and other female abductees without us showing that we had ever been pregnant in the "normal" sense. These Beings obviously have the ability to detect, in hours, what it takes our doctors much longer to detect: that a woman, more specifically, an abductee, is pregnant. This would be even more likely if the aliens are the ones fertilizing the eggs in the first place.

About two weeks later I had another atypical and rather complicated encounter. The Blonde had returned, and he seemed interested in helping me in a peculiar sort of way.

5-30-90

I'm in a huge domed-shaped building and there are many people here. Something makes me feel this place is kind of like a ship but more like an airport or a train station. No, it is more like a travel-hub. It has two levels that I can see clearly. Beings or people are moving between these two levels. These moving walkways remind me of escalators. I'm watching people move up and down between these two levels. This is a really busy place—There are many people coming and going from this station—this travel hub.

I'm walking toward a bathroom and I think Erik is right behind me— I'm in the bathroom and I think I have just delivered a baby. Something has just come out of me—It is chalky white and very small. I'm looking at it. It is not from me—It is not human. This is disgusting—

I'm leaving the bathroom and I'm back out in the open area of this station. I'm looking for Erik—I'm running now—I'm really scared— Oh! I've just seen what is behind me. It is a horrible looking male humanoid. (I-25) I'm hearing the voice of my old boyfriend from college ten years ago—He was so mentally abusive to me! His voice—It's all inside my head! I can't stand this—I still have such negative feelings for him that it makes my skin crawl to hear his voice now—The voice in my head is saying, "It's you—you're mean—you're hateful—" These are things he has really said to me—for three years I listened to him mentally cut me apart and now he is inside my head—I can't stand this! I'm running away and I'm looking for Erik. I'm calling out for Erik—I see Erik now. He observes how upset I am and he also sees the Being standing behind me.

The three of us are in a small room now. This male Being is transforming into a small, vicious little dog! It is threatening me. I have a towel or something in my hand, and whenever the dog lunges for me, I pop it with the towel. I don't really want to hurt it but I'm not going to let it bite me either. Oh God—Suddenly—the dog is transforming into a humanoid again—It's The Blonde. He is loving and caring now. Erik and I are receiving a telepathic message from him—he's telling me that he is kind and good. He loves me. He's telling me he is trying to help me—He wants me to release the hate I feel for this old boyfriend. I don't know if I can because he was so cruel to me. I've had a hard time liking myself ever since I spent those three years with him—listening to him tell me what a worthless, terrible person I was—I'm looking at The Blonde and I'm thinking about all of this and he is reading my thoughts. I tell The Blonde, "I just don't know if I can release it. Not now—I need more time."

I feel a great amount of love for The Blonde and I know he loves me. This part is over.

I'm in my cellar now—I'm back at my house. Oh! My cats! They have drowned in a large bucket of water I left in their kennel! There is something white, and it is shaped like a five gallon bucket. It is inside their kennel! They were in it!

I'm frantically trying to pump the water out of one of my cats. I'm putting my hands on his chest and I'm gently pressing down. There are two doctors in white lab coats in the cellar with me. I'm yelling at them, "Do something!" Very calmly they tell me, telepathically, "Wait a while and the cats will be okay." I'm not listening to them. I'm frantic! I have to save my cats. I'm still trying to revive my orange cat. "Who told you to do that?" One of the Beings asks me. "It's wrong—just wait." I'm becoming more and more upset—Now the doctors are very agitated with me because I won't listen to them. I'm shouting at them, "I can't! I have to save my cat!!!"

> *Suddenly, the cats are all okay and I have a distinct feeling the Beings have just brought them back. I think they took my cats and they have just brought them back!*

It would seem The Blonde is very interested in teaching me and helping me grow in a spiritual sense. I do not mean spiritually in the classic sense, but rather my experiences with him usually give me a heightened sense of duty and responsibility for people in certain situations that I myself have not been through. However, it is my ability to feel and to overtly display empathy for the animals that he is most interested in. Although he is involved with the biological aspect of my abductions, he is also very much involved in the study of my thought processes, my values, and my emotions. It would appear we are learning from one another.

The incident with my cats was traumatic for me. I know the Beings took my orange cat and possibly my other cats as well. The aliens may have performed some kind of test or experiment on them just as they do to me sometimes. The aliens know they are not to touch my cats and that I would do *anything* to protect them. I have since made this extremely clear to them. This incident angered me greatly. I didn't care then, and I don't care now, what they do to me as long as they stay away from my cats.

Approximately one week after this encounter I had a spontaneous memory surface, and although I recorded it immediately, I did not put the exact date in my journal.

6-15 to 6-20, 1990

> *I'm on the top of a building—I'm on the roof of a very tall building. There is a female and a male Being with me. They aren't human—I don't know what the male looks like but the female is about three feet tall and has very old looking skin. Her skin tone is very dark and uneven. She has very dark, straight hair. As she looks up at me I can see that her eyes are oblong-shaped and have oblong-shaped irises. They are dark brown. This female is standing to my right.* (I-9)

> *I'm looking up into the night sky. I can see many planes and helicopters flying very close to one another. I've seen them before and I always find them fascinating. So many planes flying so close to one another without crashing. It seems impossible. I've seen this three times before in my lifetime. I do not know when, but I have seen these planes flying like this before. Every time I see this I feel some disbelief that it is possible for anyone to fly planes in such a close formation without crashing into one another. I'm fixated on this thought—*

> *Suddenly, one of the little silver Cessna-type planes is breaking away from the group and it is flying down toward me—*

Now I'm holding it. It is a model and I can hear a tiny engine sound. I can't believe this is just a model. How strange—This little model was really flying, sound and all. I'm telling the short female, "I can't believe they are so small. I thought they were real." The female is amused with my statement. She is in telepathic contact with me. She has been reading my thoughts and emotions concerning these planes. I'm thinking to myself, these Beings have been deceiving me. They have been playing with me—The male is also amused with me.

Suddenly, the female simply turns away from me—she is walking away from me without any emotion or anything. I no longer have the little plane in my hand. My hand is on her shoulder and I'm telling her, "I just want you to know how much I care about you." She is looking up at me. I'm very concerned for her. I'm really worried about her and I want her to know that I really do like her. She seems totally unaffected by my feelings. She isn't responding to my caring or concern for her. She is totally void of emotion.

The feeling of deception was strong in this experience. I had seen these planes flying in the air three times in other memories, but this was the clearest memory I had of them. I always found these aircraft fascinating, but I never considered the fact they were just models. I still do not believe they were model airplanes because even model planes would crash into one another. If anything, it was a vision or a holographic image. It may have been used to entertain me or to keep my mind fixated on the planes instead of something else they did not want me to see or remember. The feelings of amusement from both the female and the male Being were not expressions on their faces, but rather expressions given to me telepathically. No words were spoken to me. The void I felt from the small female Being when I was trying to convey the feelings I had for her was profound. She was totally unaffected by my emotions. It was as if I were in telepathic contact with her and I could sense what it was like not to feel *anything*. It was as if she were transmitting this void to me so I would understand that this is what she was like inside. It was such an empty feeling. I felt so hopeless because I so much wanted her to know how much I cared for her. Although this explanation contains some contradicting statements, it is simply the best I can do to describe what I felt and sensed from her.

I have read the previous entry a few times. Each time I read about this experience or think about this small female, I remember a part of the experience I did not record in my journal. It keeps coming back to haunt me for some reason. I feel this would be an appropriate place to share the part of the experience I did not record, yet still remember as if it occurred yesterday. I am keeping it separate from the journal entry because it would be inappropriate to slip it in as a recorded memory. It was not. This is the first time I've written it down.

Prior to my being on the roof of the building with the small female and the male Being, I was flying in a craft with them. It was at night and I was looking out of a window with the female Being. I was astonished when I realized the craft we were in was flying just above a B-52 bomber. I couldn't believe it. I looked excitedly at the female and she seemed amused with my level of excitement. I saw the plane as clear as day, a figure of speech, because it was at night when this occurred. I will always remember how close we were to it and how beautiful the plane was as I was looking down at it. It isn't often you get to see a B-52 bomber flying, especially from the position I saw it from. I do not know why I didn't record this part of the memory. I also do not know why I can't seem to get it out of my mind.

The following experience contains a form of manipulation by the Being who was working on me. It is curious to me how easily I fell for the "bait."

6-28-90

I'm standing in my dining room next to the table. A short, pudgy little doctor has inserted two metal posts into my mouth. (I-15) *I'm standing here in my home and he's in front of me working with these posts or whatever they are. My mouth is open, very wide—this is awkward. Ouch!!! It feels as though these posts are going up into the top of my mouth back behind my teeth—It's really painful—Oh, now I think something is going into my brain! I can feel pain and pressure at both of my temples. Is he hammering nails into my teeth and into the roof of my mouth? This really hurts! As he is doing this I am thinking, "Please don't hit a nerve."*

They are in now. I'm becoming very emotional now—I'm having memories—They're so real! It's as if everything is happening right now—I'm supposed to be in my psychology class, but how can I be there when I'm here in my house? Oh! Now I'm performing in an orchestra—I'm in the middle of a concert—how can I play my clarinet with these things in my mouth! These memories are flooding my mind—it's all real—these are my memories—this is my life!

I'm wondering—How are they ever going to repair my teeth after this? I'm very worried about my teeth. I can't stand dentists—I don't know what to do!

The doctor is taking these posts out of my mouth now. Is he unscrewing them?

This is strange—Oh no—I don't like this—I don't like this—No, I don't like this. Something is wrong—The pudgy little doctor is telling me, telepathically, "Do not worry—they will be repaired and no one will ever know they were there." Oh good, they are going to fix my teeth. Someone else is helping him—someone else is here working with him—I'm looking at the short, pudgy doctor's face. He is trying to get the one on the right side of my mouth out. Oh! It's stuck!!! Oh no! He can't get it out! He's going outside. Where the hell is he going? To the garage? What does he need from the garage? I can't believe this! How could it be stuck? I'm frantic. I'm going to have to have emergency surgery! Yes, it is clear to me now. I've agreed to have emergency surgery to get this thing out of my mouth and out of my brain.

Suddenly, I'm in a hospital. There are a lot of people here—there's a lot going on—everyone is very busy. The pain—Oh, the pain is so bad—I think I'm passing out from the pain—I'm so dizzy—I'm lying down on the floor next to the door that leads into the operating room. I'm still wearing my long pink nightgown. I'm lying on the floor. I think I'll just sleep here. I don't care what anyone thinks—I have to lie down. I have to rest. The pain is making me tired—I have to rest.

A small voice—I'm hearing a child's voice. It is saying, "A dead human?" I'm getting up now. I'm not dead. I don't want them to think I'm dead. It's a girl with her mother. I'm standing up now. I'm waiting for someone. I'm waiting for the doctor. I've just received a telepathic message telling me I'm going to have emergency surgery to remove this device that is stuck in my mouth.

I'm walking through the doors—I'm walking into a huge room. There are a lot of people lying on tables in here. They are each surrounded by a team of doctors. It looks like a large emergency room. Is this one of our hospitals? This is incredible—I'm breathing through my mouth because I can't close it all the way with this device in it. It's really uncomfortable. I'm looking at a large black woman. She is human. She is in extreme pain and is trying to get up and away from the team that is working on her. They are sending jolts of electricity through her with a wand or something that looks like a wand. She is trying to get off the table—they are struggling with her—they are shocking her. She has fallen backwards onto her back and she is lying down on the table again.

I'm staring at the black woman. Something is familiar about all of this. I know it is wrong to hurt her, but at the same time it is necessary. It has to be done. It is somehow permissible to cause all of this pain for the greater good. Somehow, it will all be worth it in the end.

> *My thoughts shift back to myself. I'm thinking, "I hope they can perform the surgery tonight—if they can't do it tonight, then everything will be ruined—I just can't wait until the morning."*

I awakened feeling extremely dizzy and I felt as though I had been drugged. I had a slight headache and my jaw was extremely stiff and sore. I immediately felt my teeth with my tongue and wondered, "Why didn't I get them to repair my cracked tooth?" I was also running a slight temperature: 99.4 degrees. I checked the inside of my mouth with a mirror, but other than my mouth and jaw being extremely sore, I could not find any other physical evidence that the device had been in my mouth.

This short pudgy doctor was definitely in my house. There were also two other Beings watching the doctor work on my mouth. I do not believe they were interested in my mouth for any other reason than to get this device inserted properly into my brain. They were definitely stimulating the memory pathways in my brain, but their purposes for doing this are not clear to me. It would appear that it had the effect of making me want to go with them so I could have this emergency surgery performed. It seemed quite important to me that it be done that night and I could not, under any circumstances, wait until the following morning. Had that happened I would have had to go to a dentist or they would have had to keep me longer, and Erik would have surely missed me. That could have been their entire plan: to give me a reason to go with them voluntarily. There is also the possibility that something did go wrong. It is doubtful that just because they are alien Beings and are technologically advanced, they are infallible.

Seeing the black woman suffering and struggling against the team of doctors who were working on her was extremely difficult to watch. She was a large woman and I do not remember seeing any clothes on her. It pained me greatly to have to see her suffer. I knew she was in a great deal of discomfort, but I was not sure what they were doing to her. They did use a wand that transmitted a shock to her and this had the effect of rendering her unconscious. As I watched this happen I knew in my heart that all of this was being done for the greater good. What I often wonder today, now that I have distanced myself from this experience in an emotional sense, is *whose* greater good is this being done for?

6-29-90

> *I'm flying—It's at night and I'm flying—I must be on top of a large rolling object. I'm on my stomach and I can see a brick road made out of rounded bricks—I'm very close to the street and I'm going down a steep hill. The houses here look very angular—very Deco—Am I in Europe? I'm in a house now—there is a male humanoid and he is telling me which way to go. There are "others" here—*

Now I'm in my backyard and a male Being is standing next to the water with me. He is pulling a fish out of the water. Telepathically, he asks me, "What is it?" I reply, "It's an amberjack." His face has just lit up with excitement. He agrees with me. We are walking away from the water and we are near a tree. We have been communicating with one another telepathically, but I can't remember what we were just talking about.

I'm not sure what is happening now—This is some kind of test. He is letting me know, telepathically, I think—He is somehow making me feel what he is feeling toward me. I think he is mentally, trying to sexually arouse me—He's reading my thoughts again and I am thinking a message to him, "I'm very happily married." Abruptly, the feeling is gone. I'm ending this conversation—I'm walking back toward our house. Somehow I know three hours have passed.

There is obviously some memory missing from this experience, but I believe even a fragment such as this might contain some important information. I find myself wanting to believe this was The Blonde because of a vision of him I have from my mind's eye.

My traveling and being able to see the ground very close beneath my body indicates the possibility that I was floated to another destination. When I saw the Art Deco buildings, I certainly felt as though I was in another country, but this may have been a screen memory. It would appear that I am not remembering much at all about what happened after I reached the intended destination.

If this really was The Blonde, he appeared to be curious about my love for eating seafood, particularly amberjack. I felt as though he wanted to know if it was safe to eat. He may have been interested in which types of seafood are safe and which types are not. However, there is an entire telepathic conversation missing from my conscious memory during this one event by the water. I do not remember the dialogue that transpired between us that night. I simply do not have enough information to go on. However, for some unknown reason, I never ate amberjack again.

Two months passed without any visitations from the Beings. The break was welcome and it gave me a chance to relax a little and concentrate on school. Eventually, however, they always return.

8-17-90

I'm being given an opportunity to save Sandra, my best friend who died in the house fire in 1980. I'm being shown two photographs—one is of Sandra and a friend from high school who is still alive to my knowledge. The other photograph is of two other females I went to high school with and they are also alive (as of this entry).

Okay. I'm on the other side again. I've gone back in time and I am with The Blonde. He is observing me while I am trying to convince these four people of future happenings so I will be able to save their lives. It is difficult—It is emotionally draining for me to explain to them what I am trying to do and that I believe it is possible to save their lives.

Once again The Blonde was interested in knowing if I was given knowledge of the future, would I act on that knowledge? I did in this case. I knew Sandra was already dead, but I had gone back in time and in my mind and at that point in time, she was very much alive. It was very frustrating for me, but I did try to explain to her what was happening now and what would happen in her future. I'm not sure if she believed me. Somehow she seemed to know and understand that this was more of a learning experience for me rather than a true opportunity for me to save her life. She was on the other side, and it seemed as if she had all the answers. She seemed very wise and confident.

If my premise is correct, I have to wonder about the many telepathic messages and conversations I have had with them that I cannot consciously remember yet. I wonder if they have told me of future happenings and are waiting or watching to see if I will act on them. I certainly acted on the information I remembered from the vision The Blonde gave me about the lightning. By putting on the rubber-soled shoes I am alive today. By attending to my newly heightened senses, many animals were saved because I was in the right place at the right time.

I must stress that my abduction experiences have heightened my senses, but they are not why I feel the way I do about other species of animals. I came into this world with a mother, father, sister, and an array of pets. I have always had a loving, passion for animals. I believe some of the Beings may have noticed a "flicker of this flame" within me. I do not believe I was given these feelings of empathy for animals by the alien Beings. This "seed" was within me ever since I began forming conscious, long-term memories. Its cultivation began through observing and modeling my parent's behavior. As I grew into adulthood, it continued to be cultivated by watching the horrific way humans treat other species of animals. The alien Beings are extremely interested in this type of behavior. I believe my sensitivity level has been heightened by my experiences with the aliens. However, my behaviors toward and emotions for other species were not *bestowed* upon me by the aliens or anyone else.

The following experience hints at the fact that my role with the aliens might be changing. If you remember earlier in my story, I was involved in an abduction with my nephew. This time my involvement, in my opinion, would be inexcusable. I would help abduct a total stranger.

8-23-90

I'm outside at night in a wide open space. I can see grass on the ground, a hill, and some trees off in the distance about a hundred yards away. I'm with a man. He's tall, about six foot-four I think. He has short, jet black hair and highly arched eyebrows. He has brown eyes and a round pudgy face. The "leader" is on his left side, and I am on his right side. We are helping him—no, we are guiding him—We are making him walk toward a specific location—He doesn't have any clothes on and he is scared to death. He's almost in tears. He is trembling with fear. He is so frightened that he is stumbling. I feel really sorry for him. He's almost hysterically upset now. The Being on the other side of him is getting very frustrated and impatient with him. It is The Female—I know her—"Just keep walking," she says to him. "Stop Whimpering," she adds in a frustrated telepathic voice. She is almost to the point of being angry with him.

I'm still guiding him with his right arm, but this is difficult because he is trying to cover himself with his hands while he is walking. The Female Being just wants to hurry up and get this over with. I can tell. This is very obvious to me. We have to get to our destination without being seen. The Female doesn't want to be seen with him.

I'm standing in a hospital room with two beds. I don't like this. One of the beds is neatly made and the other has been used. It is in an upright position and I somehow know it is the man's bed—the man I just helped bring in. There is a light brown stain on the pillow—it looks like blood. I'm wondering why they don't change the linens. Ooo! A gruff female voice is telling me, "That's your bed now. Get in!" I'm thinking to myself that I'm not going to get into this bed or any other bed! I'm not going to be a patient—no way. I'm flopping myself down very hard into a dark blue chair. I'm not moving from here—I'm going to stay right here!

There is now a tall, glass food cart in front of me. I'm bending over to get a closer look—Some of the food has spoiled—it is rotten. I don't think I'm going to eat anything here either.

I'm still sitting in the blue chair looking around the room. This isn't a very clean hospital—I'm looking through the partially opened door. It leads out into a large hallway where a group of nurses and doctors are standing. They are all wearing surgical green or white—very appropriate for a hospital. I'm looking at a doctor who has his surgical cap over his head—oh God, I'm next.

Illustrations

1A

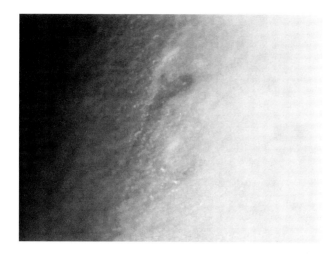

Illustration #1
Scoop mark scar next to teardrop scar on Katharina's right shin.

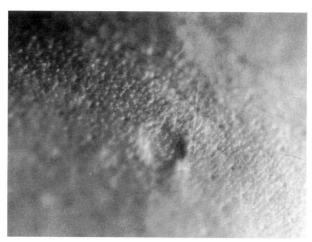

Illustration #2
Scoop mark scar on Katharina's right arm, near elbow.

Illustration #3
1967 childhood abduction.

Illustration #4
Hybrid Being: The Doctor (male)

Illustration #5
Hybrid Being: The Female (female)

Illustration #6
Hybrid Being: A Messenger (female)

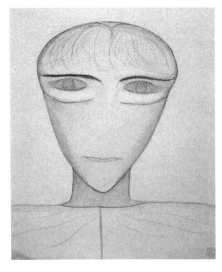

Illustration #7
Hybrid Being: The Tan Doctor (male)

Illustrations 3A

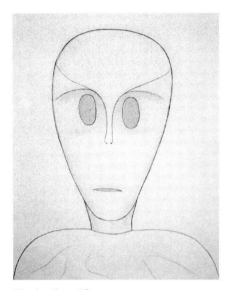

Illustration #8
Hybrid Being: The Father
(male)

Illustration #9
Hybrid Being: The Female with the
long black hair
(female)

Illustration #10
Hybrid Being: "Twenty Fingers"
(male)

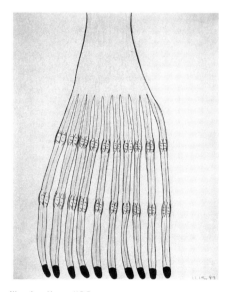

Illustration #11
"Twenty Fingers"
One of his hands

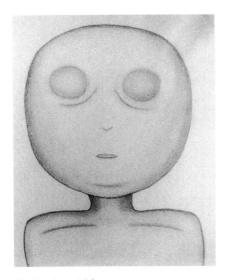

Illustration #12
Blue Being
(female)

Illustration #13
The Blonde
(male)

Illustration #14
Praying Mantis-type Being
(female)

Illustration #15
Two Type Two Greys observing the Short Pudgy Doctor inserting memory stimulating devices into my brain.
(males)

Illustrations

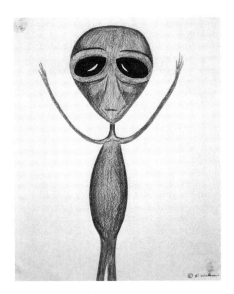

Illustration #16
Type One Grey:
"The Floating Grandfather Alien"
(male)

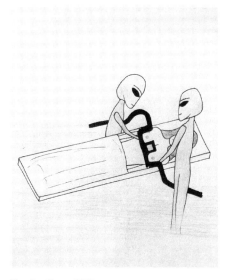

Illustration #17
Type Two Grey:
"Heart Operation"
(males)

Illustration #18
Type Three Grey:
"Pilot/Navigator of a cigar-shaped craft"
(female)

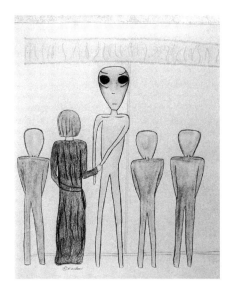

Illustration #19
Type Four Grey:
"The Diplomat" escorted by three Type Two Greys.
(males)

Illustration #20
Reptilian Tan (male)

Illustration #21
Tan Being (male)

Illustration #22
A Crystal City on "the dark side of the moon."

Illustration #23
Circular Lab Area on a mother ship

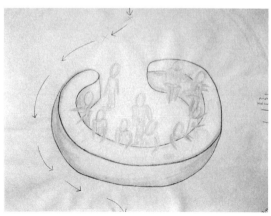

Illustrations 7A

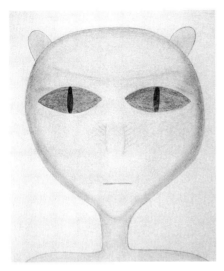

Illustration #24
An example of Camouflage: a Blue-Gray "Bobcat" (male)

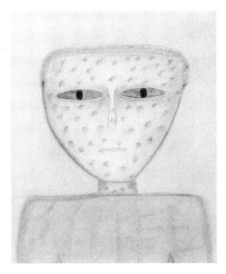

Illustration #25
An example of Camouflage: "a mean spotted Being." It is actually The Blonde during a Teaching Dream. (male)

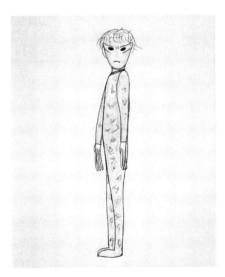

Illustration #26
An Evil Humanoid (male)

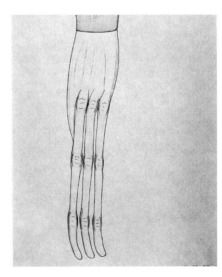

Illustration #27
Evil Humanoid's Hand

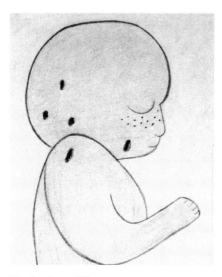

Illustration #28
The Black Baby that The Doctor was trying to convince me was mine.

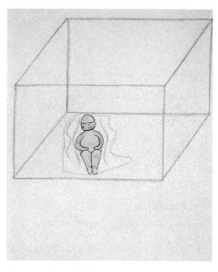

Illustration #29
The Black Baby in a glass box. The front side of the box was open.

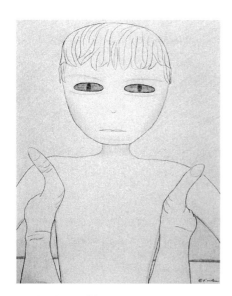

Illustration #30
The four or five year old child with golden eyes. I thought he was my child until I picked him up and saw how big he was. He was very sick.

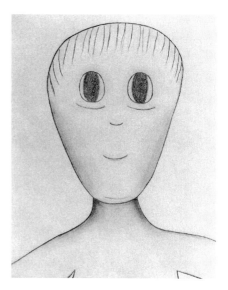

Illustration #31
A giggling, happy female child who was floating in and above a large cluster of flowers in our courtyard.

Illustrations 9A

Illustration #32
A healthy and vibrant tan-skinned infant suckling my pinkie finger.

Illustration #33
One of the many tiny spotted Beings in the small room on the military base. Only 12" to 18" tall. They closed their eyes and were very afraid of me.

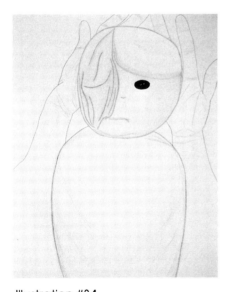

Illustration #34
This baby was handed to me after the cigar-shaped craft landed on another object in the ocean. This baby was in very bad shape.

Illustration #35
The Father and my little boy standing in our courtyard.

Illustration #36
The Beings presented me with one of my children as a way of saying "Thank you." He kept his eyes closed and was extremely frightened of me.

Illustration #37
A floating female child who was presented to me by two female Beings. They told me she was dying, but I told them I thought she would be all right. She had translucent skin and I touched her on her stomach. I thought she was beautiful and I felt an enormous amount of love for her.

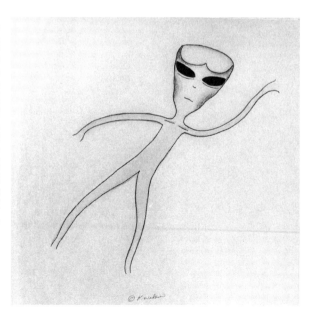

Illustrations   11A

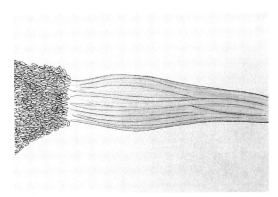

Illustration #38
Microscopic Surgery:
I watched the ovals on the end of this tissue regenerate on a view screen. A male and a female alien (doctors?) were working on me.

Illustration #39
An environmental monitoring station somewhere on this planet. The Female is standing to the right.

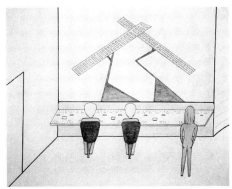

Illustration #40
A light game in a large round white room.

Illustration #41
Phone or communication device. The buttons had symbols and numbers on them.

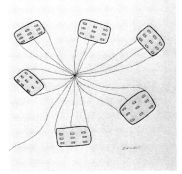

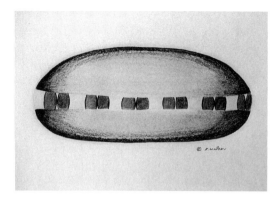

Illustration #42
"The Sighting"
One of three hamburger-shaped crafts I saw in 1976. All three crafts were silver with red, blue, and yellow lights that moved from left to right.

Illustration #43
A boomerang-shaped craft. It flew above our house for two consecutive nights. It had five dim lights on the bottom.

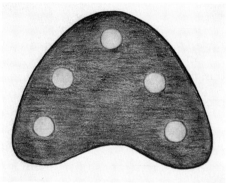

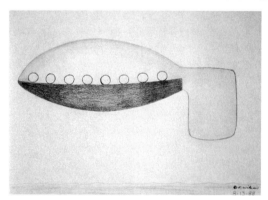

Illustration #44
A craft that rose out of the water (Gulf of Mexico) during a "dream memory."

Illustration #45
Spontaneous memory: A barrel-shaped craft with a bright light on each end. The bottom picture is what the area looked like after the craft "blinked out."

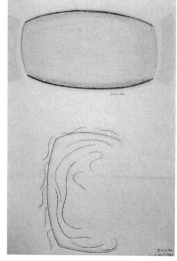

Illustrations 13A

Illustration #46
A light blue, translucent craft in the process of disappearing.

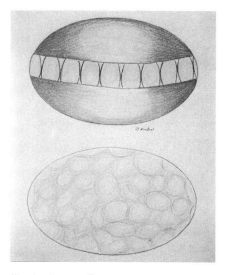

Illustration #47
Egg-shaped craft. Bottom picture shows power source.

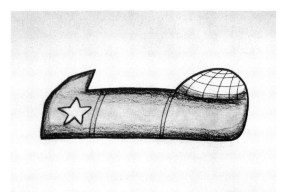

Illustration #48
An example of how the aliens alter the appearance of their crafts. This craft was altered to appear as a Coast Guard helicopter, except it had no rotors and made no sound. It came out of the water behind our house.

Illustration #49
An example of how the aliens alter the appearance of their crafts. This craft came out of the water as a white disk. As it rose into the air, wings and pontoons appeared.

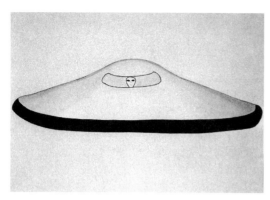

Illustration #50
A craft Erik saw when "The Sandman" came to visit.

Illustration #51
The under side of The Sandman's craft. The craft was covered with interlocking porcelain-like tiles.

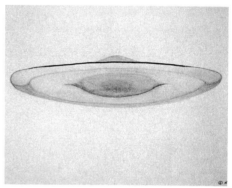

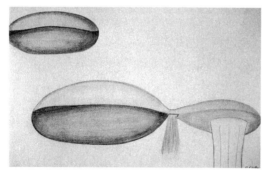

Illustration #52
3 crafts Erik remembered. Two "docked" and physically fused together. As they fused a bright flame shot down and the craft on the right emitted a blue beam of light.

Illustration #53
Five crafts flying in a "V" formation. They moved from left to right. The crafts were black, gray, and red.

Illustration #54
The orb-shaped craft I saw on a military base. It had so many angles it appeared round. It was a dull black color, and was piloted by a military person. He was dressed in a dark green flight suit and a white helmet, with a black face shield and microphone.

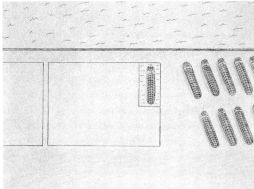

Illustration #55
View from above a military base on the water (ocean or large bay). On the left are two warehouse/hangars that extend deep underground. On the right are several cigar-shaped crafts.

Illustration #56
"The Navigator." A Type Three Grey in a cigar-shaped craft on the base above. He telepathically communicated to me, "I'm a Navigator and I'm undercover."

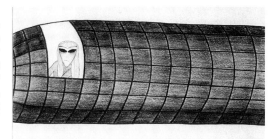

Illustration #57
I'm kicking open a window on a cigar-shaped craft as it hovers over a huge object in the ocean.

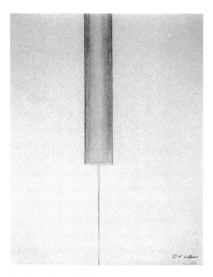

Illustration #58
A long needle The Tan Doctor used during a Laparoscopy-type procedure.

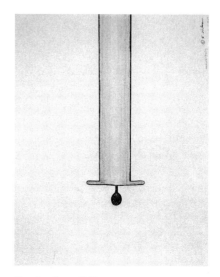

Illustration #59
An object I saw during a self-hypnosis at home. I became so frightened I came out of it very quickly. I believe it to be an implantation device.

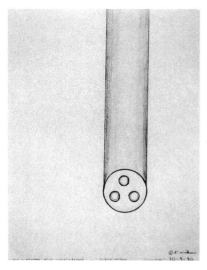

Illustration #60
A rectal probe.

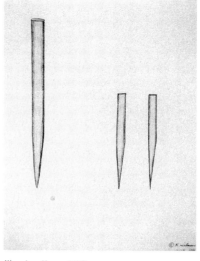

Illustration #61
The "syringe" The Doctor and The Blonde injected into my left leg. The device was 6 inches long. The smaller devices were placed into the larger. I believe something was placed in or taken out of my leg.

I immediately realized what I had just participated in. I had just helped The Female abduct a Hispanic man and I felt extremely guilty. I also thought they would leave me alone after I helped them but they didn't.

Another unusual thing about this experience was that this hospital was very much like a hospital. I saw beds not metal tables. I also clearly remember seeing pillows and sheets on the beds. There was a sliver rail along one side of the bed that the Hispanic man had been sitting up in. I was sitting in a low, dark blue cloth-covered chair. I saw a glass food cart, and the nurse was a very large woman who also had a very gruff voice. This seemed like a real hospital in every sense of the word—except for The Female Being.

An important question I now must ask is: Is it possible that just as I helped abduct the Hispanic man, there are doctors and nurses who are abductees and are using their medical knowledge to help the aliens? Perhaps there *are* humans working with some of these Beings. As you will recall, this was certainly not the first time I witnessed this team effort between aliens and humans. Although this may sound far-fetched to some, is it also possible that some of these other humans are members of a (secret) government agency? Is this experience connected to the abduction encounter when The Doctor and The Blonde drugged me and led me to the Bronco truck that was parked in the shell-covered parking lot?

Regardless of the many questions this experience left me with, I felt a strong sense of guilt at having aided in this abduction and causing so much emotional distress to this man. It was sad to see such a large man reduced to a bundle of sobs and shaky limbs as he tried to stay on his feet. How could such a man be controlled so easily, I wondered? Even though these events disturbed me greatly, I knew they *had* to be done. There were to be no questions asked. It was simply the way it had to be.

Two nights later the Beings were back. The Blonde was not involved in this encounter, and again, I noticed how different this experience felt.

8-25-90

I'm standing in the kitchen—No, this is not my kitchen. I think they want me to think I'm at home so I'll feel more comfortable about being with them. Two Beings are showing me a harp seal. A vision now—It seems as though Erik and I caught it with a little white cast net. Suddenly, I feel terrible. I feel terrible about catching the harp seal! I'm staring at the harp seal. She is lying on the counter—I feel so bad about this—I hope they don't mind—it was an accident—I feel so bad about this—These two Beings have knives in their hands. As I am thinking about how bad I feel, I receive a telepathic message—"Not as bad as it feels—" Suddenly, I can see that the harp seal is still alive! I think they are going to cut her eye out!—They have cut through the first layer of blubber! There isn't any blood yet but there will be—I'm screaming, "Let it go! Let her go! Put her back into the water at once!!" The Beings reply, "If we release it, it will only be caught again." I'm frantically thinking about all of this and then, in a pleading voice, I say to them, "At least she will have a chance at life."

I can see the ocean. I'm looking at the ocean now. I'm looking down into the water and I can see an object underwater. It is an underwater cage and it is illuminated—It must have lights on it because it is glowing a whitish-green color. It's a glowing square underwater. That is how they transported the harp seal. I knew we didn't catch her! Somehow they made me believe Erik and I did this. They have decided to release the harp seal—I'm receiving a telepathic message, "We must first take what is valuable out of the harp seal and that way no one will harm her or will want to kill her anymore." I think they are removing something from her stomach area—They have just removed a small white object—a box I think. They have handed it to me—Now I'm looking down into the water again at the glowing rectangular cage. I must be two or three stories above the water.

I'm walking up the cellar stairs back to our house. My legs are killing me! I'm standing on the stairs and I'm looking down at my right thigh. It looks strange—as though it is cramping very tightly—it looks a little knotted up. It really hurts! Is someone stimulating it in some way?

I'm still standing at the top of the stairs, but someone is behind me now—Oh! It's one of them! I'm scared—It's a female Being and she is carrying two childlike Beings. One has dark skin and the other has olive skin. This is strange—all I can see are their heads. The female Being walks by me—she is speaking to me, "These two are dying, where do you want me to put them?" Oh God—another charade—I have to go along with this—

The brown head is at the end of the hallway on the floor. Okay—it is alive—it is a living Being. I'm staring at this head—How can it be alive? The face is contorted and pudgy. It has strong features and wrinkled skin. I know it is alive, but how can it exist in this state? I must not be able to see the rest of its body—Maybe the rest of its body is underneath the floor. Maybe it's floating in the cellar.

I'm in a room with strange looking carpet. There's a bed in here, but it's really a prop. They want me to think I'm in our back bedroom, but I don't really think I am. There's Erik. We're packing a suitcase and we're planning to escape. A male Being has just walked into the room—he's looking for something. We hide the suitcase under the bed—he is walking right up to the spot we hid the suitcase! He's pulling it out and opening it up—he's taking something out of the suitcase. He knows—This Being knows that we were planning to escape.

I'm in a very small room now. There is a female Being on either side of me and we are kneeling on the floor. They have brought a child to me. She is in front of me and she is floating in the air. She is floating right in front of me. She has olive-looking skin, but her skin—it is so strange—This is the strangest skin I have ever seen. I think her skin is opaque—maybe translucent. I'm reaching out to her with my right hand—The female Beings are very concerned now—they don't want me to touch her. I'm reaching out to touch her—"She is very sick and will not live much longer—" they have just given me this telepathic message—I'm touching the child on her stomach and I tell them, "Oh, I don't know—she looks like she's going to be all right to me." The female Beings are a little surprised by my remark, but they are mostly pleased. The child's features are unusual—She has an extremely large forehead with sunken eyes, high cheek bones with hollow cheeks— very large black eyes—I should think she is really ugly but I can't. I see a small, frail, innocent, helpless child—I feel a great amount of love for her. The two female Beings are very, very protective of her. (I-37)

Now—I can't believe this—Somehow I'm outside on our deck. There are people all around me as if there's a party. I don't think I know these people. A small blonde child is walking up to me. I want to think it's my little nephew, but there is something different about him. Oh, I think he wants to play with me.

Now I'm lying on my back on the deck near the gazebo—this little child wants to play. My father is sitting in a chair and he looks as if he is asleep—He is just staring down at the ground. He is supposed to be watching the child, but he's not. Now that I am getting a good look at this man, I do not believe this is really my father anymore.

I see my gray cat. My cats are up on the deck! They're out of their kennel!—Oh, now they are in the back yard! They are all walking as though they know exactly where they are going. They are all walking with a purpose. This is strange—I'm walking down the back stairs into the back yard. I'm very concerned about my cats. There is someone I think I know in their kennel, but I don't think he knows where he is— he is a friend of mine and Erik's, and he is playing with a child—I have to get to my cats—I'm following them out into the yard. They are all walking up some kind of platform or plank in single file. My cats are walking into a big glass structure. I can see through it. It's hanging over our boat slip. It's not in the water, but rather, just above the water. It must be floating over the water. There are little boxes with pine-straw inside of them. Each one of my eight cats is getting into their own box filled with pine-straw. Someone is sliding a little door closed so they won't get out—I'm feeling better now—not so worried now—my cats are safe. I can't do anything until I know they are safe.

I'm back on the porch again. I'm looking at a female child about three or four feet tall. She is standing in the courtyard inside a large clump of flowers. She communicates with me telepathically, "Hello, how are you?" She has white hair but not enough to cover her head. Her hair is very thin. I'm compelled to speak to her in German—I'm speaking to her in German—I can't do this—My German isn't good enough. I'm embarrassed by my poor attempt to speak to her. I'm turning to go into the house, "I have to go inside now" I say to the little girl. (I-31)

"Wow" was all I could say the next morning. Erik and I immediately knew what had happened. We didn't even have to ask one another. The first thing Erik said to me was, "I remember being outside with you on the porch. We were trying to get back inside the house, but the dead bolt was locked and neither one of us had our keys. We didn't know how we got outside. I also remember being out in the garage talking to an alien and I remember being on an aircraft carrier."

Erik and I went outside on the porch and noticed the door going into the garage and the courtyard gate were wide open! These are always locked at night *and* during the day. There is no way we could have left either one of these unlocked. My perpetual checking totally eliminated the possibility of one of us forgetting to lock these doors. We went into the garage and found both televisions, the microwave, the telephone, and all the tools exactly in place. Nothing had been disturbed. In our minds that eliminated the possibility that a prowler or a burglar had been there and had left the two doors open.

Erik and I felt very drugged throughout the rest of the day. The feeling was so strong that I wrote in my journal: "We felt dizzy and lightheaded all day—It was about six o'clock in the evening before we started feeling normal again."

Thankfully, my cats were all okay! They are the first thing I check each morning when I get up. To me, it felt as though there was a party going on out in our courtyard and I felt as though there were several Beings on our porch and in our courtyard. Our courtyard was totally enclosed and the walls were seven feet tall, so it would make a convenient location for the aliens to interact with us outside without being detected by our neighbors. I believe the gate to the courtyard and the door into the garage were left open intentionally so we would have some kind of proof the aliens had been there during the night.

It seemed as though some of these events transpired in our house and some of them probably occurred on one of their crafts. The two heads the female Being brought in with her are still a mystery to me. What could they have possibly had to gain by this theatrical display of heads? The heads seemed very much alive, however, and it was their intention to have me believe this was so. I wondered if the rest of the dark skinned Being's body might have been beneath the floor. If they could move through walls, then certainly they could float halfway between two floors of a house.

The floating alien female child and the two female Beings were definitely real because I touched the child on her stomach. She had substance, as my hand did not go through her body as would be the case if she were an illusion, or a holographic image. I also felt an enormous amount of love for her and I did not want to believe she was dying. I felt as though the female Beings should have more faith and optimism about her chances at life. I was trying to show them that positive thoughts and feelings can help a person feel better even if they are sick. Believing that a person is going to die and allowing the person to know you have no hope for them is dangerous and can weaken the healing process, or possibly accelerate death. The female Beings, although deeply disturbed by my touching her, seemed pleased by the message my feelings conveyed to them. I felt the female Beings reading my thoughts and emotions telepathically.

The little child who wanted to play with me while I was outside on the porch was probably a hybrid child. I can say this with relative certainty because I saw him again in another encounter at a later date.

Did the aliens take my cats and put them in this floating glass house or see-though craft? This appeared to be the case but it could have also been an illusion in order to make sure I participated in their plan. As I stated, I was not going to be able to do anything until I knew for certain that all of my cats were safe. The closing of the little glass door to prevent my cats from getting out of this glass craft indicated to me that my cats were finally safe. I believe this is their way of holding my cats hostage, if you will, for the use of my mind and body. I have, at times, resented the aliens immensely for doing this.

The interaction with the harp seal was for teaching purposes and falls into the category I call teaching dreams. They are not actually dreams, but that is one of the words I have chosen to describe them. I cannot say for certain that this really was, or was not, a harp seal. Of course, I was devastated when they made me believe, through the use of a vision, that Erik and I were the reason the seal was caught in the first place. They used my emotional agony from my own guilt to further the lesson. When they began to cut her eye out I became even more emotional and would have probably physically forced them to stop had they not changed the direction of the lesson. They decided to do something *good* for the harp seal. They took out what was important. What I saw was a small white box, but what this represented in a symbolic sense was reproduction, and the baby that would be born and killed for its beautiful white fur. This was not news to me and I knew this was not being done for my benefit. The Beings wanted me to know that they understood the process environmentalists and animal right's activists were going through in order to protect certain species of animals from humans.

They had a reason for wanting me to understand this about them. It may be that *some* of the aliens really are trying to help protect the human species. I must emphasize the word "some." Clearly, many people are having traumatic experiences with the aliens. In addition, I am painfully aware of the thousands of animal mutilations (including people's pets) that have occurred over the years. Even though I believe many of these are done by humans, many are also done by the aliens—which aliens, I do not know. This aspect of the UFO phenomenon sickens me. I do not care why the aliens are mutilating animals. Their behavior (as well as the human beings who are mutilating animals) is unforgivable. In addition, even if the aliens are doing it to save my life, it is not their decision to make.

About a month and a half after this encounter I was taken to a very special place. It is probably clear by now that some of my experiences do not fit into the "mainstream" abductee mold, and this encounter is no exception. Here was yet another abduction experience during which I was given information about my future. Just as before, I would act on the information the aliens gave me.

10-4-90

> *I'm standing in a white room—There is a tall female here and she is in charge, but she doesn't speak. She is observing me. I want to work for them—I want to apply for an environmental position with the aliens, but I don't have any experience and I know they know this. The tall female is probing my thoughts. She knows everything I am thinking. There is a young male and a female Being with me. They seem curious and appear to want to be friendly to me. They seem very excited about the work they are doing here. They are going to show me around this facility.*

> *I'm in a monitoring room. I'm looking outside into the night. It's really dark outside. I'm looking out of a large window above a large control panel. It is a work station. There are two huge objects slowly rotating off in the distance. They look like two white, metallic ladders. They must be at least thirty feet long. They are attached to another object in the middle by a special device and they are rotating. They remind me of the metal flaps on satellites that slowly rotate in space— But these structures are much, much larger.* (I-39)

Now I am walking into the room with the tall female Being. Her expression never seems to change, and she is still probing my mind. There is a large oval table in here—like a conference table. There is a tall stack of paper work on top of the table about six inches high. All I can think about right now is how much I want to work for them—how much I want this environmental position—but I know I'm not qualified. Even though I don't have any experience I still feel I could do a good job—The tall female Being—She is reading my thoughts again—I can feel it. I'm telling her, not verbally, but with my thoughts, "I really want to work for you—I am very concerned for the environment."

Now I am outside. The younger female Being is with me. It is The Female I have seen before. I'm asking her, "Was I in space or are those things floating in space?" She seems to find my question amusing. She tells me, although I never see her speak, "No. Look—they are right over there." I'm looking and I can't believe it. I thought I might have been in space but I was in a yellowish-tan building with a flat roof. I can see the ladder-like objects still rotating slowly off in the distance behind the building. They are attached to a huge black metal "arm" of some kind. This arm is holding them up at an angle in the air. They seem to be glowing a little. Maybe there is some reflective light here.

Something—I just saw a flash out of the corner of my eye—A light. Oh! I've seen this before! I know exactly what it is. I know exactly what it is going to do. It's glowing reddish-orange and it is moving extremely fast. As the object moves across the sky it is changing to a more luminous-shaped object without a definite form. It's still round—Now—colors in the blue-green end of the spectrum—The shape is changing. It is becoming elongated. This object is moving out into space. It is leaving and it is going back out into space. It's as if it is passing through a hole or a door in the sky—It has disappeared now.

This was so fascinating and so beautiful! I feel lucky to have seen the craft even though I have seen it many times before. It is always so beautiful and fascinating to see it—It leaves me with a yearning feeling.

I am still near the yellowish-tan building—It has a flat roof. There's nothing special about the outside of this building. I'm walking along a dirt road and there is an old abandoned house to my right—a small group of old buildings that look similar to the building I was just in. There is The Female again. I'm surprised to see her—I think she has just appeared over by the abandoned house. She is waiting for me. It's really filthy here. She is smiling at me, I think. It's more in her eyes—

"Is this where you live?" I ask her. There are several cats around her. One of the cats is walking toward me—I'm bending down and I'm petting it. It is a black and white, long-haired cat. He seems to have a little skin allergy like one of my cats does—Oh, here is an interesting looking cat. I've never seen this species before. I wonder if it is deformed—It is black with orange fur around its eyes. The orange fur is curly or crinkled. I'm petting this cat too—This is a very interesting looking cat. Two other cats are heading out into the road. Oh, this isn't good. I'm picking them up and putting them back into the yard area and away from the dirt road. "No, no, no—You're not supposed to be out there." I'm telling the cats as I pick each one up and remove it from the road. The Female finds this amusing. Oh! A car is coming now and the tabby cat has gone back out into the road. My heart is racing! I turn away! I can't look. I'm scared to death for these cats—I don't think the car hit it. The female doesn't seem to be concerned about them. I'm about to have a heart attack!

Oh, now there is a dog—They are giving me a dog. It's big—I think it is a German Shepherd. No, this dog is light brown and is solid in color. It also looks the size of a Great Dane. A telepathic message, "You have to take care of this dog and you have to take it to Portland with you when you move. Make sure it gets there safely." I'm going to do this. I don't know how right now, but I'm going to do this. I've just agreed to do this. I have to take this dog with me. I've agreed to take the dog with me to Portland.

But—we're not going to move to Portland...

I was very confused about this dog. At the time we were planning to move to either Vancouver, British Columbia, or Seattle, Washington. Portland, although a possibility, was our last choice. At this point in time Erik and I did not want to move to Oregon. In fact, we very adamantly said we would never live there. The dog issue was never talked about. We had eight cats and there was never any room for a dog. It was simply out of the question. Since we didn't have a fenced in yard it was obvious we could not have a dog. I recorded this part of the experience and mentally lumped it into their apparent interest in my "caring for and saving animals" category. It was just another mental stimulus for an alien reaction test.

Interestingly enough, in September of 1991, Erik and I were driving down a highway returning from an afternoon of looking at used motor homes. We thought we saw an animal out of the corner of our eyes. Actually, I'm not even sure if I knew what I had seen. We passed the puppy, but all I remember was seeing a small, tan rib cage. Erik didn't really notice the puppy, but I asked him what it was, and after he asked me what I wanted to do, we immediately stopped. After backing the car up several yards, we found a small, tan puppy standing on the side of the road eating "road-kill." She was hardly anything but skin and bones. I quickly got out of the car and called her and she came running to me. I could tell she was scared, but before she knew what was happening we had her in the car and she was on her way to her first home. Only once in my life since that day, have I ever seen a dog this emaciated and still alive. She has since grown into a large, tan dog. We also, unexpectedly, ended up moving to Portland one month after we found her.

Initially, Erik did not want me to keep the puppy. We had an argument over her and I became very upset. I realized she was special the moment I picked her up. I remembered what the Beings told me and how I had promised to take her to Portland. I promised to take care of her and there was no way I would ever let her go. He finally relented. Today, we are both thrilled to have her as a member of our family. If the Beings could know where we would be moving before *we* did, then I thought it was very important to go with my feelings about her. She is a superb watch dog and she is extremely protective of our cats and me.

I have considered the possibility that we unconsciously made the decision to move to Portland because the Beings said we would, but I do not believe this is the case. We really didn't want to move here and we eventually ended up in Portland because the cost of living skyrocketed in Seattle so quickly that by the time we sold our house in Pensacola, we couldn't afford to live in Seattle. Portland was the only affordable place left among our three choices. Now that we have lived here for a couple of years and have since traveled back to Seattle, we both agree that we couldn't have chosen a more beautiful city to live in.

I didn't think much about the plain, flat-roofed, yellowish building the control room was situated in. It appeared as though they were working on a project to monitor our environment and I was still on Earth. Almost certainly this building was a screen memory for one of their crafts, right? At the time this experience was occurring, nothing made me feel I was on board one of their crafts. To me, it seemed I was in a remote desert location where these Beings were working. I can't prove these buildings exist yet, but I believe it is just as probable that this is an abandoned base of some kind as it is that it was a screen memory for one of their crafts. I could still see the large structures rotating behind the building and I could see a dirt road. It appeared, in every sense, to be an abandoned base of some type. I would see buildings like this in future encounters, and I would not be as uncertain about them again.

The following encounter left me feeling that I needed to devise a mental and emotional protective guard against the aliens and their game playing. It was becoming difficult for me to predict which tactic they would try next.

10-9-90

Someone has just asked me, "Who is your favorite person?" They must mean who is my favorite celebrity—my favorite entertainer. "David Bowie, yes—He is my favorite singer." Oh! There he is. He's taking my arm and he's leading me somewhere. He's taking me somewhere. I'm looking at him—This isn't right. He's too short. I'm going with him because I really believe it is David Bowie. I want to talk to him, but he has something else on his mind. There are others around but I can't see their faces. It's dark in here and we're walking somewhere together.

Now I'm in some type of oversized bathtub. Maybe this is a white box—I don't see a faucet and this is really larger than a bathtub. I feel really guilty about something—I think I had sex with that short Being that was supposed to be David Bowie—I feel terrible. I'm thinking over and over in my mind, "How could this have happened? I'm so in love with Erik." Over and over in my mind I'm saying this to myself. I feel terrible. A male humanoid with dark hair wearing a white lab coat is approaching me. He is reaching his hand out to me and is asking me, "Is this the first time this has happened?" He is communicating with me telepathically—I answer, "Yes." He replies, "I understand." He is walking away now—This is strange. He looks like the doctor who put those two metal posts into my mouth. He's the same one—the same Being!

I think I'm lying down. There is something inside me—I'm reaching for it—I can feel something inside me. It's a little uncomfortable. It's in my rectum. I think they want me to put a tampon in, but I can't with this metal thing inside me. How do they expect me to do this? I'm reaching for it so I can take it out. (I-60)

My memory ended there. I had some vaginal bleeding when I got up that morning that was not associated with menstruation. A short time after this experience I wrote in my journal that I did not feel I ovulated that month.

It was apparent to me that the person I was with was not David Bowie. Even though I knew this at some level, it was not enough to prevent me from going with him. There is an enormous amount of deception in some of these experiences and often I am aware of it while it is occurring. Unfortunately, I am not always able to prevent myself from following their preset agenda. This was a very unpleasant experience for me.

The following encounter was even more unpleasant. The physical discomfort is something I can deal with. However, when it comes to mental manipulation, that is another story. I wasn't so upset about what they did to me, it was *how* they did it.

11-9-90

> *I'm lying on my back and I have agreed to let a female Being perform some type of surgery on me. She is a doctor. There is another Being assisting her and it is a male. There is another Being assisting, but I can't see him. Oh! Now they are trying to make me believe they are my gynecologist and a psychology professor so I won't tell anyone about this—I know it's really the aliens doing this. I am sure of it—It's them—*
>
> *I feel uncomfortable, psychologically and physically. They are using mental camouflage on me and they are almost forcing me to believe this is my doctor and professor doing this to me because I know it is them. It's them. This is almost like a mental rape. I can hardly stand the mental images they are forcing into my mind.*
>
> *The female doctor is very competent and she is very sure of what she is doing. There is a pain inside me—it is very deep inside me—from my vagina all the way up to my abdomen. It's so painful. It—hurts—so—badly.*
>
> *I'm having trouble breathing—I have pain all the way down my esophagus—there is something down my throat and I think it's going all the way into my stomach. I can barely breathe and I can't swallow my own saliva.*
>
> *I'm seeing something. I'm being shown something on a view screen. I'm seeing tissue and nerve regeneration on a microscopic scale on a view screen. I've never seen anything like this before. I think they have some type of device inside me and at the same time they are performing surgery on me—I can see what they are doing inside me. They must be filming this at the same time. There's a stalk of tissue with white, creamy looking things on the end. It looks as though they are regenerating right there on the view screen. (I-38) I feel as though the doctor is satisfied with the results.*

This would have to go down as one of the most painful and most humiliating experiences out of all of my encounters. The physical pain is something that passes with the experience. However, when they tried to force these two mental images of the professor and my gynecologist into my mind, it was almost like a mental rape and it was more than I could stand. They simply could not know what they did to me in this circumstance. If they would let me know what is going on and be up front with me, and let me see them as they really look, I could deal with this entire thing so much easier. This encounter was almost excluded from this book because I found it too painful to incorporate from my original handwritten journal into the book.

If you do not understand what I mean when I use the term "mental rape," it is because it is difficult to explain the experience. It is something you have to experience to truly understand and I would not wish it on anyone. It is still difficult for me to deal with even today. Try to imagine feeling every sensation during surgery and yet be helpless to move or do anything about your situation. While at the same time, feel tubes in your nose, down your throat, in your rectum, and an object in your vagina creating pain all the way up into your abdomen. Now, try to imagine that situation being easier to handle than an alien imposing a mental image of two people you know who are doing this to you.

This may sound as if I am coming down fairly hard against the aliens. Perhaps in a way I am. However, I have to consider the fact that the aliens were not aware of how the images of these two individuals would affect me. I would have much rather have seen a large-eyed, Grey alien working on me. It would have been so much easier for me psychologically. Hindsight is twenty-twenty, perhaps even for the aliens. On the other hand, since every alien Being I have interacted with has been telepathic, I can't help but wonder how they could not have known how this was affecting me. In the end, it seems as though the aliens did this to me to make me feel so ashamed as to not want to tell anyone about it. This was probably just another form of manipulation.

About one week later I had another encounter and was thankful it was not as intense as the last one. I do not remember the entire experience so it is difficult for me to determine what really happened. Perhaps allowing me to remember the more positive aspects of my encounters and not allowing me to remember the not-so-positive aspects is a type of manipulation I can live with.

11-16-90

> *I am face to face with an alien. We must be about twelve inches away from one another. He has very tan and shiny skin, huge orange eyes with vertical pupils and a large forehead with a bone protruding around his eye sockets. Although he stands about six to six-and-a-half feet tall, we are still face to face. I'm looking up at him and we are staring into each other's eyes. He looks reptilian-like. There is another Being standing behind him. He looks similar except he has tan skin and elf ears. I'm looking back into the eyes of the Reptilian Tan who is closest to me and I'm asking him, "Why did you make him have Spock ears?" I'm chuckling too because this Being looks funny with these ears. I'm thinking he's obviously using camouflage and he looks ridiculous—*

Suddenly, the ears on the Tan Being are disappearing! They have vanished right before my eyes!

I'm looking into the eyes of the Reptilian Tan again. We are still face to face and I am looking up at him. I sense that he and the Tan Being are very nice. They are very benign Beings. I like them very much. I almost feel love for them. (I-20) (I-21)

This was a very positive experience. Today I sometimes find myself wishing I could see him again. I found both Beings to be very positive and somewhat attractive. Although I believe we may have interacted with one another since this time, this is the only journal entry about an experience with what I call a Reptilian Tan.

The following encounter resulted in much time and energy being expended while I tried to figure out what really transpired. As you will see, it was another experience involving a military base.

12-15-90

I'm standing on our deck and I believe Erik is with me—there are others here as well.

Now I'm looking at an orange flash of light in the night sky. It is surrounding a craft. I know this is an alien craft fighting one of our military planes. It's a helicopter. Yes, there are three or four helicopters fighting this alien craft. One of the helicopters has been hit and it is falling out of the sky.

Suddenly, I'm on a bus with some other people. We are on a military base.

Now I'm getting off the bus and I'm walking over to look at something.

I'm looking at a crashed cobra gunship. A military officer is telling me this is what I saw up in the air and this is what crashed and they will be starting an investigation shortly. I don't know why, but I am distrustful of him.

There are other people and they are following him away from this cobra helicopter I'm standing next to. I'm supposed to stay with the group, but I'm not going to.

I'm walking behind this crashed helicopter toward a small building. It is small, about ten to twelve feet square, maybe a little larger. It almost looks like a storage building. I'm opening the door to look inside—

There are two human females instructing a room full of tiny aliens. I have a very small, oddly shaped camera in my hands and I am clicking off pictures. These little aliens are so strange. I am overwhelmed and in awe at what these little Beings look like. I'm just standing in the doorway looking at them. One of the females is telling the room full of little aliens, "You must always remember to cover your eyes while you are here." I'm angry all of a sudden and I'm interrupting her, "No, don't ever cover up what you really look like—you're beautiful and you should never be ashamed of what you look like."

Suddenly, all of the little tiny aliens are terrified! They are terrified of me—I've frightened them. I'm reaching my hands out to them and I'm telling them, "You're wonderful, you're beautiful and I love you—I'm not going to hurt you—Don't be afraid." I'm touching them so they will know how I feel about them. They are about twelve to eighteen inches tall and have extremely round heads. They have indentations in their skin as if they have dents all over their bodies. The coloration of their skin inside these little dents is darker than the rest of their skin. They appear to have their eyes closed.

I'm holding one of the tiny aliens. (I-33) It doesn't have any clothes on and I feel as though it is calming down a little. It is very strange looking, but I love it—I love them all. The tall females don't look so human now—I sense a feeling of satisfaction from them.

Erik is standing next to me now. I'm showing him the tiny alien I'm holding and I'm telling him, "Look Erik, aren't they so cute—aren't they wonderful?" He replies in a very cautious and guarded tone, "Yeah." I feel as though I should care for them—I want to take them home with me, but I know I can't. Erik is afraid that I will bring them all home to live with us. I would if I only knew how to care for them.

I believe it is possible that the aliens wanted me to think our military had attacked one of their crafts and one of the military helicopters had crashed during the encounter. Or, perhaps the military was involved, and they wanted to make sure what I remembered seeing was a helicopter and not a spacecraft. There is also the possibility that a vision was employed to set the stage for my encounter and the aliens wanted me to think it was occurring on a military base. I felt as though I arrived on a bus with other abductees and I saw the crashed cobra gunship. I also had the distinct feeling the military officer was lying to me when he told me this is what I had seen in the sky. I felt as though he didn't want me to remember having seen one of their spacecrafts. Could this have been an alien, superimposing a military officer's image over his own, who wanted me to suspect he was covering something up, in order for me to feel the military was lying to me?

When I stood by the helicopter I saw grass on the ground and a wire fence along the perimeter of the base to my left. To my right I could see a small group of people and the dark green bus we arrived on. It looked just like a school bus, only it was painted a dark, olive green and the windows were blacked out with dark paint. Also to my right were square, light-colored buildings. It looked just like a typical military base to me. There was a reason I walked over to the little building with the small aliens in it. I never intended to stay with the group from the beginning. I knew there was something inside this small building and I wanted to see it. What I feel happened during this encounter is this: I was taken to a military base where aliens and at least one human were working together. I believe someone is interested in making me believe our government is helping the aliens. Who could it be?

It is curious that the female instructors would tell these tiny aliens "You must always remember to cover your eyes while you are here." This might suggest they were not always here and, therefore, did not live here but were simply visiting. It would also suggest the possibility that while they were here they had to keep their eyes closed, or were to cover them with something—perhaps similar to the way we cover our eyes from the sun by the use of sunglasses?

CHAPTER 10

New Beings and Another Military Base

Although Erik and I had some evenings where we expected to see the aliens, we had no conscious memories of having been visited by them until the following March.[14] That abduction contained a lot of theatrics and deception. At the end of the abduction, a Being was standing in my kitchen holding a black box with a video tape in it. He said to me, "This will teach you—Many of you believe you are having real experiences with us, when in fact, you are only having dreams about us."

I believed the Being was lying to me and was really upset because of the amount of information I was remembering from my abduction experiences.

About one week after that abduction, I had a very positive abduction experience. I would see another child and the bond between us was unmistakable.

4-8-91

I'm outside at night in what looks like a parking lot, but I know it's not really a parking lot. It is an open area and there is a cream colored building in front of me. It is square, tall, and does not have any windows. High in the sky and above me are lights with white streaks behind them. They appear to be moving vertically from my vantage point. I feel as though they are connected to the aliens. I'm really excited by these lights! They are spectacular! I feel as though I should tell someone about them.

Now, suddenly, I am with a group of people. We are together in this place, but now it looks more like a large room. I want to tell them what I just saw. I believe I just saw the alien's crafts in the sky. I'm telling a man what I saw and he is crying. I wonder if he is upset about the lights—I didn't think anyone would cry over seeing these lights in the sky. I'm shocked by his reaction.

Okay—Now I'm outside on our porch and I'm looking into the courtyard. I'm standing at the top of the stairs by the door and I am overwhelmed with amazement at what I see. I'm looking at a blonde, humanoid Being with a small male child. The child looks exactly like the father. They both have thin white hair and huge, blue eyes. The father, or male Being, is very tall and thin—They are both wearing tight fitting, white, one-piece body suits. The father was walking away from me with the small child by his side, but now they are looking at me. (I-35) The child—It is mine—Oh my God—This is my child and this is his father. They look exactly alike, but I know I am the child's mother. The male Being is very wary of me—he does not seem to trust me for reasons unknown to me. He is looking at me with an intense look of distrust on his face. (I-8)

The little boy is smiling at me! He recognizes me! He knows who I am. The male Being, the father—he is walking away now. There is a huge, floating penguin hovering above the courtyard wall—it is to my right—It is about seven feet tall and its form is slowly dissipating—The father is walking away from me and the floating penguin—The father—He has just walked through the courtyard wall—The father has disappeared through the courtyard wall!

The child is running toward me—he is smiling and he knows who I am! He is coming up the steps—I'm kneeling down and I'm extending my arms out to him. I'm picking him up—I'm holding him close to me—Oh! He has just transformed into a puppy! What is this? Now I seem to be holding a puppy that is half cocker spaniel and half Labrador retriever. I know this is still my little boy, but they want me to believe he is a puppy! I don't see this puppy, but this thought has been implanted into my mind—I'm still holding my child.

We are in the house together and there is a female authority figure in my kitchen. I want to keep my child here with me, but this female will not let me. There are others here also and in my mind they are saying, "What a cute puppy," but I know he is my little boy. The aliens do not want me to become attached to him. I've already seen what he looks like. I ask the female Being—"Can I keep him? Please?" And she replies, "No."

I feel so sad. I want the child to stay with me, but I know it is useless to argue.

This was a positive experience for me because I saw my child and the feeling I had when we were together was absolutely positive and loving. What was also so wonderful about it was that my child recognized me as his mother. It was the first time I understood what the nurturing instinct is that you hear new mothers describing. I was overwhelmed with this nurturing feeling when I saw and held my child. It seemed we had seen each other before and we remembered one another. I recognized him as the little hybrid boy who wanted me to play with him during the encounter on 8-25-90. This was the same encounter involving the teaching dream with the harp seal.

I wanted my child to stay with me more than anything, but with just a "No" from the female Being, I knew I had to accept their decision. It was final. He was such a cute little boy. He looked so much like his father it was like looking at a miniature version of The Father. There was a distinguishing feature between the two, however, and that was the obvious fact that my child exhibited feelings of happiness and seemed to trust me, while The Father exhibited a behavior that indicated he was distrustful of me.

It was absolutely amazing to me when I saw the father Being walk and then disappear through the courtyard wall. While this was happening I was aware of the penguin and I knew a penguin was not what was really there. It was a dark figure and a powerful presence that seemed to be observing us. I did not feel as though the father Being had much control over the situation. This powerful force coming from the floating penguin seemed to be controlling and manipulating all three of us—The Father, the child, and me. I felt as though it was the only Being who was in control and the three of us were merely its chess pieces. Although I describe this "floating penguin" as a controlling force, I did not sense it was negative or positive, only controlling.

The same night I was visited by the father Being and my child, Erik recalled an unusual memory from his encounter that same night.

> *We're driving down the highway near our house where the four lanes merge into two lanes. I look up and see three disk-type UFOs at tree top level. They are forty to fifty feet wide and are moving at five to ten m.p.h. They are totally silent and are white in color—a very cool white—almost iridescent. They are flying in a delta formation and while the two outside crafts are very smooth in texture, the third craft in the middle seems to be collapsing in on itself at its center. Its texture looks like a dried orange peel. They are moving out of sight toward the east and behind the trees.*
>
> *In the distance, traveling north to south, appear three sets of blue and red lights—these are police cars and they are traveling at a very high rate of speed. Well over a hundred miles per hour! They pass by the car and shake it violently—The first two police cars are bumper to bumper and the third car is only seconds behind.*
>
> *I'm looking down the highway and see that the police cars are pursuing these three crafts. I yell, "Jesus Christ! Look at that! They'll never catch those guys!" At that moment the crafts turn bright red,*

> *accelerate, and disappear—one going up and to the east and the other going up and to the west. The police cars continue driving south.*

One of the three crafts is obviously missing from this last paragraph. Apparently, the craft that appeared to be collapsing in on itself must have flown away or disappeared from view, or possibly even transformed somehow. It might have been in the process of cloaking itself, or perhaps even distorting the space around itself. Nevertheless, Erik believes it disappeared before the other two crafts did.

Erik and I both had memories of seeing crafts or lights in the sky. I suspect if we did not get into our car in the middle of the night and go for a drive, then these two portions of our memories are a screen memory implanted by the aliens. Perhaps they thought my mind would focus on the lights in the sky and I would remember nothing more about my encounter.

Two nights later the Beings, specifically the Greys, performed a classical conditioning experiment on me.

4-10-91

> *I am at a small lake and there are people fishing and lounging in and near the water. I can't see them clearly but they are here—Although I don't fish someone or something has persuaded me to try it. I'm looking at the bait and hook—there isn't a hook, it's just a straight pin and there is a white piece of fish that looks as if it has already been cooked on the end of it. Someone has already prepared my line for fishing. This is strange—Now I realize that someone has already put it out in the water for me—I don't remember them doing this. All I have to do is to hold the fishing rod and reel in whatever I catch.*
>
> *I'm out in the water a little and I feel something tugging at my line. I'm getting excited—I'm reeling it in—this must be what people enjoy about fishing—the excitement of catching something. I think I've caught something really big. I think I can understand why some people might find this fun.*
>
> *Oh my God. I've just seen what I have caught! It is a dolphin!! Oh my God—I feel terrible about this.*
>
> *I don't know how, but now I'm in a hospital. I'm not sure where I am. The walls are dark and the floor is dark too. I'm looking at a metal table with the dolphin lying on it. I'm begging for someone to help it. "Please help the dolphin!" I say to everyone who walks by. I'm frantic! I feel terrible. This is all my fault. It can't breathe and it looks dead—I'm on the verge of hysteria. I don't want it to die. "Please help the dolphin! Please help the dolphin!!" I'm screaming this over and over.*

A male is walking out of the elevator—I know him! I've seen him before. I yell, "Please help him!" He replies, "It's usually okay for the first ten minutes or so." Now there are three Beings around the dolphin. The dolphin is lying on its back and these three Beings are performing an unusual form of CPR on it. I'm watching this. I'm looking at the dolphin—He has light gray skin and is very thin. I'm wondering how he can lie on his back. I wonder about this strange position—how can a dolphin lie on his back—

Oh, I hope they will be able to save him. They are pushing on his chest using a rather strange motion I've never seen before. Finally—Finally the dolphin begins to breathe. Thank God—I'm so relieved. The dolphin is lifting itself up a little with one arm and is looking at me—Just as I look into his eyes I begin to fall—I'm falling to my knees—I'm so sick all of a sudden—I'm vomiting all over the floor.

The male Being is helping me now—he is taking me to another room. I'm in the room with this male Being—I'm fainting—

It was immediately obvious to me this was not a dolphin, but rather, a Grey, and I did not catch him with a fishing pole either. This was all orchestrated in order to make me feel responsible for his life. They convinced me that I had killed him just as they convinced me that Erik and I were responsible for catching the harp seal. My emotions were unbelievably intense over this. When he stared into my eyes it made me vomit almost immediately. I sensed that he was immensely angry with me and he intentionally made me vomit. I believe their actual intentions with this encounter were to perform a classical conditioning experiment designed to prevent me from eating seafood. Why, I do not know.

What I believe the aliens were interested in was to make me stop eating fish and it worked. After this encounter I went several months without eating fish. When I consciously made the connection and realized what was happening, I tried eating fish again. I became extremely nauseous afterwards. This happened to me on many occasions. I realize dolphin are not fish, but prior to this encounter I had recently read a study that stated fish do feel pain and suffer when they die. My eating them as a substitute for other animals made me believe I was still causing pain and suffering. This was something that, on a spiritual level, I had a difficult time accepting. These Beings wanted to emphasize that it is wrong to eat fish. They chose to use the dolphin to demonstrate this to me.

I have learned that most of our commercial fish are caught with various types of nets. Drift netting is indiscriminate as to who or what it kills. One of its many victims are dolphins. I was left with a powerful message: It was wrong for me to kill *any* other species because there was plenty of other food I could be eating which did not create pain and suffering. Remember, this message was coming from the Greys. It underscored the fact that some of these Beings have been misjudged.

Again, I must emphatically emphasize the word "some." Research, especially research by Linda Moulton Howe has shown that aliens may be responsible for many of the mutilated animals that have been discovered over the years. No matter what the Beings would like to have us believe about them, we cannot overlook either of these messages. We may find out that there really are good and bad aliens, and we may find out that the aliens are simply using positive messages to manipulate us.

6-8-91

> *I'm looking at a young girl. She is walking away from a man and she is looking up at me. She has strange eyes. They are much rounder than normal and they are very, very blue. Her hair is extremely short. It looks as though if you touched it, it would almost crinkle. It is very white too.*
>
> *I am appalled—Somehow I know that she has just had intercourse with the man she is walking away from. She looks as if she is only eight or nine years old. I'm looking at her chest—I'm hoping to see signs of a developed woman—I'm trying to justify this age discrepancy—But, she is just a child. I don't feel as though this child objected to this sexual encounter she has just had with this man—She doesn't appear to be totally human either.*
>
> *Now I'm looking at Erik and two other "people." I can't believe this! There is a small—My God—A tiny, tiny baby and I think it has heat stroke, or something is wrong with its heart—We are trying to save it. We're putting it in some water and we're performing CPR on it by pressing two of our fingers gently up and down on its chest—I'm not sure what is happening to the baby.*
>
> *Some type of instrument is being used on me to get me to relax. It looks like a wand with some little feather-type things on the end of it. Someone is tickling my back with it and it feels really good. Oh! Something—Someone has just given me a shot and it really hurt! I'm surprised that it hurt. For some reason I didn't think it would be painful.*

I awakened with some light vaginal bleeding the following morning. Later in the week I recorded the following in my journal: "For the past week I've been feeling nauseated during and after meals. I have a lot of anxiety, dizziness, and blurred vision. I feel very fatigued."

I believe this female child with the white hair was a hybrid child and the man she just had sex with was a human male. I didn't sense that he had much say in the matter. It was so strange to see her young body and to somehow know this had just happened. It goes against everything we are taught about children, but then, so many of these experiences do. Evidently, this type of early sexual behavior is not unusual for them and I have to keep in mind that this child did appear to be a hybrid, or possibly even an alien child.

The small alien infant we were performing CPR on appeared to be in trouble. I don't know if it survived or not. Because we were not trained in medical science, I do not believe we were cognizant of anything else we could have done for the baby.

Two nights later I underwent a theatrical "preparation." I was no longer just an abductee, now it seemed I was being used to abduct members of my own family. Although it had happened before, this time I was to remember much more about the experience.

6-10-91

> *Somehow I know that a man is going to hurt my little three year old nephew. This man is over six feet tall, has dark hair and dark skin. I'm frantically trying to call the police, but I can't get anyone on the phone. I'm calling 9-1-1—Someone is there, but they won't let me talk to a police officer! I'm furious and I'm screaming that I feel someone is going to hurt my little nephew.*
>
> *I'm running toward my nephew's house—I must be here now— Someone is handing me a gun and a knife. The gun is cocked. This "dark man" is standing in front of me—I think he is waiting for me to kill him. He is giving me a clear opportunity to kill him—I'm thinking—"Yes—I will kill him to protect my little nephew." I'm pressing on the trigger—*
>
> *Suddenly a male has materialized between the "dark man" and me. He is taking my weapons away from me. He says he will take care of the perpetrator, the "dark man," for me—I am relieved.*
>
> *Suddenly, I'm floating—I'm floating through the neighborhood. I am approaching a light bluish gray house. This is where my little nephew is! They—They are already there! Somehow they have found him— they found out where he lives. I'm floating toward his bedroom window. They are already here. There is a bright white light with just a hint of blue in it. This light is shining into his bedroom—I seem to be floating inside this incredibly bright white light and I'm looking into the window. My nephew is standing up in his bed and he is squinting*

> and looking into the white light—Now he is floating with his feet facing the window. He is floating, feet first—toward me. I'm thinking, "They have already found him."
>
> We are both in this intense white light—It surrounds us—I can feel it. He is lifting his little head up and he's looking at me. He looks as if he is in a trance or is drugged or something. He is looking into my eyes and I am looking into his. His little blue eyes are so pretty with this intense light shining into them.
>
> Oh! I think he recognizes me.

I think the aliens tested me before they abducted my nephew. I believe the aliens wanted to find out just how far I would go to protect my nephew. By using their familiar theatrics they determined if I had the right weapon, I would kill to protect him. That may be why they kept me floating and immobilized within the white light. They wanted me to be with him because he trusts me, but at the same time, I don't think the aliens could risk trusting me completely.

During the following abduction encounter it would appear that I was either careless when holding this child or the aliens wanted to study the thoughts and emotions associated with guilt. They couldn't have chosen a better subject for their study. After everything I've been through with them, they probably know me better than anyone.

8-7-91

> I'm in a very large, round room. I see my gray cat looking up at me and meowing. He has a square flap of skin that has been cut away and underneath it I can see his brain. There isn't any blood, only brain tissue. He doesn't seem to be in any pain. I can't believe this—I'm very upset!
>
> Now there are "others" in here with me, but I never see their faces. We seem to be sitting on these long, circular benches. My brother is here with me and he is sitting over toward my right. Someone has just told me that I have to go over to a boy on the other side of the room.
>
> I'm standing in front of him now—He has reddish-brown hair and it is very messy. He's not very tall and he looks extremely unhealthy. Oh—Now I'm holding him like a baby. I realize he is much smaller than I thought he was a minute ago. This must be a different child.
>
> I just dropped him!! He has fallen backward and onto the floor! I'm looking at his head and he doesn't seem to have any hair anymore.

> *There is a square cut into his head that looks just like the one I saw in my cat's head. I'm still upset about seeing my cat like this and I'm also upset about this little boy. I'm putting a towel on top of his head—Now I'm looking very closely at this square flap of skin—I'm lifting up the flap of skin and I can see his brain. There is no blood, only a clear fluid and his brain. I can't believe this happened. I'm putting the towel back on his head, very carefully, because I don't want to damage his brain. There are others around me and I feel as though I am being observed. All I can think is "This is terrible—Did I cause this?"*

What in the world were they up to now? First they wanted me to believe they had performed some kind of brain surgery on my cat. Then they wanted me to believe they had performed the same type of surgery on this little child. What if I remembered the events in the incorrect order? Certainly the little child didn't end up with the same flap of skin cut from his head, thereby exposing his brain, just because I dropped him onto the floor. Did they want me to believe I had caused this to happen to him? Was this a study in guilt? Carelessness? Or something else I cannot even imagine? It is possible they performed this surgery on both my cat and the alien child, but I think it's more likely that it was simply a visual deception employed to make me feel protective of my cat, and experience guilt because I dropped the alien child.

Three nights later they were back again. I still have a difficult time believing they would find me interesting, (or hopeless) enough to visit me this often! Interestingly, while this was occurring I felt as though I knew who this man was. It was as though we had met before and he seemed very familiar to me.

8-10-91

> *I'm with a black man who is fair-skinned. I know him and I remember being with him before. He is kissing me and it feels very strange— Whatever I think about this kiss, seems to happen. It's too perfect— But I am enjoying the kiss.*
>
> *He has to go back now. He has escaped from somewhere, like a prison, but it's not really a prison—he has to go back now. I have to return him to a special place, but I don't want to. I don't want him to go back.*
>
> *I've returned him, but now I feel I want to visit him because I do not like being away from him. I think I'm in a hospital. I'm taking a blanket to him. Someone is leading me through this place and into another room.*

Now I'm looking at my father. He is sitting on top of an examination table. My mother is standing next to him and she is very angry. She says, "I can't believe I recommended this hospital to anyone!"

Apparently she is not happy with the treatment my father is receiving. My father is very, very upset. His aunt is with him—I'm giving her a big hug—Oh, it's not really her—it is an alien Being. I felt it when I hugged her. They just want my father to think it's his aunt so he will calm down. Someone is behind me—I'm turning around—

There is a strange looking male—he is very tall, thin, and frail, and he has strange looking hair. He is also sitting in a wheel chair. His hair looks like a wig—very artificial. Telepathically, he asks me, "May I have photographs of your estate?" I don't live on an estate and this is all theatrics again. I suddenly feel as though I shouldn't let him know that I've figured out he is just trying to divert my attention away from my father. I'm trying to conceal my thoughts from him.

Suddenly, I am outside and I'm looking up at a light blue sky with thin wispy clouds. It is daylight and I can see several stars. This is strange—I wonder how I can see them. Oh! Now they are moving—It's them! They are moving out now—Their crafts are moving out from a central location across the sky. This is amazing!

Once again, I believe a lot of deception was being used to screen out certain aspects of this encounter. I believe I know who this black man is on an unconscious level and I care deeply for him. I am not certain if he is a prisoner or is just under the Beings' control. He seems to be a prisoner of sorts. Perhaps this was part of the deception and he was really another abductee. The kiss was peculiar. It was almost as if it were being orchestrated from outside of us. I am certain that someone was in mental contact with me during this kiss and I do not believe it was the black man I was kissing.

When I saw my father sitting on the examination table it was disturbing to me. He appeared to be upset and it hurt me so much to see him like this. One of the aliens used camouflage (by superimposing his aunt's appearance over their own) to help him calm down. It was not until I hugged her, more specifically, *touched* the Being, that I realized this was not really her. I find this very interesting because it seems to indicate that we may have a way to discover what is real in these experiences and what is illusion. Perhaps if we can somehow stop relying on our visual perceptions so much and physically interact with them, that is, by holding or touching these Beings, we can eliminate some of the false realities they seem so dependent upon when interacting with us. I approached what I saw as my great aunt with love and the desire to say hello and I love you. It was a purely human thing to do and somehow I immediately knew, not from what I saw but from what I *felt*, that this was *not* my great aunt.

When I saw my mother she appeared normal in every sense. However, in light of the camouflage technique being employed with my great aunt's image, can I say for certain that my mother was really there? Can I also infer that perhaps my father was not really there either? The fact that the alien, who appeared to be sitting in a wheel chair, was trying to distract my attention away from my father leads me to believe it probably was my father they had sitting on the examination table. There is also a good possibility that my mother may have been abducted with him for the sole purpose of keeping him calm, so she too may have really been present.

The following is only a memory fragment. It is what I remember of traveling in a beam of blue light.

8-12-91

> *I was just sitting in bed talking to Erik, but now I'm heading toward something—I'm standing upright and I'm floating toward something—I'm in a turquoise colored beam of light and I'm floating—I'm somehow moving along this beam of light. Where is Erik?—Oh—I remember now—He went before me and is already there—*

The next thing I remembered was being back in my bed. I did not feel as if I fell to sleep. I woke Erik up and tried to tell him what had happened, but he was so groggy I don't think he understood a word I said. The only fear I had about this was being unsure about the turquoise beam of light. It was a little unnerving to be moving through it while only being able to see blackness beneath me. I felt I would fall right through it, but somehow I remained floating. Unfortunately, I have not remembered anymore about this experience.

This was the month I discovered that not only did my mother not sleep well at night, she was getting up in the middle of the night and going outside. Erik and I lived with my parents for six months after we sold our house. We had reluctantly decided to move to Portland, Oregon, but it wasn't easy to find a house when we were living three thousand miles away. I'll never forget waking up one night with a peculiar feeling that something wasn't quite right in my parent's house. I walked into the kitchen and found the door leading outside partially opened. It was three o'clock in the morning. I ran to a window in the living room and looked out a window in the front of the house. Low and behold, there was my mother, still dressed in her nightgown, standing in the front yard and looking up at the sky!

It was a prime opportunity for the daughter to scold the mother. Finally, after all of these years, I had something on her! I wasn't too hard on her because her behavior did not really seem that unusual to me in light of what was occurring in our lives. I reminded my mother that she was putting herself at risk by being outside so late at night and in her nightgown no less. The following day Erik talked to her and asked her to be more careful.

My final visit of August occurred eleven days after I remembered traveling in the turquoise beam of light.

8-23-91

> *I'm flying in a craft in a low earth orbit—I can see the planet from above it. I'm a little scared—This looks a little like the space shuttle, but it's not—it is different—much smaller.*
>
> *Now I'm in the living room of my parent's house. I'm teaching someone clarinet lessons and I think her parents are here. There are two females here—definitely aliens—One is a Grey. She has clothes on and really strange looking hair. It is very sparse. She has a huge forehead, high cheekbones, hollow looking cheeks, a small pointed chin and old looking skin. Her eyes are very large. Her body is extremely thin, except for her breasts. She has large breasts and they don't look real. One of them is "uneven." It is higher than the other. I'm staring at her and studying her body. (I-6) She doesn't like this—She is uncomfortable now. She doesn't want me to study her and she doesn't seem to want to be here anymore. The little girl and her parents are gone—I think they were an illusion. Yes, they were just a distraction.*
>
> *Now—Suddenly, I am very close to a woman I know. Her name is Gertrude—she must be at least seven months pregnant. She is very upset. I ask her, "Are you pregnant? Are you okay?" She touches her stomach and says, "Yes, but I have to have an operation. I have to have the baby taken out—removed." While she is saying this she is looking up as if she is looking into the sky. Suddenly, I know the aliens are going to take her baby. That is why she is here.*

I had known this lady for twenty years. I never knew anything such as this had happened to her. I immediately blew it off and thought that, yes, the aliens had been here, but this was just more deception and theatrics. In November, that all changed. Gertrude has a daughter who is closer to my age than she is. They came out to Oregon to visit me that following November and it was then that I told her I had a "dream" about her. I related the memory to her and her daughter. They were flabbergasted. Apparently, Gertrude kept this event very much to herself. Gertrude then explained to me how she had a miscarriage during her seventh month of pregnancy. She said one day blood just started gushing down her leg. She was rushed to the emergency room where she almost died. She lost the baby. Her first question to me was, "Do you think the aliens tried to take my baby—is that what went wrong?" Naturally, I told her no. I wasn't going to speculate about something I knew so little about and which might prove to be emotionally damaging to her.

At this point, I felt compelled to ask her a few general questions and her answers led me to tell her about a few of my unusual experiences. This turned out to be quite an evening. I do not believe Gertrude's baby was taken by the aliens because she said the doctors had retrieved the seven month old fetus and that something was wrong with it. What I wondered was, did the aliens attempt to do something to the baby while it was still in the womb? Did something then go wrong? However, I could never voice this to Gertrude even after she questioned me as to whether or not I thought the aliens made her lose her baby. There simply wasn't enough information to answer this question. I believed there was a strong possibility that she and other members of her family may be involved in the abduction phenomenon. I did not tell Gertrude this until after she told me about her husband's lifelong visitations by little men who came for him in the night with a little wand in their hands. He never told her anymore than that because, as he would say, "It's better if you don't ask questions Gertrude—It's better if you don't know."

This encounter was special. I believe I had to experience this teaching dream in order to show me what Gertrude had experienced some thirty years earlier. Gertrude knew she was going to lose her baby and she seemed to believe the aliens were somehow connected to it. I felt this was a teaching dream and this experience acted as a personal kind of "awakening" for Gertrude and her family. I believe the aliens used me as a messenger to tell this family about the alien presence in their lives. I don't know why they would do this, but I feel very strongly about it. I began to realize that the "awakening," the idea that there is a time for certain people to begin consciously recalling their experiences, is indeed real.

The following experience was remembered spontaneously. It left me feeling rather uneasy and is one of those experiences that is not particularly easy to talk about.

9-9-91

> *I think The Blonde is having sex with me. He seems to be in a hurry and he is being a little rough with me. I heard him say he could only be here for five minutes. There is a large, white dog standing upright next to the bed or table I'm lying on. He is watching us—observing us. This doesn't seem right—Where am I? I'm looking around while this is happening.*

The Blonde is leaving. I can see down a dark hallway, I think. I can see what looks like a turtle standing upright. It is really scary to look at—it looks so much like a little Grey alien. I'm really scared. Its skin is light tan and it seems to sparkle when it moves around.

I'm walking down this hallway toward the turtle—I'm so scared—I'm looking at two statues now. They are completely still. There is a duck and a turtle standing upright. As still as statues—This is strange, a minute ago they were moving.

It *happened*, but when? I hoped if I was fantasizing about having sex I would feel some other emotion connected to it apart from detachment, but detachment was all that I felt emotionally. I was simply a mechanism for The Blonde. I did not feel any arousal associated with this encounter nor did I feel a sense of violation. It was a very real experience. In a way, I felt as if I was acting out of a duty to someone, and I believe The Blonde's behavior was for the same purposes.

I am positive the white dog, who stood upright and was watching us, was not a dog. Nor were the turtle and the duck what they appeared to be. Even while I was looking at the turtle, I realized that he looked more like a Grey than a turtle. There is also no reason for me to be afraid of a turtle because I have cared for and held many turtles I have relocated from various roads and highways. In fact, I quite like turtles. They are my favorite reptile and if they were not animals that belonged in the wild, I would enjoy having one as a pet.

My next visitation felt more like a violation of trust. I have a strong sense of guilt associated with it because I feel as though the Beings were successful at deceiving me again, and it left me with a feeling of helplessness.

9-18-91

I'm in my nephew's house. I am holding his hand and we are standing in his parent's room. They are asleep in their bed. He is looking up at me with such a happy face. He thinks it's fun to be in here while they are asleep. He recognizes me and is smiling and is looking up at me.

Now we are standing in what looks like the hallway between his room and his parent's room. I believe Erik is with me and there is also another child present. This child looks as if he is part alien. Perhaps he is a hybrid child. He has white skin and very large eyes. Although they are closed, I can see that his eyes are very large.

Someone is showing me a black box about six inches square. It has a rough exterior—Now I don't think this is Erik with us—this is someone else—I know it isn't Erik, but I trust this Being—I am in agreement with him. We are going to use this little black box on my nephew. I have just been told it will not harm him and I trust this Being I am with. I feel comfortable about performing this procedure.

Now the little hybrid child and my nephew look as if they have been "turned off." This black box has two tubes coming from it and they have been inserted into my nephew. One of the tubes is going into his chest over his heart and the other is going into his lower right leg. There is some blood mixed with a clear fluid in these two tubes.

Now I'm trying to make the little hybrid child watch what we are doing. He is supposed to be watching this, but he won't open his eyes. I am supposed to make him open his eyes because he is supposed to be watching this procedure.

I'm looking at these two tubes going into my little nephew's body. I am very frightened for him. I'm very angry because they told me it would not hurt him, and now I can see a little blood in the tubes and I'm afraid this must be extremely painful for him. I'm so angry now. They have deceived me. I would have never done this had I known this was what was going to happen. I'm scared—I feel as though the aliens have lied to me.

The next day my first thought was, "Oh God, what have I done?" I felt so betrayed by them. "How could they use me for something like this? They used me!" They persuaded me to believe the procedure would not hurt my little nephew.

After allowing some time to pass after this abduction I began to question what occurred. Could it be that my nephew and the little hybrid child were turned off so they would not be traumatized by the procedure? Although it was my responsibility to make sure the hybrid child watched what we were doing, I could not arouse him in any way. They were both standing, slightly slumped over, and they were clearly turned off.

What about the two tubes I saw inserted into my nephew? What did they connect to and why? Could it be possible the box was some kind of filtering device? Was it measuring something? Could the tubes have been connected from my nephew to the hybrid child? Did they need a transfusion of some sort from my nephew in order to help this hybrid child? Although there was a trace of blood in the clear fluid, it might have only been from the insertion of the tubes into his body and the clear fluid might be what they were really trying to obtain. I have to wonder if what was done that night might have helped another person or another alien. Clearly, these two children weren't placed in these circumstances because they were supposed to watch and learn. Both of the children were turned off.

Perhaps I overreacted to the entire experience. My nephew was okay the next day and I do not recall my sister saying she ever found any unusual marks on him. However, since my sister knows nothing about the abduction phenomenon, I doubt if she would have noticed if there were any physical marks left behind. She wouldn't have had any reason to look. In any event, my nephew seems normal and healthy in every way.

My husband and I were on our way to Portland, Oregon, two weeks after this encounter. Erik kept his job in Pensacola and I held down the fort in Portland until he could secure employment here. It was a difficult time, but thanks to modern conveniences like the telephone and air travel, we made it through. He came out for interviews several times and by February he had a new job and we were together again.

During our four months apart I attended school. I also became active in a local UFO group and hosted support groups a couple of times a month. Some things never change, however, and my visitations, as well as my husband's, continued even though we were three thousand miles apart. The following journal entry is an account, in my husband's words, of what happened to him on October 21, approximately one month after the experience involving my nephew and the hybrid child.

10-21-91

As the radio alarm set off with the morning news, my mind was filled with the events that I had lived in the hours before. I felt drugged and tired as if robbed of my rest. This Tuesday morning brought vivid memories and my realization that I too, was under investigation. The Sandman had come to visit.

The sky at dawn was clear and chilled as I had my first conscious sighting. An open area revealed a silver disk moving silently above the field. It had appeared over the trees and moved slowly eastward. My excitement grew. I thought of how I could tell Katharina that I'd seen one—A craft of fifty or more feet in diameter, glistening in the dawn, silent and wonderful.

I felt the presence of others to my right and turned to see. There were ten or more people around, all looking toward the craft with blank stares on their faces. I turned to walk away only to be confronted by a shockingly wonderful sight. Only feet away was a disk hovering five feet above the ground and just right of an older rust-colored Chevy pickup. This disk was beautiful. It was small, perhaps twelve feet wide and shaped similar to a bell that had been compressed. It was as white as a cloud except for the foot-wide black band around its center. A single rectangular window conformed to the very shape of the craft. **(I-50)** *This was a ship designed for one Being and that Being was* *staring at me. I wanted to touch this object and I didn't want this guy staring at me. I lifted my arms and placed my hands and forearms onto the surface of the craft. The surface was hard, yet smooth and warm. It appeared to be made up of thousands of seamless interlocking tiles. I wondered how it managed to hover. Decisively, I looked at the Being. Then with all of my strength I quickly pushed down on the craft. The craft reacted as a boat on the water. The edge dipped a foot or so in both directions before quickly stabilizing. (I-51) The Being looked at me with absolute shock. Its facial expression was one of "Why the hell did you do that?" This was the first time I have ever seen any emotion. I jumped back in fear as a Being moved toward me. "Could this be the pilot?" I questioned myself. He was floating several feet above the ground. He was a small Being, very similar to the Greys, but with a very well-defined, smooth nose and smaller eyes.*

I was given a pillow and blanket made of a very lightweight, translucent and opalescent material. The Being told me telepathically, "It is time for you to go to sleep." A primal fear set in as I pleaded for him not to do this again. As I begged, he quickly raised his left hand over my head and released a metallic powder over my face. I could taste the bitter substance that fell onto my face and lips as I drifted away and lost consciousness.

I found myself seated near the center of several other people. We were in a room with two sides. It was "L" shaped and there was a door behind me. The room had a panoramic view from the south to the west. I was seated with my back to the door. A Being came in and placed an alien infant in my arms. I had the feeling this was the pilot and then I tried to draw everyone's attention to the infant. No one seemed interested. They all just sat there and stared. I told the Being that it should take the child. I could not understand why they wanted me to hold this child and told them that children were Katharina's deal. I could feel the child's feet pushing toward my genitals. They wanted me to allow the child to fondle me. I told them that was sick and to take the child away. They did.

From our elevated view, I could see in the distance a very beautiful sight—A city situated near the horizon. A beautiful city of towering skyscrapers that may have been crystal. Around the city were tens of hundreds of spacecraft. They formed a perfect circle above the city. The ships were angled to catch the full light of sunrise. As the sun reflected from their surfaces, a golden halo was formed around this city. It was breathtaking.

In the western sky was a circle of eight to twelve soft, glowing lights. They were stationary in the dark sky.

Below me, I could see an impression in the ground perhaps fifty feet wide. The area appeared to be an old park or cemetery. It was surrounded by a metal spike picket fence. In the area was a toppled monument. One that perhaps had been an object on top of a pole. On the ground were two cherub-type statues that seemed to glow.

When Erik told me about this event over the phone I absolutely insisted that he write it down. He doesn't often write down his experiences and I had to keep insisting until he promised me he would write it down and draw some pictures. I am thankful that he did. It wasn't until the 1992 MUFON symposium in Albuquerque, New Mexico, that I saw another drawing of a craft that looked like the one Erik saw and touched. The description of a beautiful city, with perhaps crystal buildings, was another experience I had seen myself and had certainly heard of from other abductees.

I wondered if the toppled post and the glowing cherubs lying on the ground weren't possibly knocked over by the craft, and may still have been glowing from its proximity to them.

Erik was still working in Pensacola and I was still in Portland. We missed one another so very much and were excitedly looking forward to being together for Thanksgiving. Approximately two weeks before Erik came out to Portland for Thanksgiving, I had an unusual experience that was difficult to call an abduction. It was confusing to me because it had the reality and feel of an abduction, more specifically a teaching dream or a vision but I never saw alien Beings. Interestingly, when I awakened I had the distinct impression the Beings were trying to tell me something.

11-12-91

I was planting three different types of plants. As I was digging the third hole, there was a "flash" in the soil and a huge circle appeared. The circle was several inches thick. Then I saw a huge hole appear that exposed the root system of the plant I was planting. The roots were down in the ground already and when this hole appeared, the roots of this plant grew instantly, right before my eyes. Now I found myself looking at the roots of the plant and a hole that was about eight feet deep. I could see a clearish-yellow, plastic bubble under the ground with a liquid under it and I thought it might be glass. I took a shovel and punched a hole in this huge bubble and the liquid began to drain out of it.

There was a building off to my right and I went there to tell someone what I had found. When I came back to the place I had dug my three holes for my plants, there was an ocean with three ancient, nuclear power plants in it. They were almost halfway submerged under the ocean, but I could still tell what they were. The sand and water were now black and polluted. I became extremely angry. Apparently, when I dug my holes for my plants I hit an underground dome that had been built to seal off these old power plants. There were other people there and they were not concerned about this, but I was furious. I tried to get a man involved by asking him how and why this happened. He didn't seem to care. I began yelling at people, "You knew and yet you did nothing! You covered this up!" I kept yelling at various people as they would pass by. They all knew about the nuclear power plants but none of them wanted to admit it, even now as the power plants were so blatantly obvious. It was very frightening to see. I almost felt I had uncovered something from a previous civilization. I felt it was going to harm the planet.

I am sure that if five different experts analyzed this "dream" they would come up with five different explanations. The point I'm trying to make is, this "dream" had the same feel of reality to it that my abduction experiences have. It was so powerful that as I stood there looking at these old power plants, I somehow knew I was looking back into our own past. It was us. It was our human past. I was left with yet another strong feeling that something devastating will happen in our future. The aliens have shown me a war, which appeared to be a nuclear war because the sky turned a bright orange-red, and now I was looking at ancient nuclear power plants. Someone had built a dome to contain the entire structures. This was done to hide the truth from, and to supposedly protect civilization. It didn't work. I was left believing that a future civilization will not only discover them, but will also be contaminated by them as well. And they, too, will be apathetic about the discovery.

I have interpreted this event as a teaching dream. I do not look at myself as someone who is consumed with the fear of a nuclear power plant "erupting into death and destruction." I simply don't think about it unless I see something on the news. However, I don't believe in nuclear power for public energy purposes and would gladly pay the extra cost for electricity not obtained from its use. Perhaps the Beings had an interest in strengthening this attitude about nuclear power. They may have been trying to remind me about the long term dangers of nuclear power. Then again, there remains the possibility that I really did see the future.

I had been in Portland, Oregon, since October 3, 1991. Things had been relatively quiet with the exception of the teaching dream, and I was beginning to think by moving three thousand miles away I may have eluded the aliens until the night of December 4. That night, my house felt as if it were filled with an unusual energy. I felt a strong sensation of a presence associated with it. I decided at ten o'clock that night, just before going to sleep, to focus my energy and my thoughts on something positive, like trying to visualize positive energy around me. Sometimes it helps me not to be afraid when I feel that "someone is coming for me."

I was successful at reaching a comfortable state of relaxation after about twenty minutes, but I could still feel the strange energies. I was detecting a definite presence in the house.

12-4-91

Someone is here—I'm falling asleep—

I'm awake and my cats are really upset! Everyone is crying—One of my cats sounds as if he is shouting out his meows. I've just returned— I think I've just returned—I was just coming back from somewhere.

I'm going downstairs to see what is wrong with everyone—I know now—I was just out on the deck with someone! I'm running toward the family room where our porch is and where all of the cats sleep— My mind is flooded with memories—

I was just out on the porch with a Being a few minutes ago! I'm so upset—the door was open! "This is always supposed to stay closed!" I was telling him. I shut the door—Thank God my cats didn't get out. I hate it when they do this. They know this door has to stay locked— How many times do I have to tell them? I've put three locks on this door and they know better than to do this! I still feel a presence in the house.

I'm looking at my dog. She is sound asleep. How can she be asleep while the cats are all crying and upset? This is strange. I'm looking at the door—It's locked—everything is okay. I'm walking back up the stairs. I'm going to get back into bed.

I'm in bed—I still feel a presence in the house. I think I see someone by my bedroom window—I'm lifting my head up to get a better look— Paralysis—it's really strong—I know someone is in my room and I'm going to look. I'm fighting the paralysis. I remember it and I want to be stronger than it is—I'm still trying to lift my head—"I can see, I can see, I can see..." I'm telling myself over and over again. I'm still trying to lift my head because they are over by the window and I want to see them. Suddenly I'm free! I'm looking toward the window—

I'm being shown a scar—I'm looking at a scar on someone's body. Someone is showing it to me. I hear popping sounds—

Now I'm outside at night and I'm looking up at a strange looking craft. It must be a helicopter. It's about the size of a Marine CH53 but this is much more modern-looking. It is very angular, but it is still round. In some ways it reminds me of the Stealth, but this craft is round, it is not a wing. It is very angular, dark, and round. It has dark panels that fit together at angles that make me think it has an octagon shape, but it has so many angles that it appears almost round. It is very smooth and dark. It is almost black with no markings on it whatsoever. (I-54) *I'm watching this craft move at unbelievable speeds. I've just realized that I'm outside and it is dark. There are other people with me. I have moved away from the small group of people because I'm watching this craft. I am fascinated with it. It is hovering, silently, above me.*

Suddenly, it falls out of the sky! Oh my God! It's going to crash! I'm running and throwing myself onto the ground with my hands over my head. Oh, I think the pilot must be dead—It must have crashed!

I'm looking around, but I can't see the craft. It isn't on the ground and it isn't in the air anymore. I'm walking over to where I thought it was going to crash but all I can see are indentations in the grass. It must have landed and then taken off again—but how could anything move so quickly? I'm staring at the ground—Something has caught my attention. Out across a field about fifty yards away are two men. They are walking toward me. Behind these men, about one hundred and fifty yards away from me, I can see buildings that look like part of a military base. These two men don't seem to be confused about anything. They are walking toward me and I think I'm in trouble.

They are standing in front of me now. I'm telling the two men that I thought the craft I was watching crashed because it moved so quickly. I can't see it now. It must have flown away. They are looking down at the indentations in the grass. I'm really confused about them, but these men don't seem to be. They seem to be interested in the indentations—they know what they are from.

Now they are interested in why I have left the group. I think they are asking me why I left the group I was supposed to be with. I feel as though I should rejoin the small group of people I was with. I'm walking back toward them. I'm walking up a small hill and I can see my brother. He's looking at me as if "I told you so."

At this point, I was getting a little frustrated with my remembering human beings and what looked to me like military bases or military base airfields. Once was bad enough, but these memories were becoming far too frequent for me. These two men were humans. They had dark brown hair and they were wearing dark blue suits. I remember their white shirts and dark ties. I saw the buildings off in the distance behind them and I knew it was a military base. Perhaps all military bases look the same to me. I've been on several and they all look fairly generic to me to a certain extent.

Was I on a military base, or a military base airfield, to be more precise? I saw the pilot of the craft and he looked human. He was wearing a green flight suit and had a light-colored helmet on with a black microphone in front of his mouth. It looked like a one-man craft. And, if it didn't move as fast as the wink of an eye, then it cloaked itself. It was also silent and I could not feel any wind being emitted from it even though I was almost directly underneath it as I was looking up. I believe I had ample opportunity to hear a sound and feel the wind, had this craft been emitting either. It did not. Why was I on a military base airfield with a small group of other people whom I believed to be abductees? Were we being shown a special craft for some unknown purpose? Was this my government participating in this deception? Are they also involved with me and other abductees? Because of my experiences, I was beginning to believe this was exactly the case.

The only other possibility I could come up with is that the aliens are employing an enormous amount of deception with me. They are making me see entire military bases and human pilots piloting unusual, and possibly alien craft. It just wasn't making sense to me. This was an experience that I was directly involved in, not something I was watching, as is often the case when the aliens give me a vision.

I wanted to deny yet again that my government could be involved this deeply. I found myself thinking, "I know as well as anyone how difficult it would be to hide this from the public if entire military bases were aware of the alien presence." My experience with the Marine Corps showed me that the military is a tough "family" where men "rule." They are a tight-knit group of people. Yes, they have a different mind-set, but I know it would be impossible to silence hundreds of military men and women.

No matter how much I tried to deny that a liaison could exist even with one military officer, at this point, I couldn't help but wonder if a few *had* been chosen for this particular mission. It would not be unthinkable to believe the military may be providing a "playground" for certain alien-human liaisons to occur upon as long as they could keep it from the general population of the base. I had to let out a long, frustrating sigh. As confusing and frustrating as it was, I decided the aliens must be intent upon brainwashing me into believing that agencies within my own government were abducting me. At that point in time it was easier for my mind to accept.

Another abduction occurred three nights later.[15] That abduction experience contained a lot of theatrics but I did remember some interesting information. I was on a mother ship and I felt that peculiar force I sometimes feel is caused by the gravity differences on the large ships. In addition, I remembered a six inch thick, gray metallic door. I would see a door like this again and I would remember how to unlock it.

The following experience was the catalyst for my suspecting that I was being visited by several different types of Greys.

12-12-91

> *I'm standing outside at night. I think I am next to a house or a hotel. There is a row of rooms with separate entrances. There are two people in the room next to mine. I'm opening a door. A Grey alien has floated out! God! I'm terrified! My heart is racing. The Grey floated past me very quickly! In the wink of an eye it has moved out into the bushes— I can sense it—I can sense it like a dog can sense another animal. This is incredible. I'm terrified! I've never been so scared before—The fear is primal—*
>
> *I'm banging on the door and I'm screaming for these two people to come out of their room. I'm banging with my fists—The Grey is watching me do this—I'm opening the door—*
>
> *They're kissing! I was outside screaming and they're just standing there kissing! I'm so angry. I'm yelling at them to come outside— "Look over there!" I can still see the alien. It has really old and worn-looking skin. It's about three feet tall. Its entire body looks emaciated. I don't see any clothes—just old gray skin.*
>
> *I'm in my room now—the one I was supposed to stay in—The one next door to the young couple. The couple is with me and they are opening the closets and doors. They are making sure that I know I am safe. They're checking for me! They are checking to make sure the room is safe, just as I do when I feel I have to protect my cats!*

This elicited a primal fear within me that I had not felt in a very long time. There was nothing about this alien that appeared even remotely similar to us. He was the most alien looking of all the aliens I had ever seen. The way he floated was so different from anything I had seen before. It was as if he moved so fast he could have been in two places at once. I still wonder if maybe he wasn't in two places at once. It was so extraordinary how quickly and smoothly he moved.

I'm not sure what the young couple signified, nor do I know if they were really humans, as they appeared to be, or if they were simply a screen for more aliens. They were intent, in the end, upon showing me that the room I was to stay in was safe. They opened every closet door and cabinet in the little room. I was left with a very negative impression about this particular alien. He was not like the others. He was different, *very* different. It was as if he was more powerful somehow. For the first time, I had a physical form to connect with the incredibly powerful force I often felt in my room just prior to an encounter. I wondered, could this be the type of alien Being who was responsible for the paralysis, and who, therefore, had the ability to subdue me? There was no doubt in my mind anymore. I now knew there were several types of Beings interacting with me and each had their own special talents.

December was bringing another wave of visitations. I began to think one of the aliens had posted a sign on the top of my house that read, "For a good time—land here!" Three nights later I was back at the "row of rooms."

12-15-91

> *I was just driving my car. I remember being in my car—Then I went to a building with a row of rooms. Somehow—I'm leaving this row of rooms and I have just been told I have to take this man with me. He's like a little person—He's three or four feet tall. I don't trust him at all. I'm making him sit in the back seat of my car—I'm giving him a towel to sit on because I don't want him to contaminate my car.*
>
> *Oh boy—He's reading my thoughts. He knows everything I was just thinking. I'm embarrassed. I feel ashamed. I'm thinking to myself— Just because he is a different species it doesn't mean I can discriminate against him. I really wish I hadn't given him the towel. I wish I could take back my thoughts. I'm trying to send him my thoughts as a way to apologize for my previous thoughts.*
>
> *I'm driving down a desert road with this little Being in the back seat. The road curves upward and turns sharply toward the left. This road— it looks as if it is out in the desert in the middle of nowhere. I have to stop and look at a map. Somehow I know that this road goes over the city. The next mode of travel will be through space. It will be hard for me to get back if I make a mistake. I need to look at a map. I'm getting out of my car—I'm bending down to pick up the map. It is a crystal map and it is heavy. It is a solid, oddly round crystal, and it has a crystal handle. It is all one flowing piece from the handle to the round area where the map is. I'm looking at many lines overlapping one another and branching out in many different directions. Some of the lines are white and the others are red. The lines are very thin. The round part of the map is about six inches thick and it is fairly heavy. I'm holding it up and I'm looking into it.*
>
> *I'm handing the map to a male. I think it is Erik, but I can't be sure. They might just want me to think it is him so I'll believe he is with me.*

The map doesn't make much sense to me—Someone has just told me we are heading in the right direction.

Now I'm looking at a small crystal skull with golden eyes. I'm picking it up. It was near a large white object—I think I'm traveling in a large white object—maybe this is our white motor home? This crystal skull is so beautiful. It is about an inch and a half thick and two inches high. I'm really lucky to have found it. I think Erik has found two others. I'm looking at them now. The two skulls appear to be different species. They are not Homo sapiens. The crystal skulls are all very beautiful and appear to be made out of the same crystal substance the map is made out of. I feel as though I am looking at a different species of human or alien—or something.

There was no fear associated with this encounter, but again, the only Being I saw was the little man whom I made sit in the back seat of my car. He was an odd-looking Being who appeared very human-looking, but there was obviously something about his appearance that made me feel he was an alien. He had a pudgy little face and very peculiar looking, messy, brown hair. He was telepathic and seemed to be along for the ride not only to probe my thoughts, but to make sure I reached my final destination. I suspect we were not in my car for very long because when I stopped the vehicle, there was a large white object behind me. After we stopped I traveled in the large white object.

The crystal map was beautiful yet functional. It was three dimensional and it had many lines that overlapped one another. I did not read these as roads, but rather as routes, more specifically, the number of times they have traveled a particular route. I do not know if this was within one day, or one year, or the total number of times they traveled these routes. I also doubt they use our measurements of time. In any event, this map displayed the route that we were to take which would end up taking us out into space. I felt I was driving my car before I stopped to look at the map, but I can't be sure. I cannot imagine that they would allow me to pilot one of their crafts, although I feel it would be fascinating to learn. Finally, I believe the purpose of the crystal skulls was to show me representations of different types of Beings.

My last encounter in December was very positive. I will always remember this night because the aliens made me feel very special. Perhaps it was their way of saying "Merry Christmas."

12-18-91

I'm downstairs in the family room facing the sliding glass doors. There are two short Greys to my right and one to my left. They have just entered the house—They are telling me they have just come from Germany—They know I have family there.

I'm being—introduced—I think. I'm meeting someone very special. He is a different looking alien. He is about seven feet tall and is extremely thin. His head is very large and long. His eyes are huge, round, and black. His neck, shoulders, arms and torso are so thin I can hardly believe it. He must have an extra joint in his arms and legs for mobility. His entire body is gray and I do not see any clothing covering his body. (I-19) Oh—I have just been told he has come from Germany to see me. I know it is expected that I shake hands with him—I'm shaking his hand and I am very happy to finally meet him. I feel as though I have been wanting to meet him for quite some time. He is only here because of me—I'm shaking his left hand for some reason. I think I was so nervous about meeting him that I forgot to shake his proper hand. He is removing my right hand with his right hand—I think I was squeezing his hand too hard. He is smiling a little—Just a hint of a smile, as though he thinks I'm being a little silly or maybe he is even a little embarrassed by my behavior.

I'm not afraid of him at all. As a matter of fact, I feel as though it is an honor to meet him. I don't think he does the same work these shorter Greys do. He appears to be a diplomat or something. I must have requested this meeting because I feel he is only here for my benefit. It's nice to finally meet him—

Wow—He's turning around and he's walking away. His entire body moves differently than ours and the other little Greys. It's as if he has to bend over slightly as a function of walking. Strange—Did he just walk through the sliding glass door? Is he going to walk through the lattice work around our porch?

This was such an extraordinary meeting for me. My feelings toward these aliens were totally positive and trusting. There was no fear associated with these Beings. It was almost like meeting a diplomat and his entourage. It was clear that he wasn't really interested in anything other than a greeting of sorts. It was as though we were being presented to one another. I felt as though I had known about him for quite some time, that we have been working together for a common cause, and that I had been waiting a long time to meet him. Unfortunately, I do not remember his name even though I feel confident I was told who he was. It is interesting that the three other smaller Greys appeared proud as we were being introduced to one another. They were beaming with pride.

I had reached a point in my experiences where I now had a representation of three different types of Greys. The encounter on

December 12 showed me a very frightening type of Grey. On the other hand, this most recent encounter showed me three Greys who were about four to four and a half feet tall, had smooth, light-gray skin, and who appeared to be wearing body suits. Their presence was neutral and they showed an enormous amount of respect toward the tall Being. These three Greys were identical in appearance and demeanor as the two Greys who came to my house the night of 8-7-89 to repair my heart. I am not implying they are the same Beings, only the same type of Beings. Finally, there is the tall Being whom I will call The Diplomat. He was at least seven feet tall and extremely thin with a huge head and enormously round eyes. I have to wonder if I'm not seeing some physical differences due to evolution or changes due to (non-evolutionary) genetic manipulation. It is quite possible there are different races of Greys that live together on the same planet or in the same solar system. Their physical differences are extremely apparent. When I take The Doctor, The Female, and The Blonde into consideration, I am left with the belief that many, many different races of Beings are visiting this planet.

    The most interesting aspect from this latest encounter with The Diplomat was I knew, at some level, we were both working together toward a common goal. When I met The Diplomat I felt the way I might feel when meeting the President of the United States. I believe this goal we are working toward is very positive, extremely important, and long-term. I base this conclusion on a strong "feeling" I have. I knew about The Diplomat before I met him. It is as if I have so much information in my unconscious mind that sometimes pieces of information, like a feeling or other emotion, slip up into consciousness. It is just enough of a feeling to let me know the situation is okay, safe, positive, or appropriate. Of course, with other Beings, it can be enough to let me know I should distrust them.

CHAPTER 11

1992: The Year of The Government

By New Year's Day 1992, I had been on the west coast for a mere three months. I was beginning to wonder if I hadn't just entered a twilight zone of sorts. A lot of people were wearing crystals (or at least had them hanging from their mirrors in their automobiles) and were talking about the date of January 11, 1992. Some type of "time portal" was to align itself on this date. It was explained to me by friends and acquaintances that we were all supposed to be focusing our thoughts so this could occur. Our planet was entering a new dimensional plane and it needed our help.

Although I remained quite skeptical about this dimensional shift our planet was going through, I didn't want to discount it totally. I began the "what if" type of thinking. After all, there is so much we do not know about our planet and its place in the universe. I do have to admit, however, as much as I tried, I could not accept that this was actually occurring.

Nineteen ninety-two was the year everyone on the planet was going to finally find out about UFOs and the aliens. Many contactees, abductees, and even some investigators and researchers were predicting this year to be *the* year. In my opinion, as far as the grandiose visions are concerned, 1992 turned out to be *The Year That Never Was.*

Perhaps I have been too eager to say, "I told you so." What about the amazing changes that have occurred on our planet just since the late eighties? Each time I watched the Berlin wall being torn down on a news broadcast I felt a swell of emotions building up inside of me. Because of that wall, I never knew members of my own family. The collapse of the Soviet Union and the changes that followed were another unbelievable and unexpected occurrence. Sadly, we are also seeing the normal barrage of wars and environmental travesties that man is so capable of inflicting. What, except time, can show us how these occurrences have acted as catalysts for future events?

I believe it is important to view the messages that abductees and experiencers receive from the aliens very carefully. If we are waiting for the aliens to solve all of our problems we may be waiting for a very long time. If we are waiting for them to fill the skies with their presence so everyone on the planet will be able to see them, again, we may not get what we expect. These are just two scenarios that many people have been shown, or have been told, or "feel" will happen. In my opinion, it lends itself to a peculiar type of mental dependency on the aliens. Maybe this is one of the things they need from us. Perhaps the aliens need us to be looking toward them and depending upon them for the answers. Maybe this is a peculiar form of mental control. After all, how many of us haven't been consumed at one time or another with the thought that one glorious day hundreds of UFOs will appear in the sky and the entire world will be changed?

It is extremely important to consider the probability of the misinterpretation of messages and visions from the aliens. For example, research connecting the UFO phenomenon with past religious events is showing that it *may* be possible that extraterrestrial Beings seeded our planet. There is also the possibility that humanity has so distorted its own history, as well as that of the "Heavenly Beings," that we may never really know how we came to exist on this planet.

These were some of the thoughts I found myself contemplating when I came out to Oregon. I was somewhat disillusioned when I realized how many other abductees and "believers" were feeling that something incredible and wondrous was going to happen in 1992. That *this* would be the year. After the Los Angeles riots I was reminded of just how easily this particular UFO scenario could turn into a disaster.

After all is said and done, a part of me still wants to believe a form of this "belief of futuristic worldwide UFO sightings" will occur. It will occur because people will continue to talk about their experiences. The news will spread, not from viewing hundreds of UFOs in the sky, but from continued contacts and by having those contacts shared with the world through the media. There is also the possibility that none of this would have become public knowledge unless the alien Beings wanted it that way in the first place.

January 11, 1992, did turn out to be a special date even though the portals of time never opened, at least in a way that I am aware of. Three members of my support group, my husband, who was still living three-thousand miles away, and myself, all had visitations that night. If that were not enough, included in my encounter were two friends who were also MUFON investigators. They were Vicki Lyons and Patti Weatherford, and they were also three-thousand miles away at the time. Neither of my friends remembered this event having occurred and it is possible that their images were used as a screen to cover the Beings' true appearance.

1-11-92

> *I'm floating up a steep hill. It is dark and Vicki Lyons and Patti Weatherford are with me. I'm at the top of the hill now and I'm looking down at the ground—there is a flat area here with trees off in the distance. I see some grass—and something white. The ground, where there is no grass, is white. It is hard and white.*

I'm going inside something. I feel as though it is a landed craft, but I can't really see it. Patti and Vicki are making sure I reach my destination. I think Erik is waiting for me inside the craft. We make love and then I leave. I'm back outside in the dark and Patti and Vicki are still with me. They know Erik was inside this craft and that we just made love—it's okay though, it's just the way it is. We're not embarrassed or anything. We're all here for a purpose.

I'm going down this very steep hill I just came up a little while ago. I'm holding onto something that looks like silver handle bars. I'm very scared because this hill is so steep. Somehow I think I must be on a green bicycle—I'm trying to press down on the brakes to slow myself down, but I don't think there are any brakes on this thing. I'm steering toward the right. I'm so scared—Oh, finally—this is my destination.

It is a large glass building—I'm inside now and I'm here to see my doctor, but I don't want to. Patti and Vicki are waiting outside again. I guess they are my escorts or something. Oh, now the Beings are deciding what the doctor will look like. I'm looking at an illuminated screen with many small pictures on it. They are pictures of doctors—Each picture is lighting up one at a time so I can see who it is—Oh! Not him! I hate him! Yuk! They just showed me a doctor I absolutely hate—Okay—it blinked off—Another picture has illuminated—I like this doctor. He looks like my real doctor. He's very attractive—

I've just turned to my left and I'm looking at my doctor. He's walking toward me—He's walking down a hallway toward me and he's smiling very strangely. Something isn't quite right about him. I'm staring at him—He's supposed to be my doctor in Pensacola, but he isn't. His hair looks fake and his skin looks as if he has make-up on his face. His face is real shiny—

I'm feeling sick inside—I've just realized something—This is the same doctor that worked on me when I found the pen that had "Clark Air Force Base" inscribed on it. He's the same tan-skinned doctor. I don't like this—They tried to deceive me.

During my experience I felt as though I was very close to Pensacola. The hard white ground was one of the reasons for this. When I got to the top of the hill I felt as though I was very near the ocean and the white sands of the Gulf of Mexico. When I looked at the trees, they were the scrub type oaks you find in that area near the beaches. It is possible that Patti and Vicki were used to make sure I got to my destination as I have sometimes been abducted to help with other abductees, for example, the Hispanic man and my nephew.

As I stated earlier, Vicki Lyons and Patti Weatherford had no memory about this incident, which doesn't prove it didn't happen. I think most abductees remember very little on a conscious level. Of course, this certainly doesn't prove the four of us were together by any means. It is quite possible the aliens used their familiar camouflage technique to make me think I was among friends. Clearly, when I was looking at the screen with all of the doctors, the aliens wanted me to think I was seeing my real doctor. I liked him and felt more comfortable talking to him than any other doctor I had met before or since. As soon as I had the thought that my real doctor would be okay to see if I *had* to see a doctor right then, low and behold, he comes walking down the hallway. This technique, however, is not extremely effective on me. Even the first time I consciously recalled seeing this tan-skinned doctor he did not appear totally human. I described him in detail during the encounter when I thought I was on Clark Air Base. I have seen him three times that I remember and each time he looks the same.

Patti and Vicki still do not remember anything about this night, but it is interesting that Patti has spoken about one of her own experiences on television. And, Vicki may have been visited one night during her investigation of me. In the Fall of 1988, Vicki "dreamed" she ran outside in her nightgown and looked up at the night sky. She did not see anything. She then ran through her house to the back yard and found herself surrounded by five aliens who told her to stop the search for the implant. The aliens told Vicki that in time I would answer all of her questions and would share more information than she ever imagined. Vicki did not remember going back into her house, but the following morning her husband found the back door open and the porch light on. Perhaps the aliens already knew in 1988, that in the future I would write a book.

The same night (1-11-92) my husband, who was three thousand-miles away, had the following memory.

> *I found myself in an old house. I felt an evil presence and saw white flashes of light. I remembered having to save all of our cats and while this was happening, I saw a Grey. I saw its hands and described them as having a very thin thumb with three very skinny digits. The hands were large but thin. They did not have fingernails, but did have some thin webbing between the fingers. I also saw their feet, but I'm unable to describe them. At this point, I felt as though I was outside in a cobblestone courtyard and the courtyard I was standing on was moving. The Grey told me it was not moving. I then told the Grey why I thought they were here and when the Grey told me they were here to help mankind, I told him, "You're full of shit." The Grey then took me by the hand and led me somewhere.*

Four nights later, they were back.

1-15-92

I'm scared to death! There is a huge polar bear in the house and I have to save my cats from it. I have to protect them—

I'm waking up—I'm trying to look around the room, but I can hardly move—I can't even lift my head up. I'm trying to look at something— I'm trying to see—

I'm with my little nephew again. We are in my bathroom with an alien Being. I'm holding a small white instrument—I'm pulling it out of my nephew's ear. It looks similar to a Q-tip, but it is flatter and there is no cotton on the end of it. It looks as though it is made from plastic and it is about three inches long, an eighth of an inch wide, and a sixteenth of an inch thick. I've pulled this out of his ear and I'm looking at it. I'm checking it for something—It has a white substance on it and some earwax. Mostly this white substance—I think I'm handing it to someone. I think there is a Being standing next to us. I hand the ear device to him.

The following morning I received phone calls from three people in my support group and my husband. Although they all told me they were abducted the same night I was, our experiences were not similar.

Although this is just a fragment of a memory from that night, it was an extremely frightening encounter. I was beginning to see a pattern in their method of controlling me. The use of the perceived threat against my cats, that is, the polar bear, instills an enormous amount of fear in me. I would do anything to protect them. The visual image and belief that a polar bear is in the house and threatening my cats is very effective on me. In my mind, the polar bear is the most deadly land animal on the planet. It is a perfect way to control me through fear. I believe this type of deception will be my last obstacle to overcome involving the way certain aliens control me. Eventually, I hope to make them face me on more even terms. On the other hand, it may be possible that some of the aliens have to implant these beliefs and images into my mind so they can protect themselves from *me*.

The end of January brought wonderful news. Erik was on his way to Portland. He arrived on January 20. It was great to be together again! We went to bed at about 9:30 p.m. and the last thing on our minds was another alien visitation.

1-21-92

I'm sitting with three Beings—two of them are facing me and another is to my right. There is a curved glass window behind the two Beings sitting across from me. Underneath this window is a curved control panel of some type. These Beings are wearing light colored body suits—They are almost white. The Beings are telling me something very important—A message to prepare for something—I have to get ready for something—It's going to happen soon—This is such an intense feeling. This is serious—I'm mentally preparing myself for something that is going to happen—I'm sure of it. This is extremely important.

It's eleven o'clock and my dog is really upset. She is barking and barking—I'm getting up to go see—I can barely walk. I'm having trouble standing up—Erik is up now and I say to him, "I was just with them!" He replies, "I was just with them too. We were in the desert and I was teaching them how to build a fence."

We went downstairs to console our dog and to see what she was barking at, but there was no one around. Erik and I both remembered having been with the aliens and we were sure she had sensed them. The cats were all okay. It was at this point I remembered that I forgot to turn the dishwasher on before we went to bed. I turned it on before we went back to bed and Erik related to me what he just remembered about his encounter. He was teaching the aliens to build a wooden fence:

Erik would stand up a post and the aliens would walk over and draw a perfect circle around the post. The ground was very hard, so he didn't dig a hole. He said he didn't want to dig the hole and the aliens would have to do the work themselves. He showed them how to correctly measure the location for each post. Each time it was time to make a new measurement, he would come off the last measurement and the aliens would draw a new, perfect circle in the dirt around the post. They didn't have a tape measure, so they marked the distance between the location the two posts were to be positioned by making a lot of little circles side by side. They took about twenty-four measurements and then Erik told them that should be enough. Erik reminded them they had to dig the holes themselves because he did not intend to build another fence. He looked around but didn't see any buildings, just a large, flat, open area. There weren't any trees or grass but he did say he saw a few shrub-like plants.

I seriously doubt that Beings who can construct the types of crafts I have seen would need anyone to instruct them on how to build a fence, but who knows? Maybe they were trying to occupy him while I was inside the craft with the three Beings in the white body suits. Then again, maybe they were indeed interested in a wooden fence and needed someone large enough and strong enough to hold up the heavy fence posts. Even though Erik never said he remembered seeing a craft, or me for that matter, something tells me we were together, or very close by one another during our "outing" that night.

The following encounter occurred on the type of craft I compare to a three-story mall and sometimes call a mother ship. I thought the aliens overreacted a bit to my looking out of this particular window. Perhaps someone who reads this will help me to understand why.

1-27-92

I'm on a large craft with hospital-like rooms. I'm in a room with a man—he has dark hair. We must have been talking earlier because I know he has a wife and a child. He is human, just like me. He's leaving the room—I'm putting something on a shelf—A female figure is in the doorway and I say to her, "I'm not going to school today because it will be a beautiful sunny day." Oh, she's gone—

I'm walking out in the hallway—it is very wide and all white. It seems familiar to me. I feel very comfortable here and it is very warm inside this craft. It feels as though the sun is shining down on me while I'm still inside. It's like being out in the sunshine and it feels very good. I'm thinking to myself as I'm walking, "Today will be beautiful and sunny and tomorrow will be freezing rain." I'm turning to my left, still walking down this huge hallway—

I had planned to go out in the sun today, but now I know it will be dangerous for my skin—I can't do that now. I've come to a very large window—Wow—I'm in England! I'm looking out across miles of rolling hills. A typical English landscape. I know I'm in England. I've been here before and the geography is unmistakable. The sun is trying to shine, but there are too many clouds—it's misty outside too.

There are dogs outside on the grass. I'm watching them work. They are very close to the craft I'm in—This is strange—They are gray and are built like rottweilers, but they have gray wool coats on—like sheep. Are these sheep or dogs? EVIL—They see me! I really think these things are aliens! These things are aliens trying to camouflage their true appearance! They are outside and they are doing something they don't want me to see. They are doing something to the ground—One of these "dogs" is charging toward me—It hits the window and it's barking and growling ferociously at me! It shook the window! If it really wanted me, I'm sure it could have broken the window to get me! Another one is charging toward me! It's inside! It came through the window! It's in the craft looking at me! I'm scared to death! I'm not sure how this happened, but it's inside now. It looks as if it will attack me. I'm backing into a small room—slowly—to get away from it.

Suddenly, I run in and slam the door! I'm fighting with the lock—I'm trying to lock the door—Finally, it is locked. This door has a really strange lock on it—I'm looking around this small room.

I'm in this little room—I'm safe now—I wonder why the strange "dog" didn't get me? It certainly had the opportunity to. They really got upset when I looked out the window—They must have been doing something I wasn't supposed to see.

I was sharing a room with what I thought was another abductee and we had been talking about our families. The feeling of the sun out in the hallway was wonderful and warm but not in the slightest bit uncomfortable. It was just right for my body temperature. It had the feeling of warmth without being hot and was very soothing to my skin. When I thought I detected a female standing by the door, I told her I wasn't going to school today. At the time, I believed I was there for a type of school or was there because I was supposed to be learning.

The scene taking place outside the large window is anyone's guess. My first thought was: I wonder if they were making a crop circle? One has to keep a sense of humor in all of this. Another thought, one that is much more morbid, was that they might have been stealing someone's sheep and the mutilations were about to take place. Perhaps one or two of the aliens detected me and made themselves look similar to the sheep. There were several "animals" outside near the craft. I would say I saw approximately eight or ten of them. The one closest to the craft was the one that came through the window. I suppose if they can float people through walls and closed windows they can float themselves at me in an emergency situation. One thing was very clear, I was not supposed to see what they were doing, and it was important enough to them that they would scare the hell out of me in order to get me away from the window. It worked beautifully and I was duped again. On some level I knew the "rottweiler/sheep" were really aliens, but knowing this still wasn't enough to stop myself from retreating. Incidentally, it was not until I thought about this "alien/sheep/dog" coming through the window as if it really wanted to get me that it did, in fact, execute my own thoughts. Did I, by thinking of my biggest fear at that moment, give it the means by which to subdue me?

The following experience forced me to take another hard look at the government's involvement in this phenomenon and I did not like what I saw. This would be the year I finally accepted the fact that at least one agency within our government, as well as other "allied" governments, were probably more involved in the abduction phenomenon than I was.

2-10-92

I'm walking across a divided four lane road. The divider is composed of grass and trees. I'm walking toward a structure—a building. I feel as though I am in eastern Canada. I know where I am going because I've been here before. I have a definite purpose in mind. Erik is with me and we are walking rapidly toward this structure. I have strong intentions to do something. I'm on a mission and I'm not very happy about it.

I'm inside now and I feel as though I am in a deep, underground structure. I've been here before and this place is very familiar to me. It is dark down here and the only light is a dim, bluish light. Although it is dim, it is still bright enough to make out the details of this place. The walls are either concrete or stone—I'm looking at the walls now and they are definitely made out of concrete.

"I want information—I want answers!" I'm talking to some people. I am very determined. There are people here. They're humans—These people down here—I know they are working for a secret part of our government and I don't like what they are doing. I'm telling someone, "I want to see—I demand to see—" I can't recall what it is that I'm demanding to see—something or someone. I want to know something. It is extremely important. I'm looking around and I am very agitated. I'm looking at the concrete walls and a row of desks. There are wooden desks down here and some of them have paperwork on them. They are all lined up with the left side of the desks next to the concrete wall. There are about eight of them. The dim blue light is casting slight shadows that are barely visible.

I'm looking at a cart with wheels on it. Someone has rolled it into this room—It has a projector on it. I'm looking around this place—All of these people down here are with our government. Somehow I know this place—I've been here before. These people are a part of our government, but at the same time they are above the government. They don't even have to answer to the President! This infuriates me. I'm not even sure the President knows about these people. I'm very angry now—I'm remembering—I remember them from before. I want information—I want answers—I'm remembering something—

I'm looking at the projector and I realize that I'm not going to get any answers. I'm going to have to watch that damn film again and undergo indoctrination procedures again! I've had to do this before. When you don't cooperate you have to be reprogrammed again. I'm being escorted into another room. I'm extremely angry.

Now I'm sitting down with a small group of people. I think someone is trying to brainwash me into believing I'm in my living room. I'm NOT. There are about eight to ten of us and we are all here for the same reason. We are all abductees. We have to watch the film. They are all looking at me—they seem a little nervous and somewhat scared. I'm talking to one of these government people. I'm so angry it is difficult for me to control my temper. I'm shouting at a woman and two men, "Don't you know how easy it would be for someone to kill you? Anyone could kill you! As long as you have to eat you can be killed! Someone could poison your food—it would be so easy!" I know their food comes from "the outside" and I know I'm right. I'm absolutely furious with these people.

Erik is looking at me with a worried expression on his face. All of the other abductees are looking at me now and I feel as though I've really blown it this time. The other abductees are looking at me as though I'm endangering their lives by saying these things to these government jerks. Everyone just seems to want me to shut-up. I realize I've messed up this time. If anything does happen to these government people, I will most likely be blamed for being so vocal. I'm sitting down now. The government woman and the two men are looking at me as though I'm a lost cause and a trouble maker. They have a stern, hard expression on their faces. I've really blown it. I'm going to watch the film now with everyone else. Damn these people—I'm not going to get any answers.

After this experience I felt lucky to be back in my house and alive. More than anything, I felt lucky to be alive. I began the day by looking back in my journal for encounters I had which involved other humans and had hints of government or military aspects to them. I tried to explain away the burled wood pen I found that had "Clark Air Force Base" inscribed on it. I tried to deny my memory of the older looking doctor. The doctor I rode on the elevator with. The same man I remembered seeing in his military uniform as he sat with the other men around the large oval conference table, while I tried to tell them about the alien I had just seen. I tried to explain away the two men in dark blue suits that walked toward me after I strayed from the small group of people who witnessed the strange, orb-shaped craft hover and then disappear. There is no way in the world that could have really been a military base airfield in the background, could it? What about the base with the cobra helicopter and the tiny spotted, alien Beings?

What in the world were aliens and government personnel doing showing up together in my memories? Aliens and the government working together? Sure, I heard about those crazy stories and I remembered how preposterous they sounded to me. I thought about all of the times I would laughingly lump them all together, as so many other people do, into the "crazy/paranoid" category. "I, for one, am not going to believe that our government is working with aliens and they have formed some secret pact, and I will certainly not believe that my government is abducting its own citizens!" A direct quote from me to more than a few people on more than a few occasions.

"Seeing is believing" is the famous phrase that is used so often in ufology. I do not expect that many people will give my memories any more credence than I gave to others reporting the same crazy stories. I have learned the hard way that belief systems are very rigid, and only by seeing and experiencing these types of things for yourself, can you believe some of this information. I thought I was reaching a point where I could say, "Okay, I can, somewhat reluctantly, forgive an alien race for violating my rights." Now I had to deal with the possibility that my own government may be involved too. My memories were changing the way I viewed everything I ever believed in.

An unusual and very unwanted military/government twist to the abduction phenomenon is being reported by abductees. These people, just like the people reporting mainstream abduction accounts, are not paranoid or delusional. They too are simply reporting what they remember. I still do not want to believe their accounts, or even my own memories, but to quote Budd Hopkins, "I no longer have the luxury of disbelief." I know what I have experienced. I know what I have seen with my own eyes. If I am mistaken, then I ask again: Why do some of these alien Beings want me to believe that our government is deeply involved in the abduction phenomenon?

From this experience, there is no doubt in my mind that these were human beings. I did not see military uniforms in this experience, but I had been to this place before. I knew these individuals were working (literally) underground and with a secret agency. Is it possible that they are a coalition of secret agencies acting as representatives from different governments? Why are these people interested in me? Because the aliens are interested in me? I *must* ask these questions. If the only way I can draw attention to some of the more unusual anomalies in the abduction phenomenon is by risking public ridicule, then I must risk it.

Just four nights after the encounter with what felt like an "underground government," I had another unusual abduction experience.

2-14-92

> *I'm in a room in a house. The room isn't mine. The house isn't mine and the phone in the house isn't mine. I'm very frustrated because I keep receiving phone calls and they are being intercepted by others. I have no control over my communications. I even think I may be wearing someone else's clothes. This house is at least two stories, with stairs and wooden floors. There is furniture in the house. The room I'm in has a double bed and a dresser. Out in the hallway I can see other*

bedrooms and people walking around. There is a phone in here but I'm not allowed to answer it.

I'm going outside—I'm standing with Erik and we are outside together looking down a road with Federal style (architecturally constructed) homes on it. They are all abandoned and the entire road looks rather eerie. Erik is telling me that we can rent one of these and live here. I have the creeps about this. I'm looking at a long and winding road of car lights coming through part of the street. I don't want to look at them—Something tells me they are alien crafts and I don't want to look at them—I'm afraid. I don't think I'm supposed to remember them—

Erik told me he remembered the two of us lying on tables on our stomachs with some type of device inserted into our rectums. To make matters worse, both of our rectums were extremely sore immediately after this encounter. It was an uncomfortable feeling, physically as well as psychologically. The following journal entry is Erik's memory of the same night.

I was in a medical facility and I believe I was in Pensacola, Florida. I was lying on my stomach and probes were inserted into my rectum. There was a doctor to my left—I felt no pain, but I did feel probing and instrument insertion. The doctor said they were doing genetic mapping for fertilization studies. I thought this was unusual because I have had a vasectomy. I did not tell the doctor this, however. The exam lasted quite awhile, about an hour or more. During this time my brother and his wife came into the room. My brother ignored me and I tried to cover my face, but his wife recognized me. She told my brother to come over and talk to me, but he kept walking away and eventually stopped in the doorway and turned back. I told his wife not to worry. I had tried to work things out with him and now it was over. They left the room.

While I was on the table I had a vision of an ocean liner off the coast of California. I was then told California was going to fall into the ocean. "They" said I would be safe on the ocean liner. I told them "no way" because I knew the tsunami would hit the ocean liner. I then told them I would be okay in Oregon and that I had to get back there.

Also, during my exam I remember some people freaking out over radiation because they felt they had been exposed by someone who was carrying a radioactive container. They were afraid they would get cancer.

Clearly, we were both remembering something about what had occurred that night. Erik had retained more detailed memories than I had. The two most vivid things about my memory were seeing the inside of this house and feeling that my very thoughts were being intercepted by others. That would lead me to deduce that telepathy had occurred. Also, at some level I was aware that I was seeing alien crafts and that I wasn't supposed to remember seeing them. It is possible the Federal style homes were an illusion, unless the house I was in was really what it appeared to be. I felt I was in something similar to a government safe house.

Erik's memory indicates the most probable scenario of what occurred to us that night: a rectal probe and some other type of internal examination. His "memory" of his brother and sister-in-law was probably done for distraction purposes or emotional response purposes.

It is common knowledge that scientists believe "the big one" has yet to hit California. The psyche of many people living in the possible quake areas has to be somewhat differently focused than those people who do not live in an earthquake zone. This could have been a vision or a warning of what is yet to come, or it could have been demonstrated to Erik for purely psychological or behavioral reasons. I believe many of these visions we are given, whether they are true or not, are given for the purpose of studying how we will handle such information. From my experiences, I tend to view these types of visions as stimuli for emotional and behavioral responses. They may be asking themselves in their study of us: Will they act on the information we give them? How does it affect them psychologically? Emotionally? Physically? Can we effect the decisions they will make? Can we effect their future? We also have to keep in mind that the aliens could simply be taking information from our minds to use to their advantage. In addition, it could also be a form of disinformation.

The following night I was visited again. This time by a Being I had never remembered seeing before. Fortunately for me, this appeared to be a positive alien, if I can still determine who and what is positive and negative anymore.

2-15-92

I think I'm outside near a mall or a huge structure of some kind. I'm on my way to an apartment that isn't my real home, but I am familiar with it. I've used it before. It's like a home away from home. I'm being followed, very closely, by a black-skinned praying mantis-type Being. It is a female because I sense her and I can see her genitals—She has extremely dark skin and her genitals are white. She is very different looking. When she walks she has to bend over somewhat. And then her back moves in a strange coordinated fashion with her tall, thin, and lanky body. She has very long, thin legs, and she walks in a forward rocking motion. (I-14) *It is similar to the way The Diplomat walked when he went through the sliding glass door in our family room.*

Although I am not really scared, I am a little uneasy about her following me so closely. I am approaching the white apartment—I'm not certain this is really an apartment, but it is white and I have to walk up some rather steep, thin steps to get to the door. As I'm walking up these steps, I can see in my mind's eye that the Being is now a black cat. I really like cats and I sense she wants to stay with me. I think I will let her in and take care of her—I really love animals—

Oh, she isn't really a cat after all—I'm looking at her now and she wants me to think she is a cat. In reality, she is still the praying mantis-type Being. I think she wants inside. I think I will let her in because I'm feeling such positive feelings from her.

I do not remember if I let her in the white apartment. My memory ended there. The apartment was situated approximately two hundred yards away from the large structure I thought was a mall, and there was nothing else around it except darkness.

The following account is a spontaneous memory. It surfaced three nights after the experience with the praying mantis Being on February 18, 1992. I believe it occurred sometime between 1982 and 1984. I was with my ex-husband, Mark.

Okay, I'm sure I'm on a military base because I know this place! I'm with Mark. We leave the base and when we get to a busy intersection, we have sex. This is so strange. This is unbelievable.

Several hours have gone by and we are now inside a huge, cigar-shaped silver bus. I'm looking out of a window and I can see part of the silver bus up ahead of me. It's huge—I don't think this is really a bus now—It is a large, silver, cigar-shaped craft. How did I get here?

Now we are back on the base. I think we are at New River Air Station. I'm outside and it's at night. I don't have any clothes on except for a light blue hospital wrap. I don't have any shoes on either. The blue wrap I'm wearing—it opens and closes in the front and it's made out of a real light weight material. Something has made me very frustrated. I'm walking across some rocks in my bare feet.

I'm walking toward a hangar and I think I see Lt. "M." It can't be him. I don't want to think he is involved in this. Someone asks us where we've been. We have been gone for a long time. Somehow I know we have been gone for three days, but the time here on Earth was only three hours. This is nuts. I can't believe these feelings I have. We couldn't have been gone for three days. I'm looking down at the rocks on the ground. I must still be outside, but there is some kind of tent or hangar—I'm standing on small volcanic rocks. They have little holes in them and are a light color and are irregular-shaped. This is strange.

Someone has just asked us where we've been and Mark is freaking out. He's unbelievably angry. One of the other officers is freaking out too. They are both tremendously upset. The other officer is really upset and says, "I'm the one who issued the approval!" He is looking at a light blue piece of paper. It is an 8 1/2 by 11 sheet of thin blue paper that has been folded four times. I'm looking at it—It has a row of names on the left and some type of grid on the right half of the paper next to all of the names. Inside the little boxes formed by the grid are small symbols. I can only make out some small circles next to some of the names. I reach out and try to take the paper out of the officer's hands, but he jerks it away from me. He hurriedly walks away from me. I know our names were on that piece of paper—I'm watching the officer walk away from me—I'm wondering why he looks as though he can't wait to get away from me.

"My God, I can't believe this." Those were my exact words as I began to type this into my computer with very shaky hands. Mark and I were only married for about three years. All I could think about was the day he walked into the house after work and I found myself looking at a complete stranger. He then began to tell me about these strange feelings he had. He told me if one of us didn't leave, he felt he would surely kill me. He said he was consumed with thoughts of killing me. I have to wonder if, on some level, he wasn't remembering *something* unusual and he was associating it with me.

My hairstyle in this memory was also appropriate for this time frame. As to whether or not we were actually on the base, I do not know anything other than what my memories tell me. It is possible that these other two officers had been abducted also. Or, at the very least, had been manipulated to make it look like, on paper at least, that some type of permission had been granted for Mark to be away for about three hours. It was at night and if he had been on duty that night, it would have been convenient for him to have been away, although totally inappropriate. This might explain his level of anger and our being with the other officers on the base that night. Obviously, if either of the other two officers had remembered anything other than a bad dream about this night, nothing was ever stated to me. Everyone's behavior was indicative of surprise, confusion, and a need to be discreet. I cannot think of any other reason to explain why we would have been in that particular area on the base that night.

My knowing that we had been away for three days as opposed to the actual three hours was extremely vivid, and I have spoken with other abductees who believe that time is manipulated during some of their encounters.

2-24-92

> *I'm lying in bed and I'm holding my finger up in front of my face—It has three small prick marks in it. It really stings. There is a tiny bit of blood under the skin. I'm waking Erik up, "The aliens are here! Look what they did to my finger!" He is taking my hand and is looking at my finger. We can both see a little blood just under the skin—*
>
> *Some time has elapsed—Someone is giving me something to eat, but I don't want it. I really don't want to eat this—I don't want it—Oh, I have to—I eat it.*
>
> *I'm looking down at the ground. I don't feel too well. I think I'm going to be sick again. They have made me eat this before and it always makes me sick.*
>
> *I vomit whatever it was that I just ate—I'm looking down at where I got sick and it looks like sesame seeds. I don't know why I have to eat this stuff because it always makes me sick. I hate this.*
>
> *I'm traveling high above the trees. Evergreens—I must be back in the Pacific Northwest. I must be flying in the air because I'm looking down at the trees.*

The following day my index finger, the same finger I remembered having been pricked the night before, was itching and stinging very intensely. I kept looking at it to see if I could detect anything under the skin that would make it itch so badly, but I could not find anything. All I could do to relieve the itch was to massage it throughout the day. It finally stopped itching and stinging two days after the encounter. I have no idea what it was I was forced to eat. I only know that I had eaten it before and it always seemed to make me throw-up.

The next night I recorded that I felt a strange, but familiar feeling before going to bed. Every time I walked around a corner I expected to see the aliens in our house. Even after going to bed, I got up twice and looked around the house because I had a very strong feeling that someone was in our house. If I only knew what was about to take place, I would have stayed awake all night and waited by the door with my camera and a gun.

2-25-92

I'm walking down a highway near our home. I'm in the southbound, right lane. To my right is a man that I believe, for some reason, to be Daniel Ronnigan. I'm looking at him. This man is tall with medium brown hair. He is wearing a dark blue suit coat and dark gray trousers. We are walking together in the southbound lane. In the northbound lane I can see many white lights. It looks like "five o'clock" traffic— Bright headlights. This is really strange. I can't believe all of these lights I'm seeing. I'm turning around to see if there are any cars heading toward us from behind us. There is someone following us. I can't really see it, but I know it's there. It is following us as we are walking. It doesn't have any lights on and it is quiet, but I am sure it is following us. I'm looking back at the northbound lane. Something isn't right about this.

This man is talking to me now. He is telling me he just got his broker's license. He is telling me he wants me to come to work for him since I just took my real estate exam. This is strange—Daniel has been a broker for several years now—I'm looking up at this man—This is not Daniel Ronnigan. I'm studying this man's face. He's turning away from me as though he doesn't want me to see his face. Now he's taking a pair of sunglasses out of his shirt pocket and he is putting them on. I'm wondering why he needs sunglasses in the middle of the night. I sarcastically ask him, "Are those CIA issue?" Oh, he didn't like that. He is extremely uncomfortable now. He seems a little agitated with me for saying that. I think I've said something wrong—Yes, I have. I wasn't supposed to remember this. Somehow I know this man is really with the CIA and I was just hypnotized by them. They want me to think he is Daniel Ronnigan, someone I know. I know it's not Daniel. This is so strange. I wasn't supposed to remember him.

The following day, and for the first time in my life, I was expecting a visit from someone in a government agency. Then it suddenly occurred to me that maybe I had already been visited by them. What in the world was going on? Did they want me to work for a specific broker? Why? To keep tabs on me? Crazy!

The following afternoon when I was checking my messages I was astonished. I had received a message from a man who said his name was "Dave." In his message, he stuttered ever so slightly with my name. He then explained that he was a broker with a nationally known real estate company and he wanted me to come to work for him!

Strangely, I found myself compelled to call him back and take him up on the offer. I wrote his number down and then stared at my phone. I thought, "Am I supposed to work for the government?" Then I began to think. I was puzzled about this message and how this person could have retrieved my phone number. How did "Dave" get my phone number? The phone number I gave to the real estate school, which they are not supposed to give out, was an unpublished, unlisted number. Okay, you say, so what? Well, thanks to the large numbers of people moving to Portland, several thousand phone numbers had to be changed shortly after I enrolled in real estate school. Again, I got another unpublished, unlisted phone number, which I did not give to anyone in the real estate business. At that time, there were seven acquaintances who had my phone number. They were all involved in the UFO phenomenon. They were either abductees or MUFON investigators. One was a friend of an investigator. None of these people knew me by my real name and I did not tell the abductees in my support group anything about my personal life other than abduction-related information, and that I was studying for my real estate exam. When I became involved with the local UFO community I used a pseudonym for a few months until I got to know the people better. Perhaps I was being excessively cautious, but since I was the new kid on the block, I thought it would be prudent for my own protection.

A few weeks after this message from "Dave" I had access to a real estate cross directory. Our house and, therefore, our names weren't even included in the directory because the house had just been built. Therefore, there was no name or phone number listed either. The phone number wouldn't have been listed even if our names were listed because it is an unpublished, unlisted number.

Once again, either the aliens wanted me to think my own government was abducting me or someone in a government agency really was. There is the possibility that one of the few people I knew had given our number to "Dave." However, none of my friends admitted this when I asked them. To this day, I have no reason to suspect any of these people were lying to me, then or now. Therefore, I feel the only people capable of getting our phone number (and my real name) at that time would have been the phone company or a government agency.

I did attempt to work for a large real estate firm here in Portland. However, after my first caravan, I realized my heart just wasn't in it. I also decided not to follow through with the real estate business because the possible ramifications of this memory disturbed me greatly. Real estate agents are often on their own as independent contractors and often work in isolated circumstances. I did not want to become an easy target for harassment. I never called "Dave" at the company he said he worked for because I felt that is what they expected me to do. The fact that this phone call from "Dave" followed only hours after this abduction experience bothered me, to say the least.

I do not wish to believe I could be important enough for a government agency (or even one person from the government for that matter) to be interested in. After all, it would appear that thousands, perhaps even millions, of people are remembering abduction experiences. However, I cannot help but wonder if this wasn't part of a well thought out and well executed plan by people who have a lot of time and patience, and plenty of other abductees to worry about or possibly to even use. What if something had gone wrong and I accidentally remembered something I shouldn't have? I found myself wanting to believe, once again, that the *aliens* used some elaborate means to convince me I was taken by our government instead of them. Or, at the very least, that our government is working with them.

If the aliens wanted me to think I was seeing a man who worked with our government, why would this man become agitated at my realization of this? That is not how their deception works and I know this. What would have been more in line with their past behavior would have been for the man to acknowledge that he was with a government agency. Do the aliens have such subtle behavioral nuances worked out to such perfection?

I knew this man wasn't really Daniel because he made an error in his wording. He said, "I have just received my broker's license and I want you to come to work for me." It was then I realized he was not who he wanted me to believe he was and I began studying his face. When I saw his face, I knew for certain it was not Daniel. This made the man uncomfortable and he reached into his shirt pocket to retrieve a pair of dark sunglasses. Sunglasses? In the middle of the night? It would be just like me to press the issue by sarcastically asking him if his sunglasses were "CIA issue." Perhaps if I had kept my mouth shut and left well enough alone, his agitation would not have shown. It was here, at this moment, that I realized I made a mistake. I let them know I knew who they were. Or, at the very least, who they weren't. They were not aliens.

There was nothing alien about this encounter other than my sensing a presence in the house before I went to bed. In all fairness, I have to admit there is the possibility that the aliens are getting better at deceiving me. Perhaps they have conquered all of their quirks and imperfections and I was simply being deceived much better than I had ever been before. That would lead me to believe, once again, that some of the aliens have a definite purpose in wanting me to believe that my government is involved in abducting its own citizens. Finally, if the alien deception premise is correct, why would the aliens believe that I would work for Daniel Ronnigan? He lives three-thousand miles away. I could always ask the same question about the government. However, the initial effect this experience had on me was to call this broker back and, for a split second, make me feel as though I might actually want to work for the government.

3-27-92

It's three o'clock in the morning—someone is standing next to my bed. It's more than one. There's a very strong force here—A presence—I'm scared—I'm trying to look up now, but I can't move. A needle—in the right side of my neck.

Someone has just told me they need to take some blood from me. They need my blood. This is okay with me. I don't mind. I'm handing them my left hand so they can prick my finger or take it out of my arm. They always use my left arm because I have such large veins and that arm has the smaller veins, although they are still quite large—Oh, someone has just told me that won't work.

There's some kind of machine they want to use on me. I don't understand this. If they want blood—from here—Ouch!!! I'm yelling at someone. Jesus! That hurt! They just stuck me in my leg! "Why did you have to do that? Why did you have to take it from there?" I'm yelling at someone. I don't think they answer me. The pain is so intense. I wasn't expecting it at all.

The following Monday I wrote: "It is now Monday and I have had an unbelievably bad weekend. I feel as though there is something I should remember from Friday night. I think something was said to me that really scared me or upset me. I feel so miserable. I can hardly think about the aliens without thinking about the government and without feeling an intense amount of anger and resentment. I don't know what to do. I wish it would all happen so it would all be over with."

It is evident I had a strong feeling that something was going to happen. What is this "something" that is going to happen in our future? Is it Earth changes? Is it a war? Civil unrest? Chaos? Thousands of UFOs in the sky? Are they going to save our planet or destroy it? I simply cannot remember what it is they have told me. Is this for my own good? Why tell us about things that are going to happen if we cannot remember? What purpose does this serve?

Prior to falling to sleep on April 8, 1992, I thought there was something in our bedroom closet. Erik had fallen asleep already and I got up with my flashlight in hand and shined it into the closet. I didn't see anything so I went back to bed and put the flashlight between us.

4-8-92

I'm on a spaceship. There are a lot of other people here. It almost seems like a party. It is very busy here. This is very strange. I think everyone is going outside. Before I go outside, I have to find a bathroom.

I'm in a small, rectangular-shaped room with many mirrors. I'm closing several doors to cover up the mirrors. There is a toilet in here, but I can't really sit on it because the room is so narrow. There isn't enough room. Since I have to go to the bathroom I'll just have to do my best.

I think something is wrong. I think something has been done to my rectum. I'm standing up and I feel as though I'm being watched. I can't figure out how this happened. One minute I'm trying to go to the bathroom and the next minute I'm standing in the middle of a small room cleaning myself with funny looking white towels. I do not remember going to the bathroom, but everything is out of me now. How did this happen? I'm being watched. This is humiliating.

I'm finished with that and now a beautiful deer is approaching me. It is a young deer because it is only three, maybe four feet tall. It has beautiful eyes—I'm petting it—Something is making me feel uneasy. I can see a sparse amount of hair on the animal, but I can also see writing that spells out the word "lion." Should I be afraid? Is this really a lion? I'm trying to figure this out—No, it's a deer. I'm touching it again. It seems very interested in me. It has come very close to me and I am looking right into its eyes. They are glossy black—I love this animal.

Now I'm petting the deer and instead of seeing hair I can see its skin. It looks more like clay skin. This is really strange. It has lumpy skin and it looks like clay. How strange—I don't like this. I wonder if something is wrong with it. It's not behaving the way a real deer would, but it is very interested in me and I'm getting to touch it. I expected it to feel more "huggable," but instead it feels a little hard. Its movements are rather abrupt too.

Now I have to feed this deer. It is very important that I offer it food so it will stay healthy. I've found some carrots and some lettuce. I'm feeding the deer and it seems to like this food. I'm very busy now making sure the deer has plenty of food. I love this. I love feeding the animals and taking care of them. Animals are so beautiful and positive. I feel this way about all animals. I'm still offering the deer different fruits and vegetables and it is eating them.

Now, I think I've just crossed a road and it is dark outside. I can see the deer across the street with some street people. I am very afraid for the deer. There is a male Being next to me and he wants me to think he is my father, but I know he isn't. I am very afraid for the deer. I have a pear in my hand and I'm waving it in front of me so the deer will see it and come to me. It's running a little, back and forth. It's trying to decide where to cross the road. Suddenly, I am afraid! I don't want the deer to cross the road because it will get hit by a car! I'm frantic now. I realize it might die because of me and I'm no longer calling it to come over to me. I have to leave it alone. I can't have anything to do with it now. It moves off into the darkness. I feel sad. I wanted to take care of it—I'm very sad now.

Suddenly, I'm with all of those people again. I think I'm back in the ship with all of those people. We are being told to expect something fantastic to happen in the sky. Now it is daylight. We are all going outside. Suddenly, the sky turns dark as though it is night. We are all looking up. Unbelievable! The sky is dark and there is a beautiful ring of energy in the sky. It is huge. It is moving outward, and it's getting larger and larger. I think there might be more than one ring of energy. It looks as if someone dropped a pebble into the sky and the waves are moving outward. The color is metallic blue. It is brilliant yet still subtle. I can't adequately describe it because words do not come close to describing its beauty and intensity. We are all awestruck.

The sky has suddenly resumed its daylight appearance. We are going back inside into a round room—Wait—We are all going back outside—It's happening again. The same way as before—Darkness and then the beautiful metallic blue rings of energy. When it is over I ask someone, "Is that all? Is that what we've been expecting to see? Is that what we've been waiting for all of this time?" This didn't measure up to the feelings I've been having for so long. The feeling that something unbelievable would happen for the entire planet to see. I think someone else who was standing near me felt the same way as I did. The other people seem a little disappointed also. I'm not sure what I expected.

Maybe I expected to see hundreds of ships in the sky like we have seen before. This is only energy, and although it is beautiful, it does not hold the same meaning for us. We are walking back into the round room.

I will be the first to admit that some of this is so transparent it is almost funny. I'm sure I had some type of a rectal probe in the small, rectangular room with all of the little mirrors. I don't want to go into much detail, but if you've ever had one, you know what I'm talking about when I say I don't want to go into any details!

The "deer," of course, wasn't a deer. Deer are my favorite association animal for the Greys. I often wonder if this was a disguise for an alien child. I inferred from its size that it was a young deer, but perhaps there was another reason for my believing it was a child. Maybe my having to feed and care for it indicates that this was really a child. This was followed by the all too familiar, "get her to love it, get her attached to it, and then take it away" routine. In the end, with no small amount of deception and symbolism, I was made to understand that this child-deer would be harmed if I were to become too attached to it. I, very gladly, would have taken it home and cared for it as I would any animal, or alien baby, given half the chance.

The metallic, blue ring of energy may have been analogous to a treat for performing the correct behavior. I have to keep an open mind about all of these fantastic displays they are showing me. Could they simply be a reward or another bit of information to keep me coming back for more? None of these fantastic "space shows," if you will, has ever happened. Is there really going to be a fantastic display in the heavens for all of the world to see? Are there really going to be thousands of ships in the sky at once? I suppose what I am hoping for is that enough abductees and experiencers will get tired of the "treats" and demand some real food for a change. Maybe if we collectively decide to ask them, "Is this all there is? Is this what we've been waiting for?" and ask now, we will get to the truth a lot faster. That is, if we want the truth.

As difficult as it is to admit, I was duped again just seven days later. I didn't want to believe that this had occurred so recently after this last visit.

4-15-92

I'm looking in a mirror and I've gained some weight. I know in my heart that I'm pregnant. I've put on about ten pounds. (In fact, I had.)

I'm riding in some type of vehicle that is flying above a road, although I don't see a road. I think I'm with my parents, but I can't see them very well. I am going to have a baby and I'm very happy about it. I can't wait to see what it will look like. I'm so happy.

Wow! I can see many, many crafts flying very close to a mountain range. I'm straining my neck to see—we are moving away from them—They are mostly to my right and behind me. Suddenly I can see my mother but she looks like a zombie. She has a distant stare in her eyes and even though she is looking right at these crafts, I don't think she realizes what she is seeing. Oh, this is strange—Some of the crafts are transforming from saucer-shaped metallic crafts into hot air balloons! This isn't right. All of these balloons look the same. They are tan or golden. A minute ago they were saucer-shaped crafts. I don't think I'm supposed to see them, but I do see them and I know what I'm looking at. No one is going to fool me. Not anymore. I know what I'm seeing.

Some time has elapsed and I'm thinking about having my baby again. I'm wondering if it will hurt—I never thought about that before. For some reason, I didn't think I would have to have my baby like everyone else does. Now I'm afraid it will hurt. I'm telling someone next to me, "By the way, I'm not into this childbirth thing. It's not important that I feel anything associated with it. As a matter of fact, I don't want to feel or remember anything about it okay? You can give me all of the pain killers you have on hand. Just make sure I don't wake up or feel anything or remember anything." The Being I'm talking to seems to find me amusing.

I think some more time went by because now I'm in a hospital. I'm looking at another woman who is pregnant. She is human, has short dark hair and is just showing. I'm looking down at my stomach. She is much more pregnant than I. Maybe something is wrong with my baby—My baby isn't finished being formed yet and it still has a lot of growing to do.

I'm not sure how I know this, but I am really pregnant and someone has told me that my baby is dead. It is inside me, but something is wrong with it. I believe it is dead and I don't want it inside me anymore. I want them to take it out of me as fast as they can. I can't stand the thought of having a dead baby inside me.

I think it is over now—I'm really confused. Someone is handing me a really weird shaped tampon with a metal device on one end. I am holding it by this metal device. I can't let it touch anything because it has to remain sterile. I'm walking toward a bathroom, I think. This isn't really a bathroom because there aren't any doors on it. There are many other people around—a lot of women—they are going through the same thing I'm going through. Everyone is either having babies or being checked. I am just another number, so to speak. No one is really paying me any attention.

This is scary. I'm going to the bathroom and there is all of this blood coming out of me. I'm bleeding—I'm so confused. All of this time I was pregnant and I still had my periods. Does this mean that my baby is normal or deformed? I'm so worried about my baby. I'm putting this tampon thing inside me—There is a snap sound—this doesn't feel right. This isn't a tampon. This is some kind of device designed to stop the bleeding—It seems to be working.

I was really looking forward to seeing my baby and now I will never be able to see it. I don't know if it is dead or alive. What if they made me think it was dead so I would want them to take it out of me?—I would never let them take it for any other reason.

Several of my experiences have left me feeling extremely depressed and this was one of them. I felt an enormous amount of shame at even recording this the following morning. I felt dirty, and I felt I had been deceived. I have no idea what happened to this baby, or fetus, I should say. Yes, I had gained about ten pounds, but could a fetus this small survive? I can only imagine that if it did, it was placed in one of the small liquid-filled isolation tubes that I saw a baby floating in one time—an experience, which at the time, I felt was so unbelievably bizarre that I did not record it. I never thought it meant anything until I read *The Watchers*, by Raymond Fowler. These small tanks with babies suspended within the contents of them was brought out again in the CBS mini-series *Intruders*.

Whether I was pregnant or whether an egg was removed, the fact still remains that a life was probably created and was taken for purposes unknown to me. It would seem as though I saw other crafts on my way to wherever the termination of the pregnancy occurred. Apparently, this was something I was not supposed to remember. It is amazing how the aliens can change the appearance of an object and make my mind see something other than what is really there. I know I saw several crafts and these Beings did not want me to remember them. I certainly did not see them and then make myself *not* see them. I have had four conscious sightings. I was not afraid when I saw the crafts during these sightings nor did I try to make myself believe I had seen a balloon. Somehow these Beings were able to make me see hot-air balloons. Because I was aware of what they were doing, I fought it. They were never able to complete the entire image of the balloons in my mind.

Two weeks later the alien-government theme occurred during another abduction experience. It was obvious that someone was going to hit me over the head with it until I put it in writing that, "I believe! I believe! I believe!"

4-29-92

There are a lot of military personnel and others around me. I remember being here before. This is some type of military base but I'm not sure which one. Navy? Coast Guard? Probably more like a Navy base, but I'm not sure if this is our military. I know my way around and I'm walking rather rapidly through this place. A lot of us are getting into these large cigar-shaped crafts. I'm looking over to my right and I can see one of the pilots of these crafts. He has very strange eyes and a ridiculous-looking, long, blonde wig on. I'm with Erik and we are walking together. This male Being is staring at me—I'm glaring back at him contemptuously. Suddenly I "know" and I say to Erik, "He's one of the navigators and he is undercover." Everything here has a purpose. Something very important is happening here. (I-56)

We are now walking inside a structure. I think we are in a huge, underground structure. There is a place under here where water can come in. It is like a man-made river system about twenty feet wide. It is to my right. There are some military people here and they are telling us about a newly designed craft. Suddenly, one of the cigar-shaped crafts appears next to me in this area where the water is. I'm flabbergasted! Neither I nor anyone else in this place with me heard or saw this craft enter into this place—Okay—They were trying to demonstrate that it is completely silent. I think it must be able to appear and disappear quite easily. Everyone around me seems to be impressed. I am impressed too, but at the same time, I am very guarded. **(I-55)**

I've just realized Erik is gone! I think he had to go on one of the cigar-shaped crafts. Oh, this is why I'm hurrying and walking through this place—I'm looking for him. I'm so angry that they took him. I want to go on board one of these ships too, but I'm a little nervous about it. He is gone—They only took the men. Only men. This is so unfair! Why didn't they take me?

I'm walking though a restricted area. I'm cutting across a lawn and there is a mother/father/child trio approaching me. They are near me now and are trying to distract me away from this restricted area. The kid is trying to distract me by wanting to play with me. I don't pay them any attention. I have to get to this place!

I'm so worried for Erik. I have to try to get to him. I think they put him and some other men in an experimental aircraft and I have to find him. I'm afraid it will crash. I'm away from the "trio," but now I'm having difficulty walking. It's almost like being on one of their ships when the gravity difference makes it almost impossible to walk. That's what I'm feeling now. Someone is trying to distract me again. They are showing me two Japanese Lace Leaf Maple trees—a pink one and a red one—I've never seen a pink one before—

Oh—I have to go. I really like these trees, but I have to go. I have much more important things to do. I seem to have entered a garden of some type. It is strange that there could be a big circular garden inside here. I'm still underground and there is an "outside" underground, complete with trees and grass. I think I'm still underground. This is amazing. Now I have approached a door with many strange locks on it. "Do not panic." I'm telling myself. I very calmly unlock the door. I must have remembered how to unlock it. Somehow I've operated this kind of door and locking system before. This door is gray, metallic, and very thick—Good—I'm outside the garden area.

There's the craft! It's too late! They are already airborne. I'm watching and praying that it doesn't crash—Not with Erik on board. I'm scared to death for him. I'm watching this cigar-shaped craft move in the sky—It is turning on its axis, 360 degrees one way—now 360 degrees in the opposite direction. This craft is moving in ways that I thought would be impossible for it to move. It's doing a loop—now a roll—I don't think they want me to remember—this—no—I'm wrong—They do want me to remember. For some reason they want me to remember—

I awakened feeling extremely drugged. I immediately knew that they wanted me to remember this incredible event. These military personnel were wearing light gray, loose fitting uniforms. I'm not sure whose military this was, but I was very close to a body of water. There were aliens and humans here, both in abundance. At one time I thought this must be the Belgium military because something about the uniforms reminded me of Belgium. So far, I am unable to remember what it was about them that made me feel that way. The gray, loose fitting uniforms were constructed out of a material that had a heavy weave in it. They reminded me of a man's silk suit, but the weave of the material was much thicker. The weave went vertically and horizontally. These uniforms were not like the tight-fitting body suits so many of the aliens wear. I am sure the gray, loose-fitting uniforms were made out of a material that I've seen here on Earth. I also believe the only ones wearing these uniforms were humans.

The cigar-shaped crafts were about fifty to sixty feet long. They were unlike anything I had ever seen before. They were a dark charcoal color and were built out of what looked like a dark, shiny metal. The panels were twelve to sixteen inches square, and although there were lines where they were joined together, they were extremely smooth and I did not see any rivets or screws holding them together. There were no propellers or external engines either. I am confident that I am describing this type of craft accurately because I walked by one of them and I was only about ten feet away from it. When these crafts were parked, they appeared to hover about one to two feet above the ground.

The male alien telepathically communicated with me when I passed by the craft he was sitting in. I gave him a very sarcastic look because I felt he was looking at me with the same expression. In fact, it was his eyes that led me to believe he wasn't being friendly. It was my own inner prejudice that led me to believe he was unfriendly because his eyes were rather intense looking. He appeared to be a tall Grey with large black, upswept eyes and a triangular-shaped head. He was wearing a light gray, tight-fitting body suit. The yellow wig was really strange. It didn't look like real hair, but who's to say if it was really a wig. It seemed as though all of the pilots had long yellow hair. However, they do not call themselves pilots as he used the term "navigator." He also told me he was "undercover," which I find very interesting. I would imagine that they would be working undercover if they were working with so many military personnel and abductees around! The only place I remember seeing these alien navigators was when they were piloting the cigar-shaped crafts or walking to and from them.

I tend to believe the trio (mother/father/child) was probably a screen image for three Beings. They did not want me to cross into this restricted zone again. Because I knew how to operate the huge, thick gray door with the strange locking mechanism on it and knew my way around so well, I believe I had been to this area before. I have a distinct conscious memory of being outside these two warehouse-type hangars. This memory was some time prior to this experience and I did not record it because I didn't realize it was a place associated with these Beings. The first time I remembered being there I was supposed to attend a special class. These hangars are similar to buildings on top of ground, but they descend into the earth so deeply that the space they occupy exists mostly underground. It is my belief that the actual warehouse/hangar structures are only a cover to hide the fact that there are large underground areas there.

Why was I seeing, or being made to believe that I was seeing, this human-alien interaction on a base again? How many times can I deny the presence of these people? Was this a coalition of different governments? Is that why I thought the Belgium military and our Navy were somehow involved? If I didn't know better, I would say this was a submarine base. But, I know better, right?

5-7-92

> *I'm outside a landed craft with three Beings. Two of the aliens have light gray skin and appear to be wearing tight fitting body suits. The third alien has old, worn-looking skin and I cannot tell whether he has on a body suit or not. I don't think he is wearing clothes. They all have large, black eyes. They are typical Greys—I've seen them many times before.*
>
> *Something is wrong—They are lying down on the ground as if they are unconscious—I'm opening the door to their craft and I'm running inside toward a control panel. I'm activating something—The atmosphere is changing now—Oh! The old-looking alien is floating around me and is trying to make me get out of their craft!* (I-16) *I don't like him! I'm pushing him away from me with both arms—rather like shooing away a swarm of flies. I don't hurt him—I just want him away from me. The other two aliens are awake and they don't seem to mind that I'm inside their craft. They are very calm and composed. I must have done something to make them wake up—This must have been some kind of test or drill or something.*

This old alien is really bothered by my being inside their craft, but I don't care. The other two don't mind—Erik and I are with the light gray aliens and we are looking up at a large map on the wall of their craft. It must be three dimensional—it has many layers to it. Erik and I are reading the map—I'm asking the aliens, "Do these lines represent the different levels or dimensions of space?" One of the aliens replies, telepathically, "Yes." I continue, "And when you travel on this route, as opposed to this one (pointing to the map), you have to add different levels of water and (chemical unknown to me) into your fuel supply so your craft can travel through this particular type of space?" Again the alien replies telepathically, "Yes." We seem to understand everything. It makes perfect sense to us. The map has different colored lines representing the different types of space they travel through. There are black lines, but the majority of the lines are white and red.

I'm looking at Erik now. He is lying on a table in the middle of the craft. There is not much inside this craft. Just the control panel, the large map on the wall and some other controls along the interior curved walls of the craft. The table Erik is lying on must have come out of the wall or up out of the floor. I'm looking at Erik and I feel rather left out. The aliens don't seem to be interested in me. One of the aliens understands my feelings and telepathically says to me, "There is a special place in this for women. You have a special lesson to learn and a special role in this." His words comfort me and I feel better now.

I'm on a military base now. I'm walking on a sidewalk next to a yellowish-tan colored concrete, brick building. I am approaching a colonel I know. I'm not supposed to be out here with him, but I don't think he will mind. His back is to me and he has some papers in his hand and he is thinking about a speech he has to give sometime soon. I'm standing next to him. I don't say much to him, but my heart goes out to him. I say hello and I try to smile, but I can only manage a sympathetic look. I do sympathize with him. He is looking down at me because he is taller than I am. He gives me a slight nod and a barely detectable smile. His expression returns to one of sadness. He is not looking forward to this speech he has to give. We are turning around and are walking back toward the building together. This building is old and is a very simple square block design with a flat roof. It's dark outside and the door has been pulled back to remain in an open position leaving the screen door closed. We open the old screen door and go inside. This is a bar. There isn't any air-conditioning, but since it's nighttime we don't really need it. The mood inside is rather subdued. Most people are just relaxing, either drinking or playing a game of pool. It's not a very large building—I'm walking over to Lt. Colonel (name deleted). He is a friend of mine. We met back in the early eighties when I was married to Mark. It's nice to see him again. There is an air of calm inside this place. I do not hear any music playing and I see no added luxuries. Just the necessities. It is rather quiet for a bar, but under the circumstances I understand. I'm feeling the same way everyone else here is. We are just trying to relax. We're ALL involved in this. Most of these people work around here. They are either military or government personnel.

This experience left me extremely depressed for three days. I couldn't remember what could have happened to make me feel this way. The only thing I can say is the mood inside this small bar was subdued. I was overwhelmed with the knowledge that everyone in this place knew about the aliens' presence on our planet and was somehow connected to it. I did not see other abductees per se, but I believe some of these men had been contacted themselves. All of them were involved with the alien presence in one way or the other. The colonel, who was mentally preparing himself for the speech he would have to give soon, seemed almost sad. It was clearly something he was not looking forward to. I also knew him by name, but at this point, I cannot consciously remember what his name is. The Lt. Colonel is a friend of mine and I feel he is connected to the abduction phenomenon, possibly as an abductee.

One of the most perplexing things about this experience was the buildings, or more specifically, the military base. This was not Camp LeJeune or New River Air Station. I remembered having been to this base before and I believe it is in the western United States. I'm not sure if it is in the desert because I saw some grass on the ground and some bushes when I was outside with the colonel. The color and structure of the buildings were extremely similar to the small base I described when I saw the tall alien female and the large, rotating environmental measuring devices. This is also the same base I saw the hybrid Being I call The Female. Unless this was an alien implanted memory, once again, my belief is that this is a base where aliens are working side by side with our military and other government personnel.

The beginning of this experience leads me to believe I underwent some type of drill or test, much like the fire drills we all had to participate in as children and young adults in school. I knew which controls to operate to get inside the craft and what to do once I was at the control panel. This is no great knowledge or mystery to me. I simply believe it is a prudent step on their part to educate those of us who are willing to learn. The actions I took could have been as simple as basic first aid, for example, learning how to put a tourniquet on. It is also possible that being taught this knowledge was a simple reward for my participation. After all, I believe I'm learning something about them as well. These experiences are not completely one-sided, although I will have to admit, the deck isn't exactly stacked in my favor. I do not know why the older-looking alien was so against my understanding this basic knowledge and being inside the craft. Other than trying to scare me, he did not do anything to me in a physical sense to get me out of the craft. I was aware of his displeasure, but it was as if he was the one kid in a group of friends I play with who didn't like me. I wasn't going to let this one alien spoil my fun. The lighter-skinned Greys didn't appear to be bothered by my actions, but this "grandfather" alien simply could not accept my presence on board his craft. Perhaps he was the same Being who terrified me when an alien who looked exactly like him, floated very quickly out of the room during the "row of rooms" encounter. And finally, he could have been part of the drill and was acting as the distracting element, or fear-inducing element, to determine how I would function with added obstacles when boarding an alien craft in an emergency situation.

I began to read the map on the wall more as my own mental review in order to see if I could remember what I had already learned. The map appeared to be up high on one of the walls of the interior of their craft. It had depth and width and substance. The only description I could give it is to say it was embedded in the same clear, crystalline substance the small hand-held map was in during the second encounter with the "row of rooms" and the small crystal skulls. Assuming the alien was telling me the truth when he telepathically replied "yes" to my inquiries, I would guess that my knowledge of certain ship operations may be more than a mere treat thrown to the dog for the correct behavior. I believe they have a reason for wanting me to understand some basic functions of their crafts.

At the time this experience occurred, my mother and grandmother (from Germany) were visiting us in Portland. They were staying at the house with us and when I asked them if they remembered their dreams (from the same night my experience occurred), my grandmother told me that she kept dreaming about all of these little babies and did not want to elaborate on the subject. My mother told me she remembered her dreams, but she simply wasn't going to talk about them and it would be pointless for me to ask her again. "I absolutely will not talk about it, so don't even try," was the last thing she said to me. She was so adamant about not talking about it I immediately dropped the subject.

CHAPTER 12

It Continues

Nineteen ninety-two was an active year for me. Between working with abductees and our local UFO group, I was working full time in the area of alien abductions. Shortly after the following encounter occurred, I began to seriously consider writing a book. As I stated earlier, it would be my attendance at the 1992 MUFON symposium that would make me see how much a book such as this was needed.

6-17-92

I'm flying in some kind of craft again—I don't see any wings—it's not a plane. I think it's one of those cigar-shaped crafts again—The same one I saw at the military base near the water—the same one Erik was in when I had to watch from the ground—

Oh God! We're really flying fast! We're over the water! It's the Pacific— we're really flying low—I can see the waves—I'm so scared. I think I'm looking out of the front of the craft. I think I see two light colored pleasure boats in the water—they must be fishing at night—"What is that?" It is a telepathic command from the pilot. I'm looking at the fishing boats in the water and I reply very simply, "Boats."

I'm back at my seat. This crazy female pilot doesn't know what the hell she's doing! She's flying the craft all over the place—I'm afraid we're going to crash! We're flying sideways and upside down. I'm scared to death. I hate this! I hate it when they do this! Why would they fly like this over the ocean? I'm looking out of the window next to my seat—I can see the water—I can see a boat! I think we just flew over a boat in the ocean! I have to get out of here. I'm in a panic.

We have just flown over an incredibly huge object. It's in the water— We are very close to it now—I think we are over it now—I have to get out of this thing—This is my only chance to make this craft stop. I'm looking at my window. It's clear, but it isn't constructed out of glass. I'm standing up in my seat now—I'm kicking the window with my right foot. Kicking! Kicking! Kicking! **(I-57)** *I want out very badly! It's opening. The window has folded outward and away from me. There's some kind of seam in it and it's folding outward at this seam. Oh shit!*

"Decompression! Decompression! Decompression!" I'm yelling. I'm yelling this so everyone in the craft will know that I've kicked the window out. I'm scared to death. Maybe this will make them land this damn thing.

Someone is laughing at me! I'm turning around—There are two or three males at the back of this craft and they find what I have done amusing! Besides the pilot and these three males, I'm the only other person in this craft—I'm looking around the inside of this craft—I have to get out of here now. I'm going to crawl out of the window. We've landed on that large object that was in the water and I'm safe now. I'm crawling out of the window.

I'm outside now and there are a few other people around. I'm looking around to see where we have landed—I'm standing beside the large cigar-shaped craft—My God, there's the pilot! She is walking right by me and her eyes are so intense! I think she must be really angry with me for kicking the window out. Maybe not—She seems more like she was just temporarily inconvenienced by my actions. This is so strange—She looks just like the male navigator Being I saw on the military base near the water. Her hair is yellow and it's down to her waist. She is tall and thin and is wearing a tight-fitting, light gray body suit. Her eyes are huge and black. They look mean. I don't think she likes what I did to my window. She just walked past me. (I-18)

I'm looking down now. I couldn't stand for her to look at me any longer. I'm ashamed that I caused so much trouble, but I had to get out of that craft. I thought we were going to crash by the way she was piloting the thing. It seems like I'm always doing something wrong when I'm with them—

Oh Jesus—Someone just handed me a baby. Erik is facing me and is looking at me—I can't really describe what my emotions are—I've just seen this baby's face and head and I'm looking at Erik. I'm trying to block my thoughts from the Beings. This is such a terrible and hopeless situation. This baby—well, I think it should be dead—I'm amazed that it is still alive—this is a perfect case for euthanasia—Jesus Christ—I'm holding this baby away from me because it looks so horrible. I have its feet touching me and its head is away from my body—It is looking up at me with one, very black eye. Its eye is like a black liquid staring up at me. It is still alive— (I-34)

I'm looking down at the baby. Its skin is blood red as if there is blood just below its skin. Is it burned? Jesus! How can this baby be alive? I almost feel like laughing because I am so helpless to do anything for it!

The left side of the baby's face seems fairly normal except for the blood-red skin. It must be a hybrid—it has a huge bulging forehead and a very round, very black, eye. A small nose—The right side of the infant's face is totally deformed. From the forehead on down, the skull and the bone structure appear to have never formed into a hardened skull. The entire right side of its face has totally collapsed. It's as if someone forgot to put the skull in and there is only loose flesh. It is entirely caved-in. The right eye isn't there. There is an eyelid, but there is nothing underneath it. The cheek bone and chin bone have collapsed and it appears as if the skin has been burned. I wish it would have never been born. How can this be? I know it is alive because I'm holding it and it is looking up at me with its other eye. I'm trying to block my thoughts. I don't want the aliens to know how hopeless I feel—What is this? Are they joking? Why are they even trying? What can I possibly do for this baby?

I was not myself after this encounter for about five days. The following day I drew pictures of everything I remembered. When I worked on the picture of the baby, it was almost as if I was outside of myself. I was almost dissociated from myself while drawing the baby. It was so difficult for me to look at. When my husband came home for lunch I asked him what he remembered about the previous night. He said that even though he was sure they had come and taken us he couldn't remember anything. Then I showed him the picture of the baby I had drawn and he immediately told me that he felt sick and nauseous. He sat down in a chair and said, "For some reason it looks familiar to me—I don't think I can eat my lunch now."

It is difficult, even with the passage of many months, to talk or to write about this baby. However, with the passage of time many wounds can heal, and that includes emotional wounds as well. This was an emotionally wounding experience for me. I can hardly begin to put into words what seeing this baby made me feel like. I tried to explain it in my journal as the memories flooded out from my mind and onto the computer screen. There are times when I find myself writing or typing so frantically because of the flood of information and my need to document every detail. Often it is difficult to read afterwards or imagine how I could have misspelled some simple, everyday words.

Why did the aliens give me this baby to hold? From what I saw, it should have already been dead. I have realized before how important it is to try to take these experiences out of the human context. I thought if I did that with this experience it would make more sense to me.

The baby was alive and I believe it was a newborn. Perhaps that is why its skin appeared to be burned or to have blood just beneath it. At the time I believed it was a hybrid child, but it could have also been an alien child. I thought back to 1987 when Erik suggested the large, black upswept eyes were actually a protective covering for their real eyes. I wondered if this child was an alien child without the protective covering over its eye. Regardless of the species in question, if this baby was going to survive it seemed as though it was going to need some help.

I do not believe the aliens showed me this baby to induce guilt in me, to punish me, or so I could save it. They must know that simply holding a baby, while it may provide contact comfort, is certainly not going to save its life. Especially in the condition this one was in. They know I'm not a doctor or a surgeon and if they wanted a human to save it, they would have abducted a professional. I do not know if this was my child. I did not feel an emotional or biological connection to it. It was simply handed to me.

Perhaps that was it. Maybe this infant was simply handed to me to hold for a minute or so until they could take it back and do whatever they were going to do to it. I suddenly realized this baby had probably been on this craft with me. Could the aliens have been transporting the child and me back to this, huge, whatever it was, in the water? Was I taken to help calm or soothe the mother who delivered this child during its birth, as Betty Andreasson had done in one of her experiences? I think there is a strong possibility that this infant was transported on this craft and taken to this place the same time I was. I think I held the baby either for convenience sake or for the aliens to read my emotions and thoughts. Perhaps it was to determine whether we would go to the trouble to save a child in this state, or simply let it die. Remember, I was aware that I should block my thoughts from the aliens because I did not want them to know that I felt the situation was hopeless.

Something else occurred to me as I was letting time heal this emotional wound. If the aliens can perform surgery on my heart, put metal probes into my legs with just a drop of blood to show for it, take a fetus or ovum from me without leaving any physical traces (sometimes), then I believe it is quite possible that they could have surgically repaired this infant's deformities and, therefore, saved this baby's life. It is quite probable when one reviews the miraculous surgical techniques they have performed on so many abductees. If the aliens could take Betty Andreasson's eye out and put it back in, then I have to believe they were more than capable of performing reconstructive bone surgery on this infant and surgically implanting another eye.

Is it possible the aliens were saying, "Okay, look at this baby. It's in pretty rough shape, right? Well, we'll show you what we're capable of." It simply doesn't make sense that the aliens could build these incredible flying devices, perform miraculous surgical techniques, and yet have such a difficult time keeping babies alive. If they can be so exact and successful performing surgical procedures on human beings, then it would stand to reason they would be at least as capable of performing them on their own species, or even a hybrid species.

I don't mean to say that the aliens do not have their share of failures and they do not meet with difficulties when trying to crossbreed two different species. There are certainly references to this problem in the literature. I realize the importance of looking at these experiences from a perspective other than my own "human" perspective. We are simply not dealing with human beings (in most cases). Although I may not be entirely successful, I do try to understand these events from a point of view other than my own.

I have a very clear memory of what this craft looked like inside. There was a row of eight seats on each side of the craft. The seats were cushioned a little and made out of a material that looked like a medium gray vinyl. It looked similar to the same material their body suits are made out of, but it was a darker gray. The seats were designed for one human or two aliens to sit in comfortably. There was a wide space of about five feet between the two rows of seats. The floor was a dark brown metal. There was a compartment or room in the rear of the craft and I think three other Beings, or possibly even people, were back in this area. There is a strong possibility that these were humans or hybrids because I could hear one of them laughing at me when I began kicking the window. I do not recall ever hearing an alien laugh before. The area of the craft in front of the seat I was sitting in (and the same seat I stood on when I kicked out the window) was open. In front of this and about fifteen feet away from me was a dark brown, bulkhead-type wall. Through a door, or entry way into the forward section was another area that seemed to be rather spacious. This section did not have seats. There were no seats other than the two rows I described earlier. In front of this area was the cockpit and this is where the navigator was. (The female alien who was piloting the craft.) The entire craft was about fifty to sixty feet long and about twelve feet wide. I am absolutely confident in stating this was the same type of cigar-shaped craft I saw on the military base near the water. When you look at the drawings from both encounters you will have a good idea of what this craft looks like.

7-21-92

> *I'm going to see a new female gynecologist. I'm in a circular waiting room and there is a circular counter about fifteen yards away from me. This entire place is round.*
>
> *I'm at the counter now and someone is showing me a picture of a woman. Oh, this is the female doctor—they are telling me what she will look like. This isn't right—This picture doesn't match. I'm looking at the doctor and this picture doesn't match the person I'm looking at. These are definitely two different females. One is younger and has shorter hair—This is the real doctor. She is the person I really want to see. Oh—how interesting—now they are telling me that not only is she a gynecologist, but she is also a MUFON investigator. This is really something—What a stroke of luck. MUFON finally has a female doctor*

who is going to investigate abduction cases for them. This is great. I'm looking forward to meeting her.

It seems as though I've been waiting forever on this doctor. I never wait this long on doctors—I think I'm going to leave—Oh, there she is. She is coming out of a small room and several children are following her. These are really special children. Somehow I know they are extremely intelligent and they are very special children. They are all dressed up in new little outfits. It seems as though they all got them at the same store and off the same rack. Oh well, maybe they're uniforms of some type—green and white plaid—very cute outfits.

Oh no—The doctor is announcing to everyone in the waiting room that she will have to cancel all of her appointments! I'm so angry! After all of this time I've been waiting on her! It seems she has to investigate a case for MUFON, but I know that it really has something to do with these children she has spent so much time with! I'm leaving. This really infuriates me. She never intended to be my doctor. This was all a sham so she could spend so much time with the children.

I'm walking across a large open area and I'm going back to my car. I'm going to tell Erik what happened. Oh! Here's the doctor—she wants me to come back inside. I scream at her, "You are just like all of the other doctors! Take your hands off of me! Don't touch me!" I'm walking towards my car and I'm extremely angry.

Here's my car! It's parked out in the middle of the woods! How did it get way out here? Oh no—There are wasps around my car. One on the passenger side and an entire swarm is on the driver's side near the outside of the door. Maybe I can get inside before they sting me. I'm really scared now—I'm afraid the wasps will attack me—

Oh! I'm inside my car now and I'm shutting the door as fast as I can.

Here's Erik. He's getting into the car on the driver's side. He has a baby! "Where did this come from?" I ask him. He's handing the baby to me—I don't want to hold this baby—It's in some type of strange looking carrier and I'm putting the baby in the back seat of my car. I'm going to tell him what this doctor did and how mad I am—

The following morning I jumped into the shower as fast as I could. Usually I have my coffee and at least say good morning to Erik. Erik brought my coffee into the bathroom and asked, "What do you remember?" I kept showering and shouted, "What do *you* remember?" This questioning continued until I relented and explained everything I remembered. After I finished telling him about my memories I said to him, "You know, I never could figure out where you got that baby from." Erik then replied, "We got the baby from one of those containers they keep ice in. The baby was covered in ice." I looked at Erik from around the shower curtain and knew we had to talk about this.

Here is Erik's memory of the same night:

> *We got the baby from one of those containers they keep ice in. The baby was covered in ice. I was astonished to find an infant in this container because, initially, I expected to find fish or seafood. The baby blinked at me and I couldn't believe it was still alive. A little while later, you and a Being began feeding her. The two of you were just plopping the food on and into her mouth. I had to take the spoon and the food away from you and show both of you the proper way to feed an infant. After this, you took a multicolored ball about a half inch wide and put it into the baby's mouth. The baby was just lying there with its mouth open and I thought this would make the baby choke to death, but you said that it wouldn't. We stood the baby in an upright position and she chewed up and swallowed the little multicolored ball. She did not choke and she was okay.*

He said he knew it was a female baby because when he found her, she didn't have any clothes on. She was also human.

I told Erik about a sore spot I had on my left arm near my elbow. I discovered it in the shower because it was really painful when I washed it. (It was the following day before the bruise appeared.) Erik told me about an area on the top of his head that he said was sore, "Yeah, I've got a bruise right here on the top of my head." I asked him what he thought about our memories and he replied, "I guess I just had a baby dream," and I said, "Yeah, and I guess I just had an OBGYN dream." We looked at one another with cynical smiles on our faces and left for work.

Without carefully thinking this experience through, we might emotionally assume these terrible aliens placed this poor infant in ice! As a matter of fact, before I questioned Erik about how the ice felt and if the baby was cold or wet, his memories would have held a very different meaning. The substance Erik found the baby in turned out to be a substance that looked like crushed ice, but it was not cold or wet. To top it off, we still do not have a complete, uninterrupted memory. For some unknown reason they allowed Erik to find the baby on his own and in something that appeared to be ice, but wasn't. The only reason he was surprised the baby was still alive was because he thought she was really in ice. Emotionally speaking then, how many of us upon finding an infant packed in ice wouldn't naturally assume these are terrible aliens?

When I consider my own memories, it is clear that deception was the order of the night. Here they were again, trying to show me a picture of the way *they* thought I should see the female doctor. Again, I realized what the aliens were trying to do. They certainly succeeded, however, in sparking my interest about her when they told me she was a woman *and* a MUFON consultant.

This doctor was obviously more interested in the children than the other adult females or me. We were sitting together in the waiting room, which probably wasn't a waiting room at all. These children were special, however, and I can only imagine what lies ahead for them. They appeared to be human children and I believed either their mothers or their caretakers were waiting in the same room that I was waiting in.

I wondered why I associated each of these women with a child I saw exiting the small room with the female doctor. Were the children waiting for their mothers while their mothers were being examined? Could this female "doctor" have been acting as a baby sitter? Surely the children were checked over as well. Why did I feel these children were special and intelligent? Are they another generation of abductees or are they human beings who were born into an alien world?

I am confident that the children I saw exiting the small room were human and ranged from about two years old to about six or seven. They were all wearing outfits made out of the same type of green and white plaid material. When I looked at their clothing I believed all of their outfits came from the same place. I have heard a report from another abductee that, as incredible as this sounds, the aliens sent them off in search of clothing. This sounds farfetched until you consider the possibility of the interaction taking place between hybrid children and human children on this planet. Why wouldn't they want to fit in? Especially if the stories are true about the aliens sending hybrid children here to lure human children toward their crafts. In addition, I had a memory of carrying a box of clothes in the middle of the night that I retrieved from a donation drop box. It was my belief that I was to take these clothes to one of their crafts. On my way, I met a very beautiful "cat."

I am almost certain the female doctor was a female alien and they were employing their usual mental camouflage on me. The children, however, are a different matter. The children appeared to be human and they all had blonde or light-colored hair. Their hair seemed normal in every sense of the word. I don't know what this means, but I did not feel any deception was employed with their appearance. The only unusual aspect about them was the fact that they were all wearing clothes made out of the same material.

It is my belief that the wasps I saw on either side of my car were really a camouflage for aliens. I wonder at times whether I have driven out to a specific location and have been abducted from there as opposed to my house. When I see my car in these encounters, everything about it seems perfectly natural, instead of some blurry, vaguely remembered vehicle.

When I found my car out in the woods there was one wasp outside the passenger side of the car, and an entire swarm outside the driver's side. I believe the aliens wanted me to wait until Erik arrived with the baby before we left. Interestingly, the baby Erik brought with him appeared to be human to both of us. Where we went with this baby and what happened after that is anyone's guess.

On July 23, I awakened at 12:35 a.m. With difficulty, I managed to lift my head up enough to see the time on our digital clock. I could hear our neighbor's small dog barking.

7-23-92

> *I'm scared to death—I'm in space—I'm traveling high above the Earth and I can see the cloud coverage around the planet. How can I be in space? Something is following me—some kind of Being or something—It is bluish and translucent. It's coming down from above me—I'm terrified.*

The next thing I remember is hearing my neighbor's dog barking excitedly and looking at the clock. The time was now 2:13 a.m. I felt a very strong presence in the room and I got up and looked out of our bedroom window. I saw my neighbor outside in her bathrobe trying to calm her dog. At this moment our dog began to bark, which is unusual because the moment she hears her little playmate bark, she automatically barks also. Suddenly, I realized that our dog had been "turned off" by the aliens. Naturally, my eyes scanned the night sky, but I did not see anything. Erik seemed to stir a bit, but he did not wake up, which is unusual. Normally every time a dog barks on our street we both wake up.

An eerie feeling came over me after this occurred and I can only compare the feeling to what a dog or cat must feel like when they sense another animal within their territory. I sensed the presence of the aliens either in my house or very close by. I went into the bathroom and looked around, but I was too afraid to walk through the house to investigate further. The presence I was feeling was very intense. I went back to bed. Just before going back to sleep I saw a flash of white light come through our bathroom window. I must have fallen asleep after that.

I'm not sure if it is applicable to abduction research, but our dog vomited a few hours before we went to bed and the following day. Her vomit had a black substance in it, along with her food she ate. It was very unusual looking. We took her to the veterinarian later that week for a bath and had her stool checked. My veterinarian sent the sample off to a lab for a backup comparison on the results he had obtained. Everything was negative. My dog has not gotten sick since then, nor did she vomit this substance prior to my memory occurring. It may have been coincidental, but I have included the information in any case.

Five days later they were back again. Although I don't remember seeing the aliens during this encounter, the *feel* of this encounter was unmistakable. So were the aftereffects.

7-28-92

> *I'm sitting in some type of craft and I'm facing Erik. We are smiling at one another—Suddenly, we are moving really fast! I feel as though I'm flying backwards! I wasn't expecting this! Erik is still facing me—I must be sitting with my back to the front of the craft. That was really unexpected.*
>
> *The movements of this craft appear to have leveled out, or I have become accustomed to its movements. It is traveling very smoothly now—I'm looking out of a window to my left—I'm looking down at some wires—we seem to be traveling, very slowly, over high-tension wires. We are very close to them—about five to ten yards above them. Wow. This is intense. I thought high-tension wires were dangerous. We are following the path of these wires—there are many wires—these are the large ones that reach from state to state—They're so wide—*

The following day I started menstruating a week early. More interestingly, the morning after this encounter I was shocked to find my naval filled with a brownish fluid. It took three days for the fluid to stop oozing from my naval. After the soreness went away I checked my naval. I found two scrapes around the inside and across from one another, and a small puncture wound in the middle. This made me feel very uneasy. I obviously remembered very little of what happened during this encounter. Just when I thought I was getting better at dealing with these encounters and, therefore, remembering more, something such as this had to happen.

It seems that, for me anyway, "when it rains, it pours." As you read encounter after encounter, you must be wondering how I made it through this whirlwind of activity. The truth is, when I look back at some of these experiences I have to ask myself that same question. Writing the memories down is extremely helpful. But, being married to someone as wonderful as my husband really carries me through during the times I find myself questioning my sanity. He is my light at the end of the tunnel. I would not be so fortunate without his love, patience, and understanding. There are times when I feel I owe my very life to him. I cannot imagine going through this alone.

The following encounter left me believing that the aliens came to collect information from my mind to use at a later date.

8-2-92

I'm standing with Al Gore. He's in my living room and he looks as if he's only four feet tall. We are standing near the front door. There is someone to my right but I cannot see them. I'm looking at Al Gore and he is smiling at me. His smile looks kind of mechanical, as if it is frozen in place. He is wearing a dark blue suit. I must have just let him into the house. I tell him, "You know, I've never voted Republican." He laughs and smiles. Something isn't quite right about this. Someone is standing to my right but I can't see who it is.

I didn't know what to make of this fragment of memory. It seemed so real and although this may sound peculiar, it seemed as though there were two aliens in my house with at least one of them camouflaging themselves as Al Gore. I simply recorded what little memory I had of the event and went on with my day. The following night I had another visitation.

8-3-92

Okay—I'm walking though some place—I seem to know where I'm going. There are others nearby. They are two females. I should remember them because I got a clear look at them a minute ago. They were young and had dark hair. I'm going somewhere to get something.

I'm carrying what appears to be a basket with a handle on it. There are several layers of a material that looks like a cross between tissue and paper, but it is neither of these. I think there are about eight to ten layers of this light brown paper substance in here. Oh! It is surrounding a tiny alien baby. A tiny alien baby is lying on its back and it's squirming around. Its little arms are flailing out in front of it—I'm putting my pinkie finger in its mouth—it's suckling on my pinkie finger. This seems to have calmed it down some. (I-32)

There is someone in front of me and someone behind me. We are walking in single file as if we're walking on a path of some kind. Oh— I'm passing by those two females. They are complimenting me on the little baby. I hope they don't freak out from its appearance—Oh, everything is okay. They just told me how cute they think the baby is.

I'm still walking with my pinkie finger in the baby's mouth. This baby really looks small. I wonder how it can survive outside the womb at such a young age? It is tiny. It has a face—Huge black eyes, a pudgy nose, and a small mouth. It has arms and legs—little arms that are moving about. Its nose is really peculiar looking—it almost looks like a snout. This is definitely not a human baby. Its skin looks old and

> worn—it has tan skin. It looks as if it got too much sun too many times. Its skin is tan and wrinkled. I feel a great amount of love for this baby. I can't believe this baby is able to live on its own at such a young age. I just went and got it—I wonder where from?

This was a wonderful experience and I was quite taken with this tiny baby. It was more of a fascination to me than anything. I know this infant is healthy and will survive. I feel so fortunate to have had the opportunity to interact with it. I am not positive that I was carrying it in a basket, but whatever it was, it appeared similar in appearance to a basket. The tissue or paper substance surrounding the tiny infant was something I had not remembered seeing before. The many layers appeared to insulate the infant and prevent it from getting cold. It was so wonderful to see this infant. I am very pleased even now as I write about it because the infant appeared to be strong and healthy. I hope I will have the opportunity to see it again when it grows up.

As I was carrying the infant, I stated there was someone in front of me and someone behind me and I felt as though we were moving in single file. Indeed, I believe we may have actually been floating up this path I described. The two females who passed me were human. They were coming down from the direction my two companions, the infant and myself were heading. I was pleased they found the infant to be cute. I was really afraid they would think it was ugly.

The following night Erik and I got into an argument for no apparent reason. We just started bickering with one another. Nothing happened except that he kept asking me if I wanted him to go and sleep in another room. This was crazy. Of course I didn't want him to go sleep in another room. I couldn't understand what was making us so uptight. I put my head down on my pillow and the last thing I remember was Erik telling me he kept seeing these little creatures every time he closed his eyes. I told him that he should try to get rid of those thoughts and we immediately fell asleep. I believe the following encounter involves a vision replete with theatrics.

8-4-92

> I'm with Senator Gore again and we are in a large room with many people. He is organizing something. Governor Clinton must be here too—Now I'm looking directly at President Bush. He really looks tired—beaten. It looks as if someone got him out of bed in the middle of the night. He has on a gray-striped suit, a white shirt and a tie with some red in it—He doesn't have his coat on. It looks like he got up in the middle of the night. His clothes are all messy. I'm telling Senator Gore something—Oh, I'm telling him I've never voted Republican. President Bush is looking at me with a look of disgust on his face. He

doesn't like me. I think it's neat to be able to tell him to his face that I didn't vote for him. I'm proud of it. Senator Gore seems to be enjoying this. Why am I here?

Senator Gore and Governor Clinton are preparing a feast. Oh, I see what is happening now. They have started with practically nothing, no food and no money, and now they are getting many contributions. I think I'm supposed to help them raise money, but I haven't contributed anything yet. I'm looking at some white forms—some paper. These are related to raising money.

Senator Gore is carrying a plate of something—some type of food. Their feast is growing larger and larger. They are beating Bush. They started out with nothing. Their original small bowl of food is now growing into a huge feast. They are jubilant about this. I believe they will be able to help many people. We are all jubilant—except for President Bush.

Although I did not remember seeing any alien Beings associated with this encounter, it felt the same way all of my other visitations felt. It was extremely vivid and after this vision, I felt in my heart that the Clinton-Gore ticket would win the election. Since it is still October 1992 as I am writing this, it remains to be seen, but my feelings tell me this is what will happen. I decided to include this because of the four foot tall Senator Gore I was facing in my living room two nights prior to this vision. We were standing near the front door facing one another, and we were very close to one another in proximity. I feel this was a type of camouflage for a Being because his expression seemed mechanical. It also felt familiar to be staring into his eyes. I felt as though my mind was being probed. There is a strong possibility that this is exactly what was being done.

In the past I have found myself shying away from people who claim to have visions and psychic abilities. Today, I am sometimes forced into believing in psychic visions, especially when I have them. However, I still wonder if this vision and the vision involving the nuclear power plants was given to me by the aliens.

I had a vision involving President Reagan that I recorded back in June of 1985. This was well before I was consciously aware that I was being abducted by alien Beings. I recorded the vision because it was extremely vivid. I no longer doubt people who claim to have visions or psychic abilities. I may take them with a grain of salt, but I no longer totally disbelieve their messages.

June 1985

> *I saw an assembly of people, a long table, and a lectern. A woman was talking and she was introducing a man who she said was to speak about an experience that he had endured. She said to all who were listening, "With tears in his eyes, he will tell us his sad story." I was sitting in the front row and this man was sitting near me. He stood up, and when he did, I realized it was President Reagan. He walked up to the front of the room. He stood in front of all of these people to testify. He was wearing a plain brown suit that indicated to me he had lost his power and authority.*

In July of 1985, I had what I would call another vision but I do not know if it was alien-induced or not. I saw my ex-husband at an outdoor airport. It was at night and there were military planes and helicopters all around us. There were also many people around us. Mark looked older. He had gained quite a bit of weight and was wearing glasses. He seemed to be in charge of something and was holding papers and documents and was explaining something to a group of men. There were helicopters and planes flying all around.

During the Iraq war, I was writing a Lt. Colonel friend so he would get some mail while he was over in Iraq. He was up for retirement in a few months and I felt it was the least I could do for a friend and a very nice person. In one of his letters which he wrote to me while he was in Iraq, he proceeded to tell me about the time he ran into my ex-husband. He told me Mark was now wearing glasses, had put on some weight, and was working in military intelligence. I had not seen Mark since 1984 and I had not forgotten my vision from 1985.

It would be easier for me not to include material such as this from my journal, but I feel it may have something to do with the abduction phenomenon. I do not want to be considered a psychic, but I do know that many abductees feel they have more psychic abilities than they did before their encounters. I am not sure if there is a time before my experiences since they began when I was about five years old.

Perhaps this phenomenon can be explained as being highly sensitive from having your "sixth sense" used more as a simple detection mechanism, that is, feeling the alien presence just prior to an abduction. For me, this is a way for me to mentally prepare myself for the encounter. Feeling the aliens' presence gives me some control over the situation, even if only a little. I have had similar types of feelings all of my life prior to somewhat disturbing personal events. I have learned to pay attention to them and to use them to my benefit. I am beginning to suspect that our "sixth sense" really is just another one of our normal senses. Due to evolutionary and cultural reasons we have not developed it as much as our other five senses. Perhaps the abduction phenomenon is the environmental stimulus we need in order to perfect it.

I promised myself I would continue writing about my experiences through the year 1992 thereby ending the book December 31. I had hoped for another three month vacation from these experiences so I could finish the book well before Christmas. Once again the aliens showed me that their plans take precedence over my own.

9-15-92

> *I'm lying down on a table and I'm lying on my back. I'm thinking about all the different times I've undergone surgery at the hands of the aliens. It is suddenly occurring to me that I've undergone surgery more than the time I had my tonsils and adenoids removed. I'm remembering it now! They have performed surgery on me many, many times! The aliens are putting me under, just now—I can feel it. They are putting me under for another surgery. Everything is getting foggy—I'm going to sleep now. They are going to perform some type of surgery on me again—I'm not scared—just—relaxed—*

This was a peculiar experience to remember. It was shocking to remember the many different times the aliens had performed surgery on me. How could I not remember these experiences for the major portion of my life and then have them suddenly flood my mind just as I am being put under for another surgical procedure? What could the aliens be doing to me that would require my having to undergo surgery so often? It was not the first time I felt I may be part of a huge experiment. Was I similar to the cats that medical schools use when teaching nurses how to put feeding tubes into patients? The cat is put under anesthesia and the nurses practice inserting the tubes down their throats. One nurse told me it is humane because the cats are anesthetized and they don't feel anything. I wonder, do they *remember* anything?

9-22-92

> *I'm standing up with my arms slightly spread out in front of me but still close to my sides. My legs are slightly bent also. Two Beings are putting thin metal rods through the joints in my elbows. It hurts, but I'm concentrating on staying very still.*

> *Now the aliens are putting a thin metal rod through the joints in my knees and ankles. This is extremely painful at first, but after the rods go in it isn't so bad. All I know right now is that I have to remain very still and stay in this awkward position for a while. Somehow these steel rods are healing or repairing something inside my joints. This is really*

intense—I remember the aliens doing this to me before, but at that time I lost consciousness. Somehow they put me under or made me sleep during the procedure. Now they are letting me stay awake and I'm going to remember this.

On September 23, the night after this surgery was performed on me, Erik and I had another visitation. I woke up feeling angry. This is what I wrote in my journal the following morning: "Erik and I feel as though we were up all night and I am somewhat angry today. We both feel as though the aliens came during the night. He said his rectum hurt so bad that he felt he had to go to the bathroom during most of the night, but he could not go. I remember Erik getting up about four or five times during the night and I remember feeling so sorry for him. I knew he was in a lot of pain. I was up several times last night too. It was between 1:30 and 5:30 in the morning when all of this was happening. I had terrible nightmares." This is what I remember:

9-23-92

Erik and I are waiting to go somewhere. We are going to travel somewhere. There is something that resembles a bus and we are supposed to travel in it to get to our destination. We are apprehensive until we are suddenly convinced, mentally, that a professional basketball team will be traveling on the same bus with us. For an instant we have a visual image of the team players in our minds. They are all black men, and it is very exciting that we are going to have the opportunity to meet them—We are getting into the bus—

Deception. It is immediate. We have been deceived! There is no basketball team and this thing—this thing we're in—is not a bus. It's an elongated craft of some type. It is filled with people—very strange people. These people look as if they just came out of "the night of the living dead!" We're really afraid of them. They are all males and they look terrible. It's really crowded in here—I don't like this. We've been deceived to the hilt! Erik and I are sitting down next to one another—these seats are strange. They should be in isles like on a bus, but they aren't. Some of the seats are facing one another and there are other people in here with us. We are in the back and there is a curtain separating us and a few other people from whoever or whatever these Beings are. These Beings are almost like creatures. The curtain moves from time to time and I can see these "night of the living dead" creatures. It is as if their appearance and the curtain are designed in such a way so we will not want to get up and walk around inside the craft.

Suddenly, a man has run to the back of this craft where we are sitting and one of these ugly Beings is chasing him. This alien Being is throwing the man onto the floor and they are struggling. The alien is taking something—he's putting something into this man's left nostril. This is terrible! The alien is being so rough with this man! I can't stand this. Oh no! The Being is looking at me. He has picked up on my thoughts! He knows everything I was feeling and thinking as he was putting that thing into the man's left nostril. (I-26)

Suddenly I am very close to the Being. I must be standing next to him now. I think I am going to help this man on the floor. The Being and the man are struggling—Oh no! The Being's ear has fallen off! I'm looking at the side of his head and there is only a small black hole where his ear was a minute ago. The Being has picked up his ear and he is pushing it up against his head—He is glaring at me with mean, intense eyes. I'm really afraid of him. I'm terrified. He must be wearing a costume—He just pressed his ear back on—it can't be real. This is crazy. This can't be happening.

Another man has run to the back of the craft and the Being is throwing him onto the floor. He is being so violent with these poor people. The man is struggling with the Being. The Being is either taking something out or putting something into this man's nostril. The man is still struggling against the Being. This is really sick. I'm looking at this ugly Being—I'm studying him—He is at least six feet tall and is wearing a dirty and tattered body suit. It looks as if he's been wearing it for a long time. It is as if these aliens live in a very dusty place— There is dirt and dust all over his body suit and his face. These Beings must never change their clothing. I can see his left hand as his arm hangs down by his side. I can see his fingers. (I-27) *Now I'm looking up at his face again. His eyes—They are so intense. They seem almost evil. These Beings are totally unfeeling about the pain they are inflicting upon these two men. I think we made a big mistake by getting on this thing—This bus from hell.*

I am in my seat. I'm observing this tall Being. I don't think I can move anything except my eyes. I would help these men if I could, but I don't think I can move now.

Now we are in a huge round place. This looks like a large, round coliseum. Is this a concert? This is crazy. I'm sensing so much deception. Deception everywhere. This isn't right. This is all wrong. This is not a concert. They only want me to believe it is—

The following nightmare followed this memory, and I am certain I am correct when I say it was *implanted* by these alien Beings. I believe it was a way for these particular aliens to punish me for not cooperating when I tried to help the first man the Being was putting the implant into. This part of my experience was gruesome.

I'm living next to a freeway and the only thing protecting my cats from the traffic are a pair of bifold doors. I've been trying to save them and protect them all night. This has been going on all night. The aliens are repeating it over and over and over again in my mind. It is being forced into my mind. It is being dumped into my mind—I have no choice but to relive it over and over again. My cats are running onto the freeway! I keep rescuing them and they keep getting out. As soon as I save one, another has gotten out. I'm screaming, "Stop! Stop! They can't go out! They will be killed!" The Beings are looking at me as though I am a fool. I can't stand this.

There's my black and white cat! He's across the street and he has blood on his face! I'm running over to him. I'm picking him up. He is vomiting! Now I have his esophagus, heart, and liver in my hands! There is nothing I can do for him now except to hold him while he dies.

Now I'm in a bathroom. I'm washing my hands—Oh! The bar of soap—it isn't a bar of soap. I'm holding an animal heart in my hands! I'm putting it down and I'm picking up another object that I think is a bar of soap. It is an animal liver! I can't do this! I have to get out of here!

Now I have my cat again and I'm carrying him in his portable kennel—I'm walking out in the middle of some place at night. There are two polar bears in front of me sniffing the air! They smell my cat and me! They are going to eat my cat! I'm about to die. I know they will kill me too. I have to walk right by them in order to get home. I'm walking to the right of them a little. Now they are behind me and I am filled with terror. How will I ever be able to protect my cat from these two polar bears! I have to protect him—They know what I'm thinking! The polar bears are telepathic and they know what I'm thinking! They are telepathically telling me that they are going to eat my cat and I will have to watch them while they do this.

I'm almost home and one of the polar bears has reached its paw out to claw me! I felt it on the back of my leg—It hurt. He is just trying to scare me because he could have already killed me by now. I'm filled with terror. They are all around me. I have my cat in his kennel and I have the kennel on top of my head so the polar bears won't be able to reach him but I'm not tall enough! Now—I'm holding the kennel up in the air over my head—It's too heavy. I can't do it for long. The polar bears are standing on their back legs and they are much taller than I am. They are going to get my cat! I'm running inside.

I'm peeking out the door to the house and my cat is still in his kennel, but he is outside with the polar bears! They are walking toward him! I can't watch anymore! I run outside and scream and yell at them—I'm trying to scare the polar bears away with my voice and my arms, but they stand on their back legs and roar back at me. I should have saved my cat. I should have protected him!

This is probably one of the most unusual encounters ever published relating to alien abductions. Many of you will read this account and will have a difficult time believing this part of my night had anything to do with aliens or medical experiments. *It has everything to do with controlling me and punishing me.* Everything. It is a type of mental torture. It was as if these particular Beings were shoving as much fear and torture into my mind as they could. I can't imagine that they could have come up with anything more gruesome. And, I ask myself why I worry so much about protecting my pets from the aliens. Why can't I ever be certain that they will be safe? This is why. This has been done to me for years and this is why I am always checking to make sure my pets are safe.

Almost from the beginning of my experiences I had come to believe the possibility existed that I was being visited by several different types of aliens. However, in addition to that belief, I also speculated that some of these aliens were positive while others were indeed negative.

This tall Being emanated negativity. Not only was his physical appearance altered in such a way as to appear negative to me, he sent me negative energies when he glared at me. The illustration (I-26) I have of him represents the moment he swung his head toward me and glared at me. I believe some of the deception involved his grotesque appearance. The illustration I have drawn represents what I believe he really looked like and omits the deceptive parts, that is, his peeling skin and dangling ear. At that instant, I was feeling rage and had made the decision, mentally at least, to help the first young man who was being implanted with a device in his left nostril. My description of "the night of the living dead" represented a part of his physical appearance I did not illustrate. That is, the skin on this Being was torn, and it appeared as though it was peeling off. He had a sparse amount of hair and when his ear fell off, I could see what I thought was his real ear—a small hole in the side of his head. At one point, I was able to break free of his paralysis. This was when I decided to help the young man lying on the floor of the craft. This was also when I found myself face to face with this Being. After he pressed his ear back onto the side of his head I realized the enormous amount of deception he was employing. I told myself it must be a costume of some kind. At that moment, I suddenly found myself back in my seat. The Being then continued to work on the second man.

I believe this Being, or this type of Being, has been responsible for several of my encounters that involved grotesque, mental, tortuous type experiences, usually involving animals. Another example is the dream involving the slaughter of seals. I did not write the memory in my journal because it was too gruesome. The aliens in that particular encounter made me choose between the animals and my own family. I am not certain if each time these types of mental images are put into my mind it is being done for the same reasons. However, this particular time, I knew this visual imagery involving my cats was being forced, (actually dumped), into my mind as a type of punishment. It was then repeated over and over again until I emerged from REM sleep and finally awakened.

In my mind, there is no excuse or reason for this type of imagery to be forced into a person's mind by "good" Beings. It is negative and destructive. It is a type of mental torture and I can only associate it with negativity. Whether these aliens are imposing these types of images as a punishment for my not having followed their directions, or whether they simply enjoy doing this to me is irrelevant. I consider the aliens who do this to be unfriendly and negative. Indeed, I wrote in my journal the following day: "I awakened feeling miserable and fully expecting to find all of my cats dead. This is a terrible feeling. I know it was *them*."

10-1-92

I'm on board of a large ship that looks similar to both an aircraft carrier and an airplane. It is as wide as our house is long and about one hundred and fifty feet long. Maybe even longer. I thought I came on board with Erik, but I'm looking at the man I'm with. It is definitely not Erik. This young man has dark hair. I sense that this thing can fly so it must not be an aircraft carrier after all. The inside of this craft is mostly white and light gray. There is a lot of open space inside here, probably for cargo. This looks as if it could hold a lot of cargo. Toward the back of this craft are some seats for passengers, but not very many. They are arranged in a peculiar fashion. There are a few in the middle and along one side of the back part of this craft. I'm walking toward the back of this craft—I'm a little dizzy walking on this—the floors are made out of a white metal grid. For a minute I wasn't sure if I would fall through or not, but I remember walking on this metal grid before and I remember it's safe.

I'm sitting in a seat and I'm knocking on a window, and although it doesn't feel like glass, I can see through it. It is square-shaped like the window on that cigar-shaped craft was. I'm trying to get the attention of the young man with the dark hair. He is outside and this craft just began to move a little. Oh, he sees me. He's running toward the craft. We're not really moving, but we are about to. Maybe we're rolling or floating a little bit. Anyway, he's coming now and he won't be left behind. That would be terrible to be left here so far away from home— I'm looking out across a river that separates the U.S. from Canada. I can see tall apartment buildings and many green trees.

Oh, the ship is moving. Whatever this is I'm in—a ship or a craft—it feels unusual. Now it is leveling out. That is better. I'm on my way back home now. I'm going home.

The feel of this encounter was neutral and while it was occurring, I believed everything was as it should be. The only thing that felt a little awkward was walking on the white metal grid floor. I became dizzy and for a split second, I wasn't sure if it would hold me up. I believe this was an alien craft because when I looked out the window we were not floating in the river, we were just above the ground. The river was several hundred yards away and down a steep cliff or in a valley of some type. I believed we were in Canada, more specifically eastern Canada. I don't know how I knew where I was, it was just something I *knew*. Perhaps because I had been there before during another encounter. If I were to see this place again, I am sure that I would recognize it.

The young man with dark hair looked similar to a little boy I grew up with when I was between the ages of five and nine years old. I haven't seen him since I was seventeen, but it appears as if it may have been him. I do not consciously remember seeing anyone else although I felt there were other people on this craft. It is possible these other people, or aliens, were not on the same level of the craft that we were on.

The following is only a memory fragment, but it felt extremely familiar to me. I believe it demonstrates once again, the amount of deception involved in some of my encounters and the control it has over me.

10-2-92

Erik and I are about to make love. We are holding one another. Oh! There is my sister and her friend Ann! They are walking into our little room from an adjoining room. I'm really mad at them. It is so rude of them to just walk in on us at a time like this. Erik is leaving the room.

I'm partially sitting up on a bed or table. Ann is beginning to cry because I'm so mad at her and my sister. I think I'll apologize—Oooh! Ann is floating over towards me. I am amazed to see that she is only three feet tall and her skin is a spotted gray and silver. It's very pretty skin—I'm touching her stomach. Her skin is almost like glitter. I know this is not my sister and Ann, but in my mind, they are making me believe it is.

Although this is not a very detailed memory it does point to some obvious deception. Erik and I were not in our house, much less our bedroom, about to make love. We, or possibly an alien Being and I, were being observed by two other Beings. I never did see my sister and her friend in a visual sense, but I was made to believe it was them by way of their usual mental manipulation. The three foot tall Grey Being who floated toward me was not wearing any clothes and I did not see any genitals. Somehow, I knew it was a young female.

The following encounter is an example of two people who know one another being abducted together. I was very reluctant to tell my friend about what I remembered the following day, but the conversation seemed to flow in that direction. Prior to this encounter, I had three consecutive nights of very odd dreams that felt like visitations. However, I could not remember anything about them. The fourth night I was abducted and the experience felt extremely familiar to me. I was not upset, nor did I feel this was a negative experience. Like so many other encounters, it was simply the way it had to be.

10-29-92

I'm looking at Nancy. She is lying on her back on a black metallic table. There are two, thin black tubes surgically affixed into her right side near her lower back. There is a doctor with dark hair standing beside me. He has on a white lab coat and for some reason I believe he is from France. It is time for him to remove the tubes from my friend. "You will have to leave the room now," he says to me telepathically. I have to do what he says. There is no arguing. I'm looking around the room. It is a large room and there are others here. I think other people are being worked on. I'm walking away from Nancy and the doctor. Oh, she is crying a little. I knew it would hurt her when they removed the tubes. That procedure is going to aggravate her lower back. She already has back problems.

The following morning I spoke with Nancy on the phone and I asked her if she remembered her dreams from the night before. She said, "All I remember dreaming about was a black, triangular-shaped craft flying and flipping in the sky. I think I was outside and I felt as though I was being drawn toward the craft."

Nancy had an appointment with her doctor that morning for her back pain. During her examination her chiropractor asked her, "What in the world did you do to your back, Nancy? Somehow your problem has moved down into your lower back."

Nancy came home from her appointment and immediately telephoned me. Apparently her back problems had always been confined to her upper back. It was at this time that I relayed my complete memory to her. She took it fairly well. Later that day, Nancy called back to tell me she had a rash on her thighs and small marks on her arms that resembled the letter "C" inscribed on her skin. She tried to photograph them, but she said her hand was so shaky the pictures turned out to be very blurry. The marks had disappeared by the end of that day.

I have been very hesitant to share a lot of my memories with people because I believe everyone who is experiencing this phenomenon is at a different stage. We all have our own level of what we can accept and what we cannot accept regarding abductions. Most of my interaction with abductees is through a support group or a supportive phone conversation. However, Nancy is a good friend (and an animal lover) and we have a lot in common. She is a very strong woman and she has also been very supportive of me when I needed someone to talk to. Nancy found the information I gave her to be helpful and interesting.

Just when I thought it was safe to go back in the water again, another frightening thing happened. It is not as if I didn't ask for it.

10-30-92

I'm in bed and I feel their presence—I'm telling them I want to remember. "I want to remember the truth about what you look like; why you are here, everything—"

I don't feel very well. I have a sore throat and I'm also ovulating. I hate having this pain—I'm getting up to go into the bathroom to take a couple of aspirins.

I'm back in bed. I'm lying on my stomach and I'm looking toward the hallway. Suddenly, everything is black! Someone just made everything black. I can't even see the street light. Something is pulling me off of my bed! I'm stretching my arms out and I'm holding onto the covers. I'm screaming for Erik—there is no sound to my voice! A feeling of paralysis—The space around me is so foreign. I'm in a different space!

I'm trying to wake up Erik. I'm looking back at the hallway and I can see the street light again. I'm so terrified—I'm holding onto Erik. I fall asleep—

I'm in downtown Portland and everyone is lined up along the street. Oh my God—we're all supposed to sign up for military duty. What has happened? We are each receiving a dollar for taking the papers and signing our names. I'm wondering—when did things get this bad? What has happened that could make our society this bad?

I'm holding a piece of paper with instructions in six, or maybe eight languages on it. I'm looking up at an enlisted man. He is wearing a navy uniform. They want me to enlist. No way am I going to enlist. They can make me an officer, but I'm not about to enlist!

So much for remembering everything. Normally, this is the part of the abduction I rarely remember. I usually do not remember going and coming back, but I seem to remember quite a bit about what happens to me while I am with them. I felt a primal fear response when the space around me was altered. I was feeling something that I can only describe as having lived on this planet for thirty-two years and being submerged in water for the first time in my life, without ever knowing water existed in the first place. The space around me felt so different that I can only describe it as having an other-dimensional quality.

I'm not sure what to make of this dream memory. It felt to me as if the aliens were giving me information about my future again and it looked pretty bleak. Of course, this very well could have been an implanted memory to prevent me from remembering what really took place.

On the evening of November 1, I was goofing around with Erik, my dog, and my gray cat. I had my socks on and I had my gray cat in my arms. I extended my cat out in front of me and ran across the kitchen floor. Then I slid on my socks towards my dog and shouted, "Floating gray alien cat!" My dog freaked out, my cat jumped to safety, and I landed on my forehead and my knees. How I ended up in that position I'll never know. My knees were purple for two weeks. I hadn't felt that kind of pain since I stuck the metal end of an umbrella into my foot when I was five years old. Lucky for me I have tough knee caps. Nothing was broken (that I could tell) and I spent the next two days with my legs extended outward and in front of me. Two nights later the aliens came back.

11-3-92

I'm lying on my back on a table and there are several large-eyed aliens standing around me.

Ugh! I think I'm going to throw up! I'm looking at my left knee! The aliens have given me a device to use to look inside my left leg! There isn't anything inside it! I'm looking through a hole in my left knee with the device they gave me and I can't see anything! They have taken my bone out! I'm freaking out. The aliens are right beside me and they know I'm awake—and they know that I know that they know! Oh my God! I can hardly breathe. I'm getting out of control—

concentrate on breathing. Okay. "They" did this! I can't believe it. Where is my bone? Where is my knee cap? There are a few aliens on the other side of the room studying something. They look relatively tall and have light tan skin. They must have my bones! They must be working on them! I don't understand how they can do this!

The day after this memory I was experiencing so much disbelief that I didn't even look at my legs. It was too unbelievable for me to even consider taking seriously. The second day after this memory I had just finished with my shower and I was putting lotion on my legs. I had my leg up on the counter and my face was just a few inches from my left knee. It was like bending over and discovering a cockroach just inches away from your face. There, just above my left knee, at the same location I was looking into my leg using the alien device, was a hairline scar. All I could do was moan.

I went into my bedroom and tried to think about the history of that knee. It was the same knee that had a large sore on it when I was five years old. It took six months to heal and my mother and father were always asking me what I did to it. I never knew what happened. One day there was this huge sore on it and it wouldn't go away. Every time I walked, or bathed, or played, the sore would start bleeding again. I have a rather thick scar from that sore today. This thick scar is lower on my knee and is in a different location from the hairline scar.

I was still thinking about that knee. My mind drifted to the year 1990. I was visiting my brother and his wife and I had a peculiar memory surface in a dream. I was looking down at my left knee and there was something just under the skin. I think I got it out or someone else got it out. Somehow, a dark brown object shaped like a thin capsule came out of an incision on my left knee exactly where I have the thick scar today. And two inches below the newly discovered hairline scar. During the memory of this thin, brown capsule, it was so disgusting to me I thought I would vomit. I was so happy to have it out of my body. After I remembered this I told my husband about it, but I never recorded it in my journal because I found it too disgusting to write down.

I have always wondered about that scar and my mother has even asked me about it several times as an adult. "She is the mother," I would think to myself. "Doesn't *she* know where I got this scar from?" Today, I believe I know where these two scars came from although I don't know the purpose for the dark brown capsule-shaped object, or the procedure the aliens performed when they removed my knee cap and the bone in my left leg. I still find it inconceivable that they could perform these invasive surgical procedures without my finding blood, or at least some bruises. If the aliens are really capable of these types of surgical techniques, they are beyond my comprehension.

I have often wondered if maybe I didn't damage something in my left knee or left leg from my silly stunt in the kitchen. This is the only logical explanation I can come up with for their interest in my knee cap and shin bone. However, it does not explain why the aliens weren't interested in my right leg. After all, my right leg bore more of the brunt of the fall. Could they have looked at both of the bones in my legs? Perhaps I am only able to remember one of two procedures they performed on me that night. Certainly, if they had done this type of surgery to my right leg, I would have found another hairline scar on it also, but I didn't.

The following encounter was peculiar in that the behavior of this Being was totally illogical. In any case, as unusual as it may sound, I found him to be quite beautiful.

11-14-92

I'm outside with a small, slender male Being. He has black eyes and messy black hair. His eyes are pretty—they are large and black and they curve upward. He is really very pretty. (I-10) *His skin is somewhat shiny—It is very different from our skin. I don't know why but I find him attractive. Oh—he wants to mate with me. He just told me telepathically. He wants to mate with me and—I find him attractive—*

Now I know he is mentally manipulating me into feeling this way about him. It is getting stronger. I really want him now—I'm "thinking" a message to him. "I really love Erik—This is wrong." I'm wondering if he has AIDS—another good reason to resist his mental control over me.

Suddenly, we are in another place. He is manipulating me again. He is trying to make me believe he is a rock singer. He is some distance away from me. He still wants me. I'm in a halfway reclined position and I'm naked. I can feel a warm sensation coming down from above me. It is similar to sunlight only I do not see any light. I think there are others around me too. This is strange. I should be embarrassed, but I'm not. He is communicating with me telepathically. He still wants me.

Now I am standing up and I am facing this thin Being. He is telling me that all of the people think he is evil. They think he is the Devil. I'm looking around and it looks as if the ground has been charred. I wonder if there was a fire here recently. Oh, I think he wants me to believe he did this to the ground. He is trying to make me believe he is evil, but I don't want to believe it. There is something about him that is very alien, but he is not evil. He is not the Devil. Now he is handing something to me. It looks like a device with many thin black straps. It has something to do with his hands. I'm taking it from him and I am very happy to have something of his. I am grateful to have this and I will put it away so no one else will see it. I will protect him. I am taking his hands in my hands—I am holding his hands with both of my hands. Again, he is telling me that he is evil. I'm looking at his hands very carefully. I'm thinking, "Surely he is an alien but he is not evil." His hands are very thin and frail. His fingers are extremely long and skinny. I am holding them in my hands and I am counting his fingers, but I don't want him to know this. I am trying to count his fingers without staring at them too much. This is so unusual. He has ten fingers on each hand. Each finger looks as if two bones fused—there are double knuckles on each finger. There is a very thin layer of skin covering the fingers and he has black fingernails. (I-11) I'm holding both of his hands in my hands and they are very close to my face. I am very gentle with him. I'm trying to conceal my thoughts from him because I believe he is an alien and his hands appear very unusual to me. I don't want him to know that I'm thinking this. His hands are so delicate.

As strange as this may sound to many people, I felt love for this alien and I found him attractive. If I had been single, I would surely have made love with him. This may indeed be manipulation at its finest, but I believe it is important to be honest. There is some missing memory and I can only make a guess as to what happened when I was lying naked on the table and in a partially reclined position. The warm feeling I felt coming down from above me was the same warm feeling I felt when I was walking through the craft that I believed had landed in England. It was warm and comforting, but not hot.

The alien's illogical behavior stands out in this experience: his wanting to "mate" with me while at the same time wanting to make me believe he was evil. This double message I received from him made me feel as though I was being manipulated into loving someone, or protecting someone who was evil. I'm not sure why the aliens would want this done. I still do not believe he is evil. Certainly there have been some encounters, most notably the experience on 9-23-92, where I felt the Beings I was interacting with were evil or negative. But for the most part, I do not feel they are vindictive. It is a feeling that they are alien along with everything that word implies.

I drew this alien's hands immediately after this encounter because they seemed so different from anything I have ever seen or imagined before. When I was holding his hands, I believed my feelings of how strange they seemed to me should be shielded from his mind. I did not want to offend him. It is my belief that the thin black straps were some kind of device he wore over his hands to make them appear differently. I believe he wanted me to know I was special by showing me his hands. At the time, I felt that not very many people were allowed to see his hands while they were uncovered.

On December 6, I had a memory surface in a dream. I had been having a recurring dream that involved flying underneath a canopy of trees. That is where the memory always ended until now.

12-6-92

> *I'm flying in a craft. There is a large window above me and I can see upwards and outside. We are flying underneath a canopy of trees. It is fall and the leaves are all golden and beautiful. These must be large trees because we are flying underneath them. We must be in one of those neighborhoods with tall trees that make a tunnel along the street.*
>
> *I wonder how can we fly so low without hitting the trees?*
>
> *We are exiting the canopy of trees. Suddenly, there is a cliff and I can see a city. It is Syracuse, New York. There is a tall white building—the city is off to my left.*
>
> *Now we are banking sharply to the right, and we are moving upwards at a very steep angle. I think the pilot must be having trouble since we were flying underneath the trees a minute ago. Now we are going down—we are going down rather quickly. We have landed.*
>
> *We are all getting out of the craft. I don't remember seeing an airplane and now I don't believe we were ever in an airplane. Erik is with me and we are going to a hotel. I think I see telephones in my mind's eye, and I tell Erik to get us another flight out of here. "I don't care what time it leaves or what kind of plane it is, just get us out of here." Erik is going to try to make some telephone calls and get us out of here. I think I'm going to our room. We have to get out of here. We can't be gone any longer than 24 hours. We have to get back to the house to take care of our family—our pets. They can't be away from us any longer than twenty-four hours.*
>
> *I think I'm in our hotel room and there is a strange looking male in here with me—*
>
> *Now I'm not sure where I am. I think there is some deception going on here. He is trying to make me believe I'm in Pensacola at my old house. He is trying to create a conflict in my mind. I know I'm not really there. We are outside now and he is asking me what a particular structure is. He is trying to create a mental conflict in my mind, but I'm not going to let him. I'm going to fight him on this.*
> *"What is this?" He asks me forcefully.*

> *"I don't know." I reply.*
> *I'm looking down into a large hole that is about six to eight feet wide and about thirty feet deep. It is made out of newly poured concrete. It looks like a new missile silo—Now—suddenly, I'm sinking. I'm sinking! I think I'm sinking down into wet concrete. This male Being is looking at me and he is pleased. I feel as though I'm going to drown in wet concrete and this male Being is looking at me and he is pleased! It seems as though he can feel my terror. I feel as though I am going to die. This feeling amuses him. I think I'm crying out for Erik.*

The flight in the craft is fairly straightforward. I believe I was in a craft and we were indeed flying through a neighborhood. Again, I seemed to know that I was in Syracuse, New York, although I have never been there before. I'm not sure if I should put too much emphasis on the events that occurred after we got off the craft. It seemed this male Being did in fact do something to me that made me feel I was going to drown in a thick liquid substance. Parts of this memory may also be a screen memory.

Two nights later I found myself at a training camp again, and if I'm not mistaken, I saw The Doctor again too.

12-8-92

> *I'm at a training camp. There are several males with dark skin standing next to me. We are all lined up and we are training. We are moving our legs in a peculiar fashion. Another male is being corrected. He was marching and the way we are supposed to move is not supposed to look like a march. Another male is demonstrating how this is to be done. We are supposed to slowly lift our legs, bend our knees, and move each leg slowly outward and away from our bodies. This requires more energy than I thought it would. I feel as though this is a type of an aerobic exercise as well as a coordination building exercise. We are training for something and this is a warm-up exercise to help get us into shape. We have been training for about an hour or so.*

> *Now we are finished with this part of the training. Most of the males are getting ready to go to bed. We each have a small room that consists of a door, a small room, and a bed. It is only large enough for two people to stand side by side. The bed is for one person only. Above the exterior of the door is a shelf for our personal belongings. I want to get out of here really badly. I don't want to sleep here and I'm going to leave. I'm taking off the clothes they gave me to wear and I'm naked now. I'm reaching up to the little shelf for my nightgown and I'm putting it back on. I'm very agitated. There is a four foot tall, very petite female standing next to me. She has large, round, brown eyes.*

"I have never seen those before," she says to me while staring at my breasts.
"Well, wherever you're from—" and then I pause and say, "That doesn't surprise me."

I'm putting my nightgown over my head thinking how stupid this little female is. She is really irritating me.

I'm haphazardly shoving my things into a white bag. I have mostly toiletries: tampons, a toothbrush, dental floss, and some jewelry, although I don't recognize the jewelry. There was the clothing they gave me to wear while I was there—that went into the bag too. This is like a group dormitory. The petite, female Being and I are the only two females in our group. The rest of the occupants are males with dark skin. One is definitely an African-American. He was standing next to me during the exercises. He is very muscular and attractive. I've decided to leave, and I'm walking out of the room with my bag.

I'm standing in a huge elevator now. I have the white bag on the floor in front of me and I'm wearing my blue bathrobe over my nightgown now. At least one, or maybe all, of the elevator walls are transparent.

Oh no—I've just seen our group leader and he has seen me. It's The Doctor. It has been a long time since I've seen him.

I'm trying to look away from him. I don't want him to know that I'm leaving. I'm looking down, and I'm trying to hide my face. He begins to communicate with me telepathically, "So, you're going to leave."

I'm looking away from him and I feel terrible that he saw me. Again, telepathy, "Go ahead and leave. Just leave. I don't care."
I feel terrible. I've disappointed him tremendously. I don't want to leave now because it will reflect on him and my entire group. I've made a commitment to do something and I can't back out now. I'm getting off the elevator and I'm running through a little garden area inside this place. My trainer, my group leader—I think it's The Doctor—he is walking away from me and I'm trying to catch up with him. He is angry with me. I'm telling him, "I'm not going to leave. I'm not leaving, see? I'm here."

Now I'm being escorted by a female. She is taking me into another room. It has soda drinks, alcohol, snacks, and some other foods from Earth. She tells me, "See, we have special things here too. You can have the same things here that you have at home—"

> *I'm so angry now. I feel as if she is trying to bribe me with food! I'm thinking to myself, "I don't want this! This isn't why I'm here! I'm going to stay for the right reasons! Not for this stuff!"*
>
> *The Doctor—is he my group leader? We are together and he is explaining something to me. He must have known I felt uncomfortable with all of the males and the petite female Being during our training session. He is telling me, telepathically, "You were put with that group because you are all in relatively the same physical shape. It was done to help facilitate your training." His words make me feel somewhat better. I feel extremely committed to him and this cause.*

I awakened feeling extremely fatigued and my vision was particularly blurry again. I recorded this memory and how I felt in my journal, and continued my daily routine. It was a difficult day because my vision was so distorted. This type of visual distortion has become somewhat common for me after an experience. I also felt as if I had been up all night.

The first thing I wondered about was if I had finally seen The Doctor again. It had been a long time since I had seen him or The Blonde, and I assumed they were either finished with me or had decided not to let me remember seeing them anymore. It was unusual when I looked at him. Although I felt embarrassed that he had seen me, it was more so because he was probing my thoughts. He instantly knew what I was thinking and that I was planning to leave. I wonder what it is that I have committed myself to? What kind of project could require that I go through training in a physical sense?

The petite female Being was definitely alien. She was about four feet tall, had a round face with large round and very brown eyes. I do not know for certain but I believe she may have been a hybrid. She looked alien, but she had some human qualities also. She had medium brown hair which did not seem unusual to me. That is to say, it did not look messy or artificial as if it were a wig. She also had emotions because when she said "I have never seen those before" she was very curious and almost like a child. I am not sure why her presence aggravated me so. I may have been in an aggravated state because I knew I was away from my home and I knew I couldn't sleep there with the rest of my group. I very much wanted to get home. Although it is impossible to say whether or not I am correct, I feel I am close to understanding or remembering what it was I was doing there.

12-18-92

> *This is strange. I'm looking for a phone. I've been told I'm supposed to call Andrew, an old friend from high school. I do not know why they want me to call him. We have not kept in touch with one another. We never really got along with one another either. I think this is*

manipulation. I'm looking for a phone. I think I see one, but it is unusual looking. I think I'm supposed to put my I.D. card in it in order for it to work, but I don't have an I.D. card.

I'm looking for another phone. Now someone is giving me a telephone number. It's in my head: 2-4-X-7-6-6-X—Over and over again. Someone wants me to call this number very badly. It just keeps repeating over and over inside my head. It is as if it is being beamed into my mind.

Oh—now I'm getting into a strange vehicle. Someone is sliding a panel over to me. The panel is in front of me now. A female is sliding a view screen over the top of this panel. I can see myself in it. It looks very modern looking. It looks like a screen made out of a transparent material, but I can see myself in it. The female says to me, "Here is the phone. We have to start moving in order for it to work."

Now we are moving and I'm wondering why this phone can only operate while we are moving. It is a very elaborate phone. I think someone can see me through the view screen. Maybe this is one of those new phones we're going to have one day. The kind everyone will have in their homes one day. This must be the type of phone you talk on, and the person on the other side can see your image while you are talking. I wonder why I have to ride in this vehicle for it to work?

Oh! Now I think I'm really inside one their crafts! We are moving very close to the ground. I can see it. I feel as if I have butterflies in my stomach. The craft is making sudden dips and turns. I should be afraid because we are flying very close to the ground. We are following the contour of the ground very closely! We are flying over a rocky area and I can see a little stream. I wonder how we can fly so close to the ground and follow every contour without having an accident? This is an unusual craft—Oh, someone is to my left. I think Erik is to my left. The female is piloting the craft and Erik is here with me. He is looking at me and he's smiling. Although he looks somewhat surprised, I think he is enjoying riding in this craft.

Now we are doing some maneuvers over the water. I almost feel as if we are floating on top of a stream that has a fast current, but I'm not getting wet. I think I'm still inside the craft. Although I'm not sure how we can fly like this, I'm having fun.

Okay, now I'm looking for another phone. The number 2-4-X-7-6-6-X—I'm repeating it over and over in my mind. They want me to call

Andrew, but I don't want to. I don't really like him. This number is being repeated over and over again.

I'm standing in a long line to use a phone. There is a young male—He is going to let me use the phone ahead of everyone else. This is strange. I don't think I know how to use this phone. I should be able to use this phone, but I do not know how.

What could be the significance of this number? Clearly it is a telephone number. The prefix is a prefix right here in Portland. (I have intentionally omitted two numbers for the publication of this book.) It is quite possible the 2-4-X prefix is probably a prefix in many different cities as well as Portland. The following day, my curiosity got the best of me and I dialed the telephone number. An elderly lady answered the phone and although I did not have the nerve to tell her the aliens gave me her telephone number, I did ask for a fictitious name. She in turn said I had the wrong number and when I asked her if this was 2-4-X-7-6-6-X she said no it wasn't. Smart lady. But, I called back and when she answered again, I knew I had dialed the number correctly. I apologized for bothering her a second time and hung up the phone. I then sent the aliens a strong mental communiqué: If you're going to ask me to contact someone, you are going to have to give me a little more to go on. I do not know if they ever received my message, of course. It was only a thought. I could have done some research to find out which city Andrew is living in to see if the prefix matched, but I am of the opinion that, since the aliens know me so well, they can darn sure be more specific if they want me to telephone someone.

This leads me to believe the part of my memory that involved the phone and the phone number were probably part of a screen memory. It was the first and last thing I remembered about this encounter. A phone was even used to get me on board the craft in the first place, and it could not operate properly unless the craft was moving.

It is probable that the only true memory about this encounter was when Erik and I were flying in the craft very close to the ground and the stream.

My last encounter of 1992 left me with more questions than answers. Because the aliens follow their own agenda very strictly, I do not have a final experience that neatly ties all the loose ends up for this book. December 30 was my last visitation of 1992. All I wanted was some time to finish the manuscript.

12-30-92

Oh, great. I was visited again. I am sure they were here, but I don't remember that much about the experience. I was hoping they would leave me alone. I can't believe this. I know I felt their presence, but that is all. I am very depressed today. I always become depressed when they visit me and do not let me remember the encounter. All I know is today, the morning after their visit, I have started menstruating ten days early, and I do not know what they did to me to make this happen.

Recently, I have felt as though I have been having long and involved conversations with the Beings about my book. It is almost as if they are grilling me for reasons and explanations. All I remember about the conversations is that they are extremely intense and much dialogue transpires during the conversations. I do not know why they are doing this. I do not know if they are guiding me or not. I've always recorded what I remembered, whether I understood it or not. They rarely explain things to me. If they have given me answers to my questions, then it is their wish that I not remember them at this time.

All I wanted was some time out from them so I could finish this book. I know they know I am writing this. Why else would they make this last visit so obvious?

It is evident I would have liked to have remembered this last encounter, but this may have been another one of their great ironies. My last visit of 1992, the last journal entry for my book, and no memory.

CHAPTER 13

The Guys

My nickname for the aliens who have been visiting me is "The Guys." I thought this would be an appropriate name for this chapter since the following descriptions represent what I have learned about the different Beings who have interacted with me. I will describe each type and will explain what my interaction with them was like. I have chosen designations such as "Type One" or "Type Two" for my own convenience because this is how I perceive them. I have not researched other people's work into these category types because I wanted to base my conclusions on my interactions with the alien Beings and not from other people's research.

Hybrid Beings: These Beings sometimes appear very human looking but have unusual eyes and skull shapes. Their skin color ranges from orange-tan, to brown-tan, to gray, to a chalk-white. It is possible that these Beings were created from a combination of genetic material from a Grey, Tan, or white-skinned alien and a human being, or a Being who is physiologically similar to humans. They communicate by way of telepathy, and I am able to communicate with them using my speaking voice and by sending them my thoughts. They are able to understand me using both of these types of communication. The shape of their eyes, their height, and their bone structure vary greatly, and this is apparent in my illustrations. I almost always observe vertical pupils within either black eyes, dark brown eyes, vivid blue eyes, or orange eyes. I have never seen anything on the side of their heads that looked like ears and they all have hair on the tops of their heads. They walk as we do and I have never seen a hybrid levitate. The clothing they wear normally consists of a light or neutral-colored body suit, sometimes with a white lab coat over it and other times without the lab coat. It is possible that some of the hybrids I have interacted with are not the first generation born from a cross between humans or human appearing Beings. It is also important to consider the possibility that Beings with similar physical characteristics to ours exist on other planets and possibly in other dimensions.

In my experiences with the hybrids they almost always appear to be working on an important project and are simply doing their job. I have rarely observed hybrids in a command position. They usually behave as scientists who are on an important mission. I believe the hybrids are working for another race of aliens and *possibly* certain elements of our government. In some of my experiences they were seen with the Greys.

Most all of the hybrid adults have exhibited some form of emotion while interacting with me. Usually it is amusement, frustration, distrust, or surprise.

They have probed my mind and have implanted false visual images in order to try to camouflage their appearance. They have performed laparoscopy-type procedures on me to remove eggs or to implant what I believe to be genetic material, or enzymes or chemicals that I feel might effect my genetic make-up. They have taken skin samples, blood samples, hair samples, measurements of my body and have performed brain stimulation or brain mapping procedures on me. They are also interested in my thoughts, emotions and beliefs. Examples from my illustrations: The Doctor, The Female, A Messenger, The Tan Doctor, The Father, The Female with the Long Black Hair, and The Hybrid with Twenty Fingers. It is my belief that The Pudgy Doctor is also a hybrid and he is pictured on a separate page with two Type Two Greys.

Type One Grey: Of the four types of Greys I have seen, the most unusual is the three to three-and-a-half foot tall Grey. Sometimes they have skin that appears so old and worn I observe tones of brown instead of gray. These Beings appear to move about by floating or levitating themselves through the air. I have never seen one of these Beings walk or stand as humans do. They have very small bodies with thin arms and legs and no noticeable musculature. Their fingers are very thin and since I have never focused on their feet, I have never seen their toes. They are hairless and have triangular-shaped or oblong-shaped heads. They also have very large black eyes which are oval-shaped and sometimes have a slight curve or tapered point at the outer corners. Their noses are barely detectable and I have never noticed any ears. Their mouths are very small and slight usually appearing as a thin line. I have never seen one of these Greys wearing clothing, nor have I observed genitals.

It was apparent from my encounter with this type of Grey, that I was terrified the first time I saw one. It was not its appearance that made me feel this way but rather the presence or energy that was associated with it. It is my belief that this particular type of Grey has the ability to paralyze and levitate me. It may also be possible they have the ability to use their thought processes alone, or a combination of thought and technology to physically alter and manipulate my body during an encounter.

I do not remember communicating with this type of Grey, however, they appear to be capable of reading my thoughts. They are normally in a position of observation and control. I also feel they may be at the top of the command structure. I do not feel as if these Greys can relate to my emotions in the manner that the hybrids can, but even the hybrids seem to lack patience when dealing with my emotions. I have a tendency to refer to these Greys as "grandfather" aliens because they seem so old and are apparently respected by the second type of Grey, which I will describe next.

During my encounters with the Type One Greys I have observed them acting as observers, controllers, and "mind probers." These types of Greys may also be responsible for mentally implanting thoughts and images into my mind. I would like to stress that they *feel* the most alien of all the Beings I have ever encountered because of their presence. An example from my illustrations is The Floating Grandfather Alien.

Type Two Grey: The second type of Grey is slightly taller than the Type One Grey: about four feet tall. During my experiences they wear light gray, tight-fitting body suits. Their skin is also light gray. They are hairless and have large heads that are triangular or oblong-shaped with a pointed chin. They have large, black, upswept eyes with no detectable pupil, and their noses are very slight. Their lips are thin and appear almost like a straight line. These types of Greys tend to look very much alike. They appear to stand on their feet, unlike the Type One Grey. They have minimal emotions, however, I have noticed a few instances when they seemed surprised or puzzled by my behavior. They are task-oriented individuals who work dutifully and are not easily distracted. During my encounters I am never afraid of them and the feelings I receive from the Type Two Greys are neutral. Their behavior leads me to conclude they are scientists and biological technicians. There is one exception: I am still unable to explain the reasons why the Type Two Grey (who raised his arms as if to say "boo!") was being held in the see-through room by men wearing military uniforms.

These aliens have performed surgery on me, have (possibly) helped me interact with babies, and have taught me about their travel routes and the operations of some of their crafts. They are capable of telepathic communication and are able to understand me when I speak to them or "think" messages to them. An example from my illustrations is The Heart Operation.

Type Three Grey: The third type of Grey I have interacted with is about five and a half feet to six feet tall. The shapes of their heads, eyes, and faces are similar to the Type Two Grey I described above, except that they have a bony ridge around their eyes and forehead area. They also wear light gray, tight-fitting body suits. The differentiating characteristics with these Greys are their height and their "missions." They also have hair on the tops of their heads although it looks unusual. I sometimes feel they are wearing wigs, but the idea of real hair should not be ruled out. I believe these types of Greys have the ability to deal with our emotions more easily than the Type One Greys or the Type Two Greys.

I have observed the Type Three Greys working alongside humans that I feel are either in the military, or in some other government capacity. They are normally navigating, that is, piloting the cigar-shaped crafts. I also feel they may be responsible for more of the behind-the-scenes operations. These Greys have communicated with me telepathically but usually only when they feel it is necessary. They do not appear to be interested in me in a biological sense and I do not believe they are scientists. What I feel about them most strongly is that they are similar to pilots in our military. I believe they may be pilots and test pilots and are the Beings who fly some of these "missions." I have experienced neutral feelings and being somewhat happily excited when I'm with them. This usually occurs because I'm on the base where they are working and I am able to view their, or "our," very unusual crafts. Examples from my drawings are The Blonde Female Grey (pilot/navigator), and The Navigator inside a cigar-shaped craft.

Type Four Grey: This type of Grey is about seven feet tall. I believe I have seen a female and a male. I have only seen them one time each that I remember. They have very large heads and very round, large, black eyes without pupils. They do not have ears, and their lips are very thin. Their bodies appear extremely thin and they have very long arms and extremely long, thin legs. When they walk they must bend over slightly to facilitate locomotion. I believe this has something to do with their extreme height and the structure of their backbones. During my experiences with the Type Four Greys, I could not detect any clothing and I could not see any genitals. Their skin was a medium gray color.

I had only brief experiences with this type of Grey, but during those experiences they were highly admired and respected by the Type Two Greys, The Female, and myself. I have concluded that these aliens are at the top of the hierarchy. They came across to me as very serious individuals. I felt I was either being checked on, as one would check a progress report, or I was being tested by them. An example from my drawings is The Diplomat.

White-skinned Alien Beings: This type of alien looks extremely similar to the Type Two Grey described earlier with the exception of their skin. It is possible they are the same type of Being and the only difference is their skin color. Their skin is chalk-white in appearance and they usually wear white body suits instead of gray ones. I have not had much interaction with them, but the experience I remembered was intense. I was on their craft and they told me I should prepare for something which they felt was extremely important. After they telepathically communicated this information, I believed this event was supposed to happen in the near future. Although the information I received left me with a feeling of impending doom, these Beings themselves were pleasant.

Reptilian Tan Being: My experiences with a Reptilian Tan showed me they are somewhat similar looking to the Greys. The most notable differences are their eyes and skin color. Their skin color ranges from an orange color to a tan color. Their eye sockets are large like the Greys but the Reptilian Tans have golden to orange eyes with vertical pupils. Their skin is sometimes extremely shiny and smooth. The Reptilian Tan I saw had a rather large bony ridge that protruded around his eye sockets and forehead area. The Reptilian was approximately six feet (possibly six and a half feet) tall. He communicated by way of telepathy and I communicated with him by way of telepathy also. I found him to be more muscular than the other Beings with the exception of The Blonde. The Blonde's and The Reptilian's physique are approximately equal. I found the Reptilian Tan's presence to be positive or pleasant. I also found him pleasing to look at.

Praying Mantis-type Being: I have had one encounter with an ebony-skinned, Praying Mantis-type Being. She was approximately six feet tall and although she was quite unusual looking, I was not really afraid of her. She did not wear any clothing and I saw something which was extremely white where our genitals are located. During the encounter, I assumed these were her genitals. She was capable of telepathic communication and mentally implanting visual images in my mind. I felt she was kind and positive and did not intend to harm me in any way. When she walked she moved like the Type Four Grey I described earlier. She had to bend over, and then her back would move in an unusual manner when she would move her legs. When this movement occurred, this is when I could see what I thought were her genitals. She was extremely thin and it almost appeared as if she were literally skin and bones, (possibly an exoskeleton). I did not see enough muscle anywhere on her body to lead me to believe that she was anything but a skeletal structure covered in a beautiful ebony-colored skin.

Blue-skinned Being: This type of Being has very beautiful, pale blue skin. The Being who was interacting with me was a female and at the time I thought she was a child. Today I believe she may have been an adult. While I was interacting with her I thought she was a most spectacularly wise Being. She was the first alien Being I remembered. She had a very round head, large round eyes, a small nose, and a small round mouth. The Being I saw was about four feet tall with a petite body build. Her eyes were the same color as her skin. She had no hair anywhere on her body and I did not detect any clothing, nor did I see any genitals. My feelings during the time I was with her were of profound love. She communicated with me telepathically and I believed her to be exceptionally spiritually advanced. During our contact with one another we were being observed by the Greys or possibly the Tans. It is possible she may have been forced to interact with me and may have been held against her will, or perhaps she interacted with the Greys in order to fulfill a more important mission of her own. She appeared much wiser (almost "all-knowing") than any other alien Being I have encountered.

The Blonde: The particular type of Blonde Being in my experiences may not require a physical body all of the time. The Blonde I have had experiences with appears to be a minimum of six feet tall and has an attractive build. He has beautiful blue eyes and I have observed vertical pupils in them. I am not certain if I have ever seen his ears or if he even has any. His nose is slender and his lips are also slender, however, they have much more shape to them than the Greys'. He has blonde hair and it is usually messy. When he is in physical form, I believe his hair is as real as his body, that is, it is not a wig. I have never sensed anything but positive feelings from this Being when he appears as a Blonde. I also have extremely positive feelings for him. Indeed, the first time I drew a picture of him, I inadvertently drew a yellow halo or aura around his head because I felt such positive feelings from him, as well as for him.

During my experiences with The Blonde, he seems interested in my welfare and has sometimes apologized ahead of time for some of the things he was about to do. He is also very interested in my spiritual advancement and my ability to feel empathy for other animals, including humans. The Blonde has also worked alongside The Doctor and he appears to be subordinate to him. Sometimes I believed he was working with The Doctor and the Greys so he could be in a position to interact with me for teaching purposes. He has aided the doctor in taking blood and/or bone marrow samples from my leg. He has also performed gynecological procedures on me, and I believe our interactions together have been observed by the Greys. If I did not know better, I would say that I have time-traveled with The Blonde and other Beings in order for them to teach me certain lessons. If I did not time-travel with him, then I would say he has taken me into other dimensions. We may, however, find out one day that time-travel and moving through or into other dimensions are the same thing. I have seen him transform from a cat into a large beam of white energy and then back into himself (as a Blonde), and from a spotted-skinned Being into a dog, and then back into himself (again as a Blonde). I believe all of these transformations were done for teaching purposes.

Tan Being: I have seen several Tan Beings who appeared similar looking to the Greys with one exception: the color of their skin is a light tan or sometimes a pale yellow-tan. They range in height from about four feet to six feet tall. Their facial features are similar to the Type Two Greys and the Type Three Greys. I do not recall ever seeing this type of Being wearing clothes, nor do I remember seeing any genitals. The experience I remember most clearly when I saw a Tan Being involved the Reptilian Tan. The Tan Being was standing behind the Reptilian Tan and was also the Being employing the camouflage, that is, the elf ears. I felt a positive presence associated with both of these Beings and found their strong facial features and their tall height very attractive.

Green-Gray Grey: This particular type of Being is also similar in appearance to the Type Two Greys except for their skin color. Their skin is a very dark gray-green. Erik saw this particular Being during an encounter with what he termed "the Greys" and stated that his face and head were somewhat longer than the others (meaning other Greys).

Spotted Tiny Beings: These are the small aliens I saw in the room with the taller female instructor types, when I thought I may have been on a military base. These Beings are tiny, about twelve to eighteen inches tall. They have very round heads, round eyes, tiny noses, and mouths. I do not know if I saw their eyes or not. It appeared to me that they had their eyes closed. It looked as though an eyelid or something that was the same color as their flesh was covering their eyes. However, this is what I thought about the Blue Being (9-12-87) and the hybrid child (1-27-89). It may be that their eyes did not have pupils and were indeed the same color as their skin (or a slightly lighter shade).

These tiny Beings have a light tan to a yellowish color skin. Evenly distributed throughout the skin are indentations which look similar to uneven scoop mark scars. These indentations are a brown and tan color and are a darker pigment than their skin. When the Blonde transformed his image to appear as a frightful looking Being during the encounter on 5-30-90, his skin appeared identical to that of these tiny spotted aliens. Although I believe their overall form and size are probably true to what I saw, I believe they, or the tall females who were instructing them, were employing a defense mechanism. They may have altered their skin in such a way as to make me think they were ugly or frightful. If you will remember, they were terrified of me when I opened the door and stood in the doorway. The only defense they may have had against me was to make me fear them. Perhaps they thought I would find their skin ugly to look at and would not want to touch them or pick them up.

Humanoids: This is a general term that relates to anything human looking with a head, torso, two arms, and two legs. Although I have tried to keep the two categories separate, it is possible that the categories called "Humanoid" and "Hybrid" might overlap sometimes. When I saw a Being I considered to be a hybrid, it is because it appeared to be a composite of two or more Beings. It really looked like a hybrid Being to me. When I use the term "humanoid" it is because it had a humanoid appearance, but I do not remember exactly what the Being looked like, or it resembled a human, but I didn't retain a clear image in my memory.

Now that I have explained my definition of a humanoid, I have to contradict myself just this once. The exception is the category "evil humanoids" or the Beings I described as "the night of the living dead" creatures. I saw at least one of them clearly enough to draw. When you look at the drawing you might want to say he is really a hybrid. He was tall and wore a tattered body suit. He had small, glossy black eyes, four long, bony fingers, and was telepathic. He also commanded a strong negative or fearful

presence and
was able to paralyze me with what I perceived to be nothing more than a look.

The Children: I have seen many infants and children during my experiences. Their appearance varies greatly, probably due to the many different species and races of their parents. I have included illustrations of the children I have seen or held and remember most clearly. My emotions with the children have run the full spectrum. I do not recall ever having negative feelings toward an infant or child simply because of who they were or what they were doing. If these emotions were apparent, they were due to my reaction to the circumstances or physical condition of the infant or child.

CHAPTER 14

Why Are They Here?

After I realized I had been having abduction experiences I made an intentional effort not to read much about UFOs, the alien abduction phenomenon or phenomena related to it. I did not want what I read to influence my memories and conclusions about my abduction experiences. I will, therefore, draw mostly from my own experiences when covering information relating to why the aliens are here.

The question most commonly asked of me is: Why are the aliens here and what are they doing? My experiences have shown me certain things that might enable me to add a piece or two to this corner of the alien jigsaw puzzle.

Because of certain geological, historical, and anthropological evidence, I believe it is *possible* that alien Beings have been visiting this planet for thousands of years. The aliens appear to be conducting a longitudinal study on specific human lineages. In the field of psychology, a longitudinal study evaluates a group of subjects at several points in time, over a number of years, or even decades as may be the case with the aliens. This type of study can assess how certain characteristics or behaviors change during the course of development.

My experiences have shown me that the aliens are interested in human psychology. This is evident in my encounters that involve theatrical concepts, teaching dreams, and visions. Stimuli have been presented to me through a variety of methods and the aliens have observed, and perhaps recorded my reactions. Regarding this recording process, telepathy may offer an alien species the opportunity to learn and experience along with the abductee and the Being who is in direct contact with the abductee.

The aliens have studied my psychological reactions and thought processes involving several different emotions. However, they seem most interested in my ability to feel empathy. They have studied my ability to feel empathy towards animals (including food and exotic animals) and human beings (including infants and children), and they have tested my feelings and thoughts about vegetarianism and animals' rights. In addition, they have shown some interest in our environment and how I respond to the concept of war and disaster, and sometimes even "future" events.

It is my belief that some of the aliens have used my reproductive organs to obtain genetic material in order to create life. I do not remember experiencing a "missing fetus" after having been examined by a human doctor and told I was pregnant. However, I have memories of similar events occurring with hybrid or alien doctors during an abduction. My mother, however, experienced a "missing fetus" that occurred just prior to her pregnancy with me. I can only speculate that either I was removed by the aliens and placed back into the womb for purposes that relate to my role as an abductee, or I have a sibling living somewhere on this planet, or on another planet, or possibly on a spaceship. There have also been times during my life when I felt I was pregnant, but I did not go to a doctor. Because of my abduction experiences, I have a tendency to avoid doctors whenever possible. It is impossible to say what a doctor would have discovered had they examined me or given me a pregnancy test immediately after an abduction experience.

I have had encounters during which the following events occurred: laparoscopy-type procedures, leaving behind scrapes, cuts, and blood in my naval; blood and possibly bone marrow extraction which left blood on my sheets and severe pain in my leg; skin scrapings and hair clippings being taken; tubes or other devices inserted into my nostrils, throat and down into the esophagus; rectal and vaginal probes; long needles or rods being inserted into my joints; a wand with a feather-like device on the end of it that was used to help me relax; and injections of drugs in various parts of my body, most commonly my neck.

In addition to psychological and behavioral studies, I believe genetic (molecular) studies are also of great interest to the aliens. Because I have been shown children and infants who look completely human, completely alien, and everything in-between, I strongly believe a portion of the longitudinal study is directed toward a massive breeding program. As far as this breeding program is concerned, I must emphasize that *my* experiences have shown me the following: (1) I do not believe the aliens are creating babies in order to use them as food. I have never seen any indication that this is occurring, nor have I ever seen a dead baby or child. There have been several times when the aliens told me a baby was sick or a child was dying, but that child or infant was always alive during my encounter with it. (2) I have rarely observed aliens abusing or not providing care for the children they have shown me. During the few encounters where I observed this type of behavior, I was never quite sure if the children, or their extreme situations were real or not. This is extremely important to understand. We must consider the possibility that the aliens employ visual imagery when attempting to understand certain concepts about us. An example is the encounter involving the babies lying on the floor in filthy conditions prior to the baby shower. It is my belief that visions and holographic representations are used frequently, often times as learning tools. These are tools that teach humans as well as aliens. (3) I believe the aliens care a great deal for the children they are creating. I have seen first hand that the aliens want us to feel for *their* children the way we feel for *our* children. Unfortunately, many humans have children for selfish reasons and often show the opposite of a loving and nurturing behavior toward their children.

It is probable that these extreme inconsistencies in our behavior are what the aliens are trying to understand. In addition, if millions of adult Americans are being abducted, then many of these alien children may be related to human beings on this planet. It is important that we try to understand this and the implications, and begin to look at a broader view of the abduction phenomenon. Perhaps instead of reacting as victims, we can consider the broader ramifications of their activities. It might behoove us to act in a proactive manner and respond as concerned parents and teachers.

I believe my husband and I have children who were created from a combination of our genetic material and an alien's genetic material, or even another human's genetic material. Whether these children are living on enormous spaceships, artificially or naturally created planets, or in other dimensions, I do not know.

There have been times when I questioned whether the aliens were simply using me as an experimental animal in a laboratory experiment. While I think it is highly probable that some of the procedures they have performed on me are of this nature, I am also inclined to believe that I, and other abductees, are playing a much broader role. It is possible the aliens are attempting to alter me physiologically and this alteration is occurring on a molecular level. Perhaps there is a role I am to perform in the future that requires this physical alteration. It is also possible that because the planet I live on is being drastically altered in an environmental sense, my physiology must also be altered in order for the aliens to continue to obtain what they require from me.

CHAPTER 15

Government Agencies, the Military, and the Aliens

You have read my accounts involving military and government personnel in some of my abduction encounters. For years it was extremely hard for me to accept what I was seeing. Today I realize I am not alone. Other abductees have remembered seeing military personnel during their encounters.[16] This is an issue ufology needs to seriously address, and soon.

I have stated many times that either the government and the military are involved, or the aliens have a reason for wanting me to believe they are working together. Recently, (in 1993) my husband relayed his first memory of an abduction encounter involving a white, human male, who stood approximately five feet, six inches tall. He was wearing a dark green, military uniform. Erik felt extremely uncomfortable when he told me he saw this military man during his experience. What was even more difficult to accept was seeing him standing next to a human doctor and a Grey. The trio were standing at the foot of a metallic table or bed in which my husband was lying and they were staring down at him. Abductees and researchers should not ignore the military/government connection simply because it does not fit in with what has been published so far, or because they are too afraid of being ridiculed by their peers.

If the aliens are intent upon making me and other abductees believe our government is working with them, then it is important to ask why. Are the aliens trying to perpetuate fear and distrust among those whom the government is governing? It is already evident that the public's trust in its government, at least in this country, is at an all-time low. It seems as though in the last fifteen years we have seen more corruption and deceit at the highest levels of our government than ever before. One major lesson we learned during the Reagan and Bush administrations was that white-collar crime pays, and extremely well. Do we really need the aliens telling us something we already know? I do not believe so.

I believe UFO propulsion studies, alien abductions, and government-alien bases are the most closely guarded secret our government has. They very well could fall into the top three most important black projects our government is currently working on.

On the other hand, there is no reason to assume that just because someone is in the military or is a high ranking official they are going to be left alone and not be abducted with the rest of us. This, in turn, opens up another possibility that ufology and the public must consider. Perhaps some of the military and government personnel that abductees are seeing are also being abducted. They are simply performing their role as both an abductee and as an inadvertent government onlooker. It is also possible the military men some abductees are reporting in their encounters are military health care professionals. Their expertise as physicians and nurses is simply being used during their abduction in much the same way as I have been used to provide psychological comfort and security to my nephew.

Any ufologist, researcher, or mental health professional who automatically discounts the reports about the military and the government working with the aliens is inviting the possibility of another holocaust upon those they consider to be "different." Even though the German citizens were told what was happening to the Jews, Poles, Gypsies, the mentally ill, and whoever else the Nazi regime found inferior, they could not believe the information. Their minds simply would not allow them to accept the idea that their government could be responsible for such atrocities. Do not discount what I and other abductees are reporting simply because your mind will not allow you to believe there is a connection between some members of our government and some of these aliens. Do not discount what I am reporting because you automatically lump all such information into your government conspiracy category. I am not a government agent disseminating disinformation. And finally, do not ignore what I am reporting because you have made a stand in the past and you are not about to back down now. It would be dangerous for anyone studying, or directly involved in this phenomenon not to ever change their opinion as to what they believe is occurring. I have to remain open to the idea, although it is *extremely* difficult for me, that our government may in fact be trading alien technology for genetic material, or at least is aware of what is being done to us and has chosen to look the other way.

While some of you may scoff at this idea, I will agree that it sounds somewhat surreal. When I use the term "military" I do not mean the military as an entity. It is more likely that a very select few military groups with specific psychological profiles and security clearances are working on these types of projects. It is doubtful that our military, as an entity, could ever contain itself about something as explosive as the UFO phenomenon. The military's role comes more into focus when looking at the *playgrounds* that military bases provide. For example, who can really say what is going on northwest of Las Vegas, Nevada, next to the nuclear test site, except those who have worked there? Commercial aircraft and non-designated military aircraft cannot even fly over the area. And most importantly, anyone who thinks this is the only "playground" of this type that the government has is fooling himself.

The government, as an entity, can be viewed in much the same way. It is doubtful that Congress is aware of the specifics of these kinds of black projects. However, there are agencies within agencies, and a very effective way of dealing with sensitive information called compartmentalization. (I might also add that it appears the aliens are also familiar with the process of compartmentalization.) With the books that have been published on the CIA, and other books tying the military and the government in with UFOs, I have a hard time believing that many people, including me, would have ever had a difficult time accepting the possibility that this liaison could exist. We may find out one day, quite by accident of course, that just as bread and butter go so well together, so do UFOs and our government.

When I realized during my experience involving the reprogramming film that "these people do not even have to answer to the President," I knew without a doubt what I was up against. I was virtually powerless then and probably still am. The only thing I could do was to write this book, knowing full well that it will only reach a minute portion of our population. The preceding experience did not involve alien Beings, nor did my encounter with the man from the CIA who tried to convince me to work for a specific broker. What am I and other abductees to make of these experiences? How many screen memories can be in place at one time? Who is to say these were alien-related experiences? Who is to say that someone from a secret government agency did not come into my home, drug me, abduct me, hypnotize me, and then fill in the gaps with their own screen memory? As so many debunkers are quick to ask: Why are advanced alien Beings performing such crude, human-types of experiments on abductees?

People have to reach their own conclusions about the UFO phenomenon. All I can do is report what I remember. However, I hope the experiences of other abductees, as well as my abduction experiences, will not be ignored or discounted just because they do not fit in neatly with other published accounts. Many abductees are terrified from their encounters with alien Beings. Seeing military or government personnel working alongside the aliens only makes these feelings worse.

CHAPTER 16

Earth Changes

Discussions about UFOs and abductions can become quite thought-provoking and sometimes very confusing. This is because in addition to the aliens' agenda, the government's role, and animal mutilations, the topic of Earth changes is bound to come up during a discussion of why the aliens are here. Earth changes are very real and they occur on a daily basis. There is nothing "new age" about them. Our planet has been undergoing geologic changes for millions of years.

Most people focus on earthquakes when they think about Earth changes. Not only is the planet we live on unpredictable, we also have dangers from space to consider. According to the book *Agents of Chaos*, "On March 23, 1989, an asteroid half a mile in diameter zipped past Earth at 50,000 miles per hour, missing our planet by a mere 500,000 miles. If this asteroid had hit our planet, astronomers estimate that the impact would have been equivalent to the explosion of 20,000 hydrogen bombs. A direct hit on land would have opened a crater five to ten miles across which would have been large enough to obliterate an entire city. Astronomers estimate that about 1,500 asteroids and comets large enough to decimate the Earth are careening through the solar system."[17]

Earth changes are real, and according to scientists, not psychics or abductees, they *will* occur. "Sudden and commonly violent intrusions of disorder, such as meteorite impacts, mass extinctions, catastrophic earthquakes, and ice ages have repeatedly transformed our planet. These chaotic forces that destroy and reshape land forms typically occur at irregular intervals over long eons of geologic time."[18]

After some of my encounters with the aliens, I was left with a feeling of impending doom. Sometimes I was left believing there is going to be a global war in my lifetime. Other times I was left feeling it may be catastrophic Earth changes on a global scale that are going to occur. Some of the aliens appear to want me to know that *something* global is going to happen and they want me to be prepared for it. Such as the night when I was on the dark side or opposite side of the moon and was being trained to fight. I felt that one day, I would have to defend myself in some type of guerrilla warfare. In another encounter, I was in an underground structure observing dirty and dusty caverns and I felt that one day, hundreds of people would have to live down there. I was shown the lightning incident followed by my being in an earthquake. During this experience I felt that natural disasters were happening all over the planet. These are just a few examples that you have already read about. They have left me feeling as though the aliens are trying to tell me that something is indeed going to happen during my lifetime.

These events either will happen, or they will not. Past predictions such as the catastrophic Earth movements that were predicted for the sixties and seventies never came to pass. Predictions made at several UFO conferences and symposiums about UFOs coming to our planet by the thousands in 1992 so everyone would find out about them, did not come true either.

Perhaps another asteroid capable of extinguishing most forms of life on our planet is heading toward Earth. I believe there is a much greater probability of this occurring than the other "prophetic" warnings that have been put forth thus far. Let us suppose for a moment, that the aliens are technologically advanced enough to have calculated the trajectory of the asteroid and have determined that it is heading for Earth. Can we rule out the possibility that the aliens may want to help us in some way? Even if it is to keep an experiment going? Environmentalists are trying to save many species of animals from extinction, are they not? If it is not an asteroid and it is indeed Earth movements (or a combination of an asteroid followed by enormous geologic changes), the possibility remains that the aliens have a way to predict what our scientists cannot: that catastrophic Earth changes are going to occur soon.

I am positive catastrophic Earth changes are going to happen because of what history and science has taught me. As far as the predictions of Earth changes by psychics, abductees, or aliens, *interpretation* is everything. It would be interesting to have the visual images and physical descriptions put in writing by the people who predict Earth changes. This would give many different people the opportunity to read the information and interpret it themselves. In this way, the information might yield different conclusions. If we all arrived at the same conclusions independently, then there might be more emphasis put on the predictions of Earth changes.

According to *Agents of Chaos*, "When a volcano, whether in the Cascades, the Mono Lake region, or elsewhere, gives signs of an impending eruption, the wisest course is to move out of the area until after the activity is safely over. The common American tendency to pursue business as usual, to regard a familiar land form as a non-threat and to ignore geologist's warnings, is likely to produce many unnecessary deaths and injuries."[19]

Perhaps by listening to people who have a high accuracy rate at predicting Earth changes, like geologists (and perhaps even some psychics) we can at least prevent our loved ones from suffering needlessly.

CHAPTER 17

So You Think You're More Aware?

I was born into this world a female human being. I was born into a loving family. I was not physically or sexually abused, or harmed in any way by any member of my family. I am married to a loving and kind man who is also my best friend. We have what we consider to be a wonderful family. We are extremely happy together. I have never had to go without any of my basic needs being met, and I have always had more than I really needed to get by in life. I wish all human beings were as fortunate as I have been.

Even though I am blessed with all of this, my life is sometimes unpleasant because of my abduction experiences. However, what is even more painful are the actions of my own species. It is the inability of my fellow human beings to behave as thinking, *feeling*, creatures that I find most disappointing.

I have been to several UFO conferences and have hosted many abductee support groups. There has not been one of these where an abductee, whether they were a Ph.D. psychologist or a clerk in a store did not profess, "I am so aware now because of my alien encounters." In addition, when I hear abduction researchers and abductees speak about the cruelty the aliens are inflicting upon them or their "victims," I cannot contain my amazement at their double standards. In almost every case, these individuals wear leather, eat meat, buy products that have been cruelly tested on animals, and believe that animals' lives are not as important as humans' lives. If you agree with these statements, then think about this possibility: perhaps humans' lives are not as important as the aliens' lives.

I would like to recommend the book *Diet For A New America* by John Robbins. In it, you will learn how the everyday behavior of humans is inflicting pain and suffering upon millions of animals. Simple changes in humanity's behavior could prevent this suffering *overnight*. Our behavior may be why cows are the most commonly found mutilated animal. Our society holds no respect for cows whatsoever. Why should the aliens? How often do we think about the cow as the social animal research has shown it to be? Has it ever crossed our minds that cows might be sentient, conscious beings? What if humans are viewed with the same status by the aliens? Apparently, it has never crossed many people's minds that they should consider themselves lucky. Indeed, we should be thankful the aliens are not playing by the same rules humans use with the other species we share our planet with.

Does your cat meow to you when it is hungry? Does your dog whine at the door when it needs to go outside to use the bathroom? Perhaps I gave the aliens permission to abduct me. You see, *I* can say I may have given the aliens permission because I can communicate with them and the aliens understand me. Humans do not try to understand pigs, cows, chickens, or any other animals for that matter. They are simply a commodity to be used and consumed in any manner humans see fit.

When considering the many viewpoints on animal experimentation, I found the following information very interesting: "The real choice is not between dogs and children, it is between good science and bad science; between methods that directly relate to humans and those that do not."[20] "At this very moment, what is being done to animals in laboratories cannot be legally done to our worst enemies in times of war. We can't see the irradiated monkeys and rats, electrode-implanted cats, burned beagles and pigs, rabbits in "Elizabethan" collars, eyes oozing from oven cleaner and livers bursting from alcohol infusions—but, to paraphrase the English writer John Bryant, "If suffering were a smell, the stench—from laboratories would be unbearable."[21]

"Animal experimentation, like tobacco and drugs, is big business. It is supported in this country by an estimated $15 billion a year in federal and state taxes, donations to charities, and private industry. That money allows experimenters to cage, hurt, and kill 65-100 million animals every year. They claim that harming animals is all *necessary.*"[22] That last sentence sounds very familiar to me. I wonder, where have we heard that before?

I have had positive, as well as neutral and negative abduction experiences. Many different types of alien Beings have chosen to interact with me. *Some* of these aliens have actually experimented on me. Even though I was treated far better than any lab or food animal on our planet, I still found several of my abduction experiences difficult to endure. However, there is not a day that goes by that I don't think about how lucky I really am. I wish more than anything that my fellow human beings could open their hearts and allow themselves to feel empathy for other species.

The time has come for humanity to consider the rights of animals and to treat them as sentient, conscious beings. When people finally realize that humans are being experimented on by superior beings, perhaps they will be cognizant of their own behavior and will choose to stop the suffering.

Epilogue

In 1987, when I was twenty-seven years old, I became consciously aware of the alien presence in my life. I was overcome with anxiety and fear due to my inability to understand what was happening to me and why. Government and religion produced a culture that prohibited me from understanding what was occurring.

My experiences are continuing, so like most abductees my story has no ending. This is life's adventure for me. I have learned much from studying my abduction experiences, but I have suffered much also. Humans will not change unless that change is forced upon them. I am no exception. My experiences have changed me. I look around everyday at people with a part of myself wishing I could just be normal, like them. But another part of me knows that I was born into this world as an abductee, and until society acknowledges the existence of alien Beings, I will never be considered normal. I will always be different.

Our life experiences make us who we are. I did not want this to happen to me and I do not apologize for what I am remembering. Sadly, and what is most amazing to me in all of this, are the "believers" who ridicule or do not believe abductees simply because they do not agree with how our experiences make us feel. I wonder if it has ever occurred to anyone that the aliens may have "control groups." Some individuals may be subjected to only positive stimuli; others may be subjected to only negative stimuli; a third group may be subjected to both positive and negative stimuli; and a fourth group may be subjected to only neutral stimuli. What a great disservice we do to one another by labeling and attacking each other because we have had different types of experiences. I am happy for those experiencers who have had only positive abduction experiences. You give me hope. I feel a great sadness for those abductees who have only had negative experiences, and I can relate, somewhat, to both groups of individuals.

I have learned much about the many different types of Beings interacting with us, however, I do not pretend to have all the answers. No one of us does. I am only one piece of the puzzle. I continue to press forward because I am not afraid of the truth. To understand what is happening to all life on our planet, human beings will have to embrace the unthinkable, the unimaginable, and the unbelievable.

The Painting

One cold and dreary February afternoon in 1993 I wrote the following prose. I was thinking about the many abduction experiences I have had and how tired I was of it all. Although I did not know what lay around the corner for me I knew something was about to change in my life. Nineteen ninety-three turned out to be a difficult year for me—a year that tested my patience.

Writing this book and reliving these experiences has been very difficult for me, but it has also been very cathartic. I no longer have to worry if I have a key piece to the puzzle that makes all the others fit. I have shared everything I know until this point in my life.

Although my experiences are continuing, I still have hope for the future. I feel that 1994 will be as exciting as 1993 was trying. I hope that each one of you who is seeking the truth will find it, and it is with this hope I wish to leave you with.

I am standing before a vast expanse of canvas. I can see an area of the picture that represents the physical world in which I exist. I see the past, although it is somewhat distorted because of humanity's view of itself. The one aspect of our past that has remained constant has been our ability to deceive ourselves. No matter how far back in time we go, we are always warring, destroying, and re-creating ourselves. It is the same each time because we have yet to learn from our past. I briefly observe my individual past upon this canvas. Because the canvas is so large, it appears only as a speck of dust.

I lose my balance for a moment and I have to take a step backward. Suddenly, the paranormal, ufology, and the alien abduction phenomenon are coming into view. How extraordinary and complicated this is to gaze upon. My mind feels as if it is being consumed by a whirlwind. This part of the canvas is rearranging every aspect of my reality. Even as my eyes are immersed in this part of the picture I cannot understand what it is I am looking at. I am dizzy, tired, and confused. Why didn't they teach me about this in school? Why didn't they teach me about this in church? Where is the government I trusted in? Where are my parents to protect me?

I feel as though I am falling into an abyss from which I will never return. Nothing will be the same anymore. My reality is being recreated.

Finally, after many years, I am facing the canvas again. I cannot stand in the location I was standing in before. I've been there and I remember the whirlwind. I must stand some distance away from that location. I could not see the complete canvas from there and I do not want to be swept up by the whirlwind again. It only leads to confusion, which in turn leads to fear. I have moved beyond the fear.

I think I am moving a few more steps backward. Yes, that is it. That little voice in my mind, my higher self, my Guardian Angel, or perhaps my God has told me to take a few more steps backward. Yes, I think I understand now. I am considering something I have denied and ridiculed all of my life. I never thought this would help me move forward. These few steps backward have enabled me to view much more of the canvas than I ever could before. I never thought I would find myself here in this place.

I am looking at a place I closed my mind off to ever since I left my childhood. It is wondrous and filled with the colors of the rainbow. My physical body is standing quite a distance away from the canvas and at the same time, I am floating within the canvas. I do not understand where I am, but it is exciting. Another door is opening and I am on the verge of a new awakening.

Katharina Wilson, Portland, Oregon 1993.

Correspondence

If you are interested in specific types of information relating to my case that were not covered in this book you may want to purchase *The Alien Jigsaw Supplement*. It was published separately because not all of my information could be included in one book. The supplement includes journal entries that were deleted from *The Alien Jigsaw*, transcripts of the hypnosis sessions that were summarized for the book, and information about symbols and unusual writing I have seen. As a personal research project, I designed a relational grid that compares my experiences with several theories and important questions about the abduction phenomenon. Additional data acquired from my research grid is also included in the supplement.

If you would like to write to the author* or if you wish to order *The Alien Jigsaw Supplement*** please address your correspondence to:

Katharina Wilson
Puzzle Publishing
P.O. Box 230023
Portland, OR 97281-0023

*If you would like a reply to your letter, please enclose a self addressed stamped envelope.

**Please enclose a check or money order for $16.95 (postpaid) payable to Katharina Wilson. *The Alien Jigsaw Supplement* will be available May 1, 1994.

Notes

1. Budd Hopkins, Javid Jacobs, Ron Westrum, *The UFO Abduction Syndrome*, Unusual Personal Experiences: An Analysis Of The Data From Three National Surveys (Las Vegas, NV: The Roper Organization, 1992) 21-22, 48.

2. Laurence Steinberg, *Adolescence* (New York, NY: Knopf, 1989) 30, 32.

3. For clarification purposes please refer to journal entry 9-12-87 of *The Alien Jigsaw*.

4. Katharina Wilson, *The Alien Jigsaw Supplement* (Portland, OR: Puzzle Publishing, 1993) Occurrences of Missing Time.

5. Katharina Wilson, *The Alien Jigsaw* (Portland, OR: Puzzle Publishing, 1993) Appendix C.

6. Katharina Wilson, *The Alien Jigsaw Supplement* (Portland, OR: Puzzle Publishing, 1993) Hypnosis Sessions: 8-1-88.

7. Wilson, Hypnosis Sessions: 8-8-88.

8. Wilson, Hypnosis Sessions: 8-8-88.

9. Wilson, Hypnosis Sessions: 8-8-88.

10. Wilson, Hypnosis Sessions: 9-8-88.

11. Wilson, Hypnosis Sessions: 10-5-88.

12. Wilson, Hypnosis Sessions: 10-26-88.

13. *Communion*, The Movie (Pheasantry Films in association with Allied Vision and The Picture Property Company, 1989) Based on the book, *Communion: A True Story* by Whitley Strieber (New York, NY: Avon, 1987)

14. Katharina Wilson, *The Alien Jigsaw Supplement* (Portland, OR: Puzzle Publishing, 1993) Journal Entries Omitted From *The Alien Jigsaw*: 3-30-91.

15. Wilson, Journal Entries Omitted From *The Alien Jigsaw*: 12-7-91.

16. Leah A. Haley, *Lost Was The Key* (Greenleaf Publications, 1993) Karla Turner, Ph.D. *Into the Fringe* (The Berkley Publishing Group, 1992) The two main themes of these cases are abductions by alien Beings and abductions (and harrassment tactics) carried out by government and/or military personnel.

17. Stephen L. Harris, *Agents Of Chaos* (Missoula, MT: Mountain Press, 1990) 221.

18. Harris, 223.

19. Harris, 226.

20. "Arguing The Issue: A PETA* Special Report," *PETA News* Fall, 1991: 13. A quote by Robert Sharpe, Ph.D., *The Cruel Deception*.

21. "Arguing The Issue: A PETA Special Report," *PETA News* Fall, 1991: 12.

22. PETA, 12.

* PETA—People for the Ethical Treatment of Animals
P.O. Box 42516, Washington, DC 20015-0516 (301) 770-PETA

Appendix A

Physiological and Psychological Effects

The following list contains common physiological effects that my husband and I have felt prior to, or immediately following an abduction experience.

- A ringing, fluttering, or buzzing sound in one or both ears.

- High electrostatic field in our house, car, and places we go, such as the grocery store. This usually occurs just prior to an abduction, but sometimes afterward also. These effects are felt as a physical shock when touching one another, our pets, and all types of objects, whether they be metallic, plastic, or cardboard.

- A strong feeling of being drugged (always following an experience) after one or both of us have been abducted. Although neither of us takes tranquilizers or sleeping aids, we can only speculate this may be what the aftereffects feel like. It can also be compared to the feeling one has after staying up all night, or most of the night. This feeling has lasted as long as twenty-four hours after an abduction.

- Sensing or feeling a presence near us or in our house, usually at night and just prior to an abduction. A similar occurrence I also experience is feeling as though someone is mentally "tuning" into me while I am going about my normal activities. It is as if the aliens are telepathically tuning into my reality to check on me or to monitor me.

- We have discovered round scoop mark scars and straight line scars after a few abduction experiences. There have been times, of course, when we did not have any memory of the abduction experience and awakened to find unusual scars. Sometimes drops of blood have been found on the sheets after an abduction.

- I have awakened with a sore naval, only to find blood or a brownish fluid in it. I have also awakened with scrapes and puncture wounds inside my naval. These sometimes take three days to stop bleeding, and about a week to heal completely.

- Puncture wounds or marks on the neck (over jugular artery) and in an arm over a vein.

- My husband and myself have experienced rectal pain after an encounter. I have, on occasion, experienced vaginal pain also. We have both experienced soreness inside one of our nostrils all the way up to the eye, and I have experienced sudden and very intense migraine headaches immediately after an abduction.

- Extremely blurred vision and disorientation lasting up to one week. I have been diagnosed with binocular convergence disorder. Even though it became pronounced after several abduction experiences back to back, I am not sure if this is directly related to these experiences. However, my doctor could not tell me how or why people get this disorder.

- After abduction encounters, having feelings of everything from euphoria to extreme depression, depending on the nature of the encounter. Sometimes these feelings have lasted up to five days.

- An aversion to certain foods immediately after an abduction experience. Normally this involves a sudden dislike of something I enjoyed the taste of the day before. There is the possibility of psychological conditioning associated with these sudden dislikes of food. My husband and I stopped eating all animal products (except for occasional dairy) in 1986, one year before we were aware of our abduction experiences. Therefore, the types of foods I have had an aversion to are certain types of seafood, which incidentally, were my favorite food. I have been able to document two experiences involving immediate aversions to certain types of fish.

- Some of the procedures the aliens do to me physically have caused me to begin menstruating early. I have been under extreme stress (death of a loved one, divorce, relocation, loss of job) at different times in my life, and I have never started menstruating early because of these events. Therefore, I do not believe it is the stress of the abduction that is causing this to happen. It may be occurring because the aliens are removing eggs or are altering them in some way. Without the alien interaction, my body operates on a regular cycle of every twenty-five to twenty-eight days.

- I have suffered from chronic urinary tract infections for most of my life. However, as a child, I would never tell my mother because I feared she would take me to a doctor. Again, the doctors do not know what is causing them.

- It is difficult to say if my limited psychic abilities are due to my abduction experiences since both have been occurring for most of my life. I am a much more sensitized individual today than I was ten years ago, and I believe there probably is a connection with my abduction experiences.

- Although we believe Erik was abducted prior to having a vasectomy, after this operation the aliens still appeared to be interested in collecting sperm samples from him. Several times over the past five years, he has awakened with small lumps in his scrotum. These have coincided with Erik awakening feeling extremely drugged, or with either Erik or me, or both of us remembering an abduction experience from the previous night. He has twice been to see a physician about this, but the physician did not know what could have caused it. Once he was given medication for it. The soreness and the small lumps disappear after about two weeks. We have deduced that the aliens are still able to retrieve sperm from him.

- Erik has been questioned by his doctor as to whether or not he ever broke both of his arms. Since he has never broken either of his arms Erik asked his doctor why he would ask this question. His doctor told him that his arms did not hang properly and appeared as though they had been broken and reset.

Appendix B

With the exception of Katharina Wilson, Budd Hopkins, Vicki Lyons, Patti Weatherford, and Dan Overlade, Ph.D., the names in this book have been changed to protect the identities of individuals written about in this story. All experiences described in this book are true.

Appendix C

Dan C. Overlade, Ph.D., practiced clinical psychology for over thirty-five years. He worked with several abductees in and around the Pensacola, Florida, area from 1988 until his death in 1990. He earned his bachelor's and master's degrees in psychology from Utah State University and a Ph.D. from Purdue University in 1954. He held appointments as adjunct professor of psychology with the University of Florida and the University of West Florida. He was a past president of the Florida Council of Clinic Directors, a past president of the Florida Psychological Association, a past president of the Florida State Board of Examiners of Psychology, and a past president of Forensic Psychologists, Inc. Dr. Overlade held diplomas in clinical psychology and forensic psychology of the American Board of Professional Psychology and the diploma in clinical hypnosis of the American Board of Psychological Hypnosis.

References

Baron, Robert A. and Don Byrne. *Social Psychology: Understanding Human Interaction*. 5th ed. Newton: Allyn and Bacon, 1987.

Carson, Robert C., James N. Butcher, and James C. Coleman. *Abnormal Psychology and Modern Life*. 8th ed. Glenview: Scott, Foresman and Company, 1988.

Crooks, Robert and Jean Stein. *Psychology: Science, Behavior and Life*. New York: Holt, Rinehart and Winston, 1988.

Ferster, Charles B. and Stuart A. Culbertson. *Behavior Principles*. 3rd edition. Englewood: Prentice Hall, 1982.

Fowler, Raymond E. *The Watchers: The Secret Design Behind UFO Abduction*. New York: Bantam Books, 1990.

Friedman, Stanton T. and Don Berliner. *Crash At Corona*. New York: Paragon House, 1992.

Fuller, John G. *The Interrupted Journey*. New York: Dial Press, 1966.

Groves, Philip M. and George V. Rebec. *Introduction to Biological Psychology*. 3rd edition. Dubuque: William C. Brown, 1988.

Haley, Leah A. *Lost Was The Key*. Tuscaloosa: Greenleaf Publications, 1993.

Harris, Stephen L. *Agents Of Chaos*. Missoula: Mountain Press, 1990.

Hastings, Arthur. *With the Tongues of Men and Angels*. New York: Holt, Rinehart and Winston, 1991.

Hopkins, Budd. *Missing Time*. New York: Ballantine Books, 1981.

Hopkins, Budd. *Intruders: The Incredible Visitations At Copley Woods*. New York: Random House, 1987.

Jacobs, David M. *Secret Life: Firsthand Accounts Of UFO Abductions*. New York: Simon and Schuster, 1992.

Marchetti, Victor and John D. Marks. *The CIA and the Cult of Intelligence.* New York: Knopf, 1974.

Marks, John D. *The Search for the "Manchurian Candidate."* New York: Times Books, 1979.

Olds, Sally B., Marcia L. London, Patricia A. Ladewig, and Sharon V. Davidson. *Obstetric Nursing.* Menlo Park: Addison-Wesley, 1980.

Randle, Kevin D. *The UFO Casebook.* New York: Warner Books, 1989.

Robbins, John. *Diet For A New America.* New Hampshire: Stillpoint, 1987.

The Roper Organization, *Unusual Personal Experiences: An Analysis Of The Data From Three National Surveys.* Hopkins, Budd and Jacobs, David M. and Westrum, Ron. "The UFO Abduction Syndrome." Las Vegas: Bigelow Holding Corporation, 1992.

Steinberg, Laurence. *Adolescence.* 2nd ed. New York: Knopf, 1989.

Vankin, Jonathan. *Conspiracies, Cover-ups and Crimes: Political Manipulation and Mind Control in America.* New York: Paragon House, 1992.

INDEX

A
agency 126, 161, 212, 215, 221, 222, 285
Air Force 81, 82, 124, 125, 131, 133, 207, 214
Andreasson, Betty (Betty Luca) 98, 240
animal(s) 32, 42, 49, 56, 57, 84, 105, 106, 108, 116, 132, 136, 153, 159, 166, 168, 181, 190, 199, 209, 212, 218, 225, 226, 227, 245, 254, 256, 259, 276, 279, 281, 287, 288, 289, 290, 300
automobile 140

B
baby 36, 37, 39, 46, 47, 48, 51, 52, 53, 62, 63, 64, 65, 66, 67, 83, 88, 94, 95, 98, 135, 150, 151, 166, 182, 184, 188, 189, 227, 228, 238, 239, 240, 242, 243, 244, 245, 247, 280
behavior 24, 25, 26, 38, 39, 44, 45, 53, 66, 67, 69, 71, 72, 99, 101, 108, 130, 137, 159, 166, 183, 187, 190, 202, 217, 219, 223, 227, 235, 262, 263, 273, 279, 280, 289, 290
Belgium 231, 232
birds 117
bleeding 91, 95, 140, 170, 228, 261, 299
Blonde, The 70, 87, 91, 107, 120, 127, 128, 131, 134, 135, 139, 140, 146, 151, 152, 153, 158, 159, 161, 189, 203, 267, 275, 276, 277
blood 52, 67, 72, 92, 106, 109, 129, 140, 160, 161, 184, 188, 191, 220, 224, 228, 238, 239, 240, 254, 261, 272, 276, 280, 299
blue beam 118, 143, 144
blue light 96, 118, 187, 213
blue-skinned Being 48, 66, 109, 275
    alien female 109
    baby 48
    female baby 66
body suit(s) 55, 57, 78, 79, 114, 115, 145, 203, 210, 232, 241, 253, 271, 273
bone(s) 104, 106, 109, 129, 140, 163, 169, 172, 188, 239, 240, 260, 261, 262, 271, 275, 276, 280
Budd (Hopkins) 24, 35, 45, 47, 48, 49, 50, 53, 59, 215, 303
Bush, George (President) 248, 283

C
camouflage 32, 57, 72, 91, 108, 137, 144, 171, 172, 187, 208, 211, 244, 249, 272, 276
Camp LeJeune 35, 39, 125, 234
Canada 213, 257
cat 55, 82, 87, 88, 89, 110, 122, 123, 128, 133, 135, 137, 141, 152, 153, 163, 168, 184, 185, 218, 244, 251, 254, 260, 276, 290
CAT scan 41, 71, 91

child 21, 22, 23, 25, 26, 43, 47, 49, 51, 54, 61, 63, 64, 66, 73, 74, 75, 84, 95, 101, 112, 120, 130, 134, 135, 136, 147, 148, 156, 162, 163, 165, 177, 178, 182, 184, 185, 190, 191, 192, 193, 211, 226, 230, 232, 239, 244, 267, 275, 277, 278, 280, 300
children 21, 23, 26, 29, 30, 37, 49, 51, 63, 68, 80, 84, 97, 99, 109, 120, 183, 191, 193, 234, 242, 244, 278, 280, 290
CIA 221, 223, 285
Clark Air Force Base 124, 125, 131, 207
clinic 46, 305
Clinton, Bill (Governor) 248, 249
college 21, 30, 33, 34, 54, 81, 82, 86, 152
Communion (The movie) 103
crab 121, 122
craft 23, 29, 42, 45, 56, 57, 71, 80, 93, 94, 112, 114, 131, 132, 133, 134, 136, 140, 141, 142, 144, 145, 146, 148, 149, 150, 155, 165, 167, 169, 173, 174, 177, 179, 186, 188, 192, 193, 194, 197, 201, 207, 210, 211, 212, 214, 216, 217, 218, 227, 229, 230, 231, 232, 234, 237, 240, 241, 244, 246, 252, 253, 255, 256, 258, 263, 264, 265, 268, 269, 273, 274

D

dark side of the moon 115
deer 32, 135, 136, 225, 226
dimension 53, 115, 117, 119, 205, 233, 260, 271, 276, 281
Doctor, The 63, 64, 74, 75, 89, 97, 119, 133, 139, 140, 147, 161, 203, 265, 266, 267, 272, 276
dog 100, 105, 106, 152, 168, 169, 189, 196, 199, 210, 211, 245, 260, 276, 290
dolphin 180, 181
dream 69, 72, 80, 82, 86, 111, 121, 138, 177, 195, 208, 219, 235, 256, 258, 261, 264
dream memory 260

E

embryo 110
energy 87, 89, 119, 195, 226, 272, 276
England 211, 263
exam 130, 216, 221, 222
examination 27, 71, 95, 107, 108, 131, 186, 187, 217, 258

F

Father, The 179, 272
Female, The 120, 149, 160, 161, 167, 168, 203, 234, 272, 274
floating 22, 23, 32, 43, 44, 45, 97, 98, 99, 100, 101, 111, 116, 123, 128, 131, 138, 141, 145, 148, 163, 164, 165, 167, 178, 179, 183, 184, 187, 193, 206, 229, 248, 257, 260, 268, 272, 273
Florida 26, 32, 33, 87, 216, 305

Fowler, Raymond 229

G
Germany 70, 71, 202, 235
glass box 63, 66
Gore, Al (Senator) 247, 248, 249
government 79, 81, 90, 113, 125, 126, 161, 175, 198, 212, 213, 214, 215, 221, 222, 223, 224, 229, 234, 271, 273, 283, 284, 285, 287
Greys
  Green-Gray 276
  Type One 271, 272, 273
  Type Two 271, 273, 274, 276
  Type Three 273, 276
  Type Four 274, 275

H
Hopkins, Budd 24, 35, 45, 47, 48, 49, 50, 53, 59, 215, 303
hospital 30, 39, 41, 46, 62, 70, 88, 122, 124, 150, 156, 160, 180, 185, 211, 218, 228
Howe, Linda Moulton 121, 182
hybrid 53, 98, 101, 120, 165, 179, 183, 190, 191, 192, 234, 239, 240, 244, 267, 271, 272, 277, 280
hypnosis 21, 24, 37, 48, 50, 55, 59, 60, 61, 62, 64, 68, 72, 79, 82, 83, 100, 101, 305

I
implant 129, 208, 254, 272
infant(s) 52, 74, 98, 122, 183, 193, 239, 240, 243, 248, 278, 279, 280
Intruders: The Incredible Visitations at Copley Woods 45, 79, 103, 229

J
Jacobs, David 122
joints 104, 251, 202, 280

K
kill 38, 88, 115, 137, 138, 162, 169, 181, 183, 184, 214, 219, 254, 290
killed 38, 85, 127, 128, 133, 138, 149, 166, 181, 254
killing 36, 79

L
laparoscopy 133, 272, 280
lion 56, 57, 137, 225
love 35, 49, 96, 97, 106, 108, 110, 132, 134, 135, 150, 152, 158, 163, 165, 170, 173, 174, 186, 207, 218, 225, 227, 246, 248, 257, 258, 262, 263, 275

loved 42, 288, 300
loves 123, 152
Lyons, Vicki 48, 49, 59, 71, 206, 208, 303

M
machine gun 114
mall 57, 150, 211, 217, 218
manipulation 39, 131, 147, 155, 170, 172, 203, 258, 263, 268
map 200, 201, 233, 235
menstruation 25, 170
Messenger, A 272
military 33, 35, 89, 90, 124, 125, 173, 174, 175, 197, 198, 214, 215, 218, 229, 230, 231, 232, 233, 234, 237, 238, 241, 250, 259, 273, 277, 283, 284
missing time 53, 54, 68, 75, 96
Monet 82
Monet cat 141

N
Navigator, The 231, 238, 241, 274
New River Air Station 35, 125, 218, 234
New York 59, 112, 264, 265
Norfolk 36
North Carolina 35, 45

O
ovary 27
Overlade, Dan (Ph.D.) 59, 61, 64, 65, 67, 68, 69, 71, 79, 80, 82, 84, 93, 94, 101, 103, 303, 305
ovulated 170

P
pain 30, 34, 35, 41, 48, 71, 72, 91, 92, 94, 99, 100, 101, 104, 106, 109, 122, 125, 129, 134, 139, 140, 155, 156, 171, 181, 184, 216, 224, 228, 252, 253, 258, 259, 260, 280, 289, 300
paralysis 23, 99, 145, 196, 200, 255, 259
penguin 178, 179
Pensacola 26, 30, 33, 38, 41, 48, 50, 86, 87, 125, 127, 149, 150, 169, 192, 194, 207, 216, 264, 305
Portland 35, 106, 168, 169, 187, 192, 194, 195, 209, 222, 235, 259, 269
Praying Mantis-type Being 217, 218
presence 22, 33, 35, 45, 51, 90, 91, 95, 103, 110, 142, 179, 189, 192, 195, 196, 198, 203, 205, 208, 223, 232, 234, 235, 245, 250, 259, 267, 270, 272, 273, 275, 276, 277, 299
psychological testing 50, 59
puberty 24, 25

Pudgy Doctor, The 155, 156, 157

R
Reagan, Ronald (President) 249, 283
Reptilian Tan Being 172, 274, 276

S
scar 129, 140, 196, 261, 262
school 23, 30, 31, 33, 35, 41, 42, 72, 80, 87, 106, 111, 117, 125, 128, 130, 131, 158, 175, 192, 211, 212, 222, 234, 268
screen memory 32, 45, 56, 71, 131, 140, 158, 169, 180, 265, 269, 285
seals 116, 256
Secret Life 122
Slater, Elizabeth (M.D.) 59
spontaneous memory 72, 96, 130, 142, 153, 218
Strieber, Whitley 103
surgery 156, 157, 171, 172, 185, 240, 251, 252, 262, 273

T
Tan Doctor, The 131, 272
Tan Being 276
teaching dream 85, 86, 115, 116, 147, 179, 189, 194, 195
telepathic 21, 23, 44, 86, 101, 105, 132, 137, 139, 143, 152, 154, 156, 158, 159, 160, 161, 163, 168, 172, 201, 237, 254, 273, 275, 277
Telepathy 44, 84, 88, 92, 97, 113, 124, 133, 141, 142, 150 217, 266, 271, 275, 279
tiger 137
travel 94, 119, 136, 137, 146, 276
turtle 190
"Twenty Fingers" 263

U
underground 77, 84, 118, 119, 195, 213, 215, 230, 232, 287
underwater 43, 162
university 31, 34, 56, 305

V
Vehicles,
    automobile 140
    barrel-shaped craft 142
    box-shaped craft 132
    cigar-shaped craft 218, 229, 230, 231, 232, 237, 238, 241, 256, 273
    delta formation 112, 144, 179
    hamburger-shaped craft 29, 42
    lights 26, 86, 87

    mother ship 150, 198, 211
    ring of lights 87
    saucer-shaped craft 227
    spinning shuttle craft 150
    underwater cage 162
    white car craft 44
vision 47, 77, 78, 79, 85, 87, 90, 108, 127, 128, 158, 159, 165, 174, 194, 198, 205, 206, 216, 248, 249, 250, 279, 280

W
war 77, 78, 79, 115, 119, 128, 195, 224, 250, 279, 287, 290
Watchers, The (Ramond Fowler) 229
Weatherford, Patricia (Patti) 206, 208, 303

Y
yellowish-tan building 167, 169, 233

Z
zoo 55, 57, 116, 117